Photos courtesy of Savogran Co.

DO YOU HAVE AN OLD CHAIR or dresser out in the garage that could be restored to daily use if you refinished it? Taking off the old finish is the first step, properly preparing the surface for a new finish is next. The final appearance depends on how well you do this step. You'll find information on the subject on page 2089

THE SECRET of fine studio photography, and especially of taking formal portraits, is good lighting. If you know how many lights you need and how to place them, you can take portraits with a professional flair. The article on page 1986 gives you hints on how to control shadows, highlight features and avoid hotspots

THERE IS a propeller for every outboard use, from trolling to water skiing. See page 2029

FOR MORE FUN in your game room, put in a pool table. You can build one from plans on page 1962

Courtesy of Bernz-O-matic Corp.

IF YOU OWN your own home, you should know what plumbing is all about, because you'll probably have to repair it from time to time. And one of these days you may want to remodel, coming up with a lovely new bathroom like the one above. Whether you do it yourself or call a plumber, it will pay you to read the articles on pages 1934 and 1940

THERE'S NO TOOL like a good tool, and a propane torch is one of the better ones. It's convenient to use in a hundred jobs around the house, from repairing a leaky gutter to laying floor tile. See the article on page 2025

Popular Mechanics
Do-It-Yourself Encyclopedia

in 16 volumes

A complete guide to

- home maintenance
- home improvement
- hand-tool skills
- craft projects
- power-tool know-how
- hobbies
- automotive upkeep
- automotive repair
- shop shortcuts
- boating
- fishing
- hunting
- model making
- outdoor living
- radio, TV and electronics

Volume 11

Book Division, Hearst Magazines, New York, N.Y. 10019

Printed in the United States of America

VOLUME 11

How to use your Encyclopedia

Browse. Glance through this volume, or any other volume of the Encyclopedia. Likely you will find the solution to a particular home-maintenance problem that has been bothering you, or a shop project so appealing that you will immediately head for your bench. Browsing not only is enjoyable, but is a source of ideas.

Seek specific information. Perhaps you want to find out how to cure that leak in your basement, how to keep the exterior paint from peeling, or how to tune and set the carburetor on your car.

Four reader aids, all cross-referenced, will enable you to find specific information:

1. *Alphabetical headings.* Located at the top of the page, these headings cover broad classifications of information. If you are looking for information on how to keep paint from peeling, for example, look up "Paints" alphabetically, then find the particular section dealing with peeling paint.

2. *Alphabetical cross-references.* These are shown in a box at the bottom of the page. Some material can logically be classified under more than one alphabetical heading, so if you don't find what you are seeking alphabetically (as described above), be sure to check the *alphabetical cross-references* at the bottom of the page; there you may find precisely the classification you are seeking. For example, you and your son decide to build a model airplane, and are looking for plans. You look up "Model airplanes" and find nothing under that alphabetical heading. However, if you glance at the bottom *of that same page* you will find an alphabetical cross-reference that reads: **model airplanes,** see airplane models.

3. *See also references.* These are shown at the end of many articles. They refer you to related articles which may also be of interest.

4. *Instant index.* Located at the end of Volume 16, it is thoroughly cross-referenced to help you find information under any heading.

1 *Alphabetical headings*

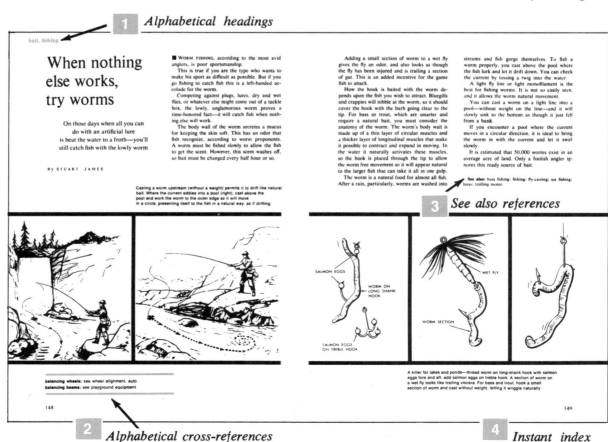

2 *Alphabetical cross-references*

3 *See also references*

4 *Instant index*

Playhouse in a shoe

BY RODMAN W. SHUTT

continued

■ THIS PLAYHOUSE is a fairy story made real—the "Old Woman Who Lived in a Shoe."

As a playhouse it has everything. The body of the shoe forms a long room—"cave" to the kids—and there's a door, windows without glass and a loft reached by a ladder through an opening in the plywood floor.

Construction begins with a platform which serves as a foundation. On this you build a rough 2 x 4 framework. Contours of the shoe are obtained by nailing plywood ribs and ordinary lath or lattice strips to the rough frame. The plywood ribs are cut with one edge curved, the radii varying with the curvature desired.

Finally, chicken wire is stapled over the whole thing to form a foundation for a weatherproof covering of either Celastic or fiberglass, whichever you use. As the covering goes on, flaps for the laces are formed. Note that these have five eyelets each, made by gluing hardboard or plywood rings to the fabric flaps. Lacing is ⅜ or ½-in. hemp rope. After the covering material of either type has been applied, finish with an undercoater and two coats of outside paint in the color desired. The original shoe was painted a bright yellow with brown for the shoe sole and eyelets. The windows, shutters and door were painted green. The roof consists of wood shingles laid over ¾-in. plywood and then painted a bright red.

See also: children's furniture; dollhouses; dolls; games, children's; kitchen, play; tree houses.

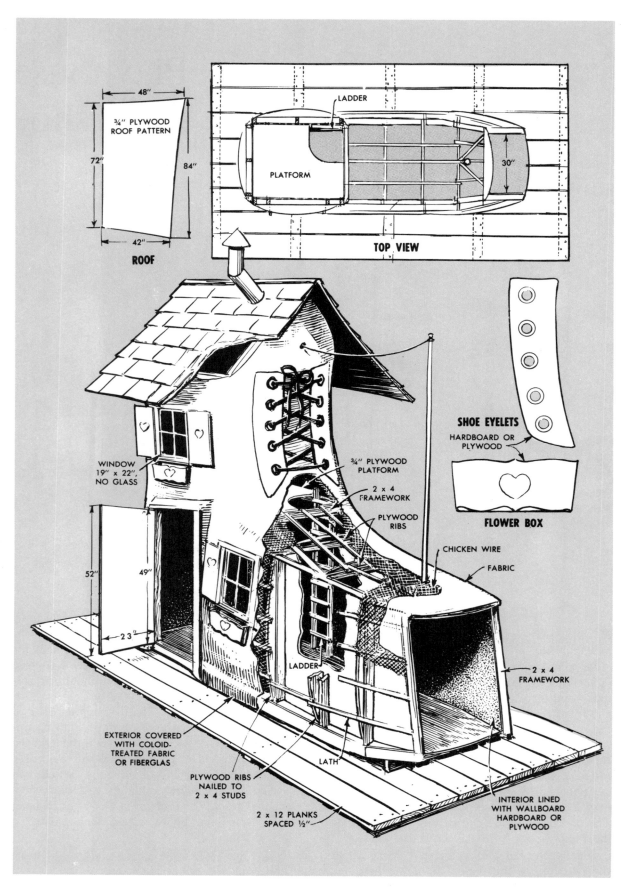

48″

¾″ PLYWOOD
ROOF PATTERN

72″

84″

42″

ROOF

LADDER

PLATFORM

30″

TOP VIEW

SHOE EYELETS

HARDBOARD OR
PLYWOOD

FLOWER BOX

WINDOW
19″ x 22″,
NO GLASS

¾″ PLYWOOD
PLATFORM

2 x 4
FRAMEWORK

PLYWOOD
RIBS

CHICKEN WIRE

FABRIC

52″

49″

23″

2 x 4
FRAMEWORK

LADDER

LATH

EXTERIOR COVERED
WITH COLOID-
TREATED FABRIC
OR FIBERGLAS

PLYWOOD RIBS
NAILED TO
2 x 4 STUDS

2 x 12 PLANKS
SPACED ½″

INTERIOR LINED
WITH WALLBOARD
HARDBOARD OR
PLYWOOD

Without the special equipment ordinarily used, it's no simple trick to form a truly round ring of medium-heavy wire to a given size. But if you construct the setup pictured, using a length of pipe slightly smaller in diameter than that of the ring needed, you'll find it an easy matter to turn perfect coils every time. Make a bender of ⅛-in. steel rod, drill a small hole in the pipe to catch the end of the wire to be bent and you're all set to form any number of rings of the same diameter. Be sure to keep the wire you are winding taut. This will wind it tightly around the post and give you more uniform rings.

You know, of course, what a messy job it is to knead solvent into a paintbrush. It's rough on your hands, too. But it's the only sure way to get a brush clean so it won't harden when stored between painting jobs. Instead, pour the solvent (except lacquer reducer, as this will soften some plastics) into a plastic bag, drop the brush in the bag, and then hold it as illustrated, or snap a rubber band over the brush handle and the top of the bag. Kneading can then be done more efficiently than by other methods, and you keep both hands out of the mess from start to finish of the cleaning job.

PLASTIC BAG

Strips cut from a newspaper and immersed in water until soaked through make good masking "tape" for use when painting sash. Cut the strips about 1½ in. wide with one straight edge, wet them thoroughly, allow excess water to drain off and then place them along sash rails, stiles and muntins as pictured. The wet paper will adhere to the glass long enough to permit painting to be finished on one small sash. Be sure, however, to peel off the paper before the paint is thoroughly dry, or you may run into a problem with the newspaper sticking.

Take-apart playhouse

BY DAVE SWARTWOUT

■ WONDERING WHAT TO MAKE THE KIDS in your "spare" time? You can't go wrong with a playhouse, especially this one. They'll have fun with it all year long for it is small enough to set up indoors for winter play. Measuring only 4 ft. square, it comes apart in 5 flat panels by removing just 8 wood screws. Best of all, it's easy to build, especially if you have a circular saw to run the grooves in the frame members.

As for materials, you'll need two sheets of ⅛-in. tempered hardboard, eight 8-ft. and two 6-ft. lengths of 1 x 2, two doz. cadmium-plated #10 x 1¼-in. wood screws and a ¼-in. dowel 12 in. long. If you plan to have a perforated wall in the rear, as shown above, you'll need a 4 x 4-ft. panel of ⅛-in. perforated hardboard and a 4 x 6-ft. panel of tempered hardboard to replace one of the 4 x 8-ft. panels.

To groove the 1 x 2 frame pieces, set your

circular saw to make a ¼-in.-deep cut, as shown in the detail at the bottom of the page. You'll have to make two passes in order to make the grooves wide enough to accept the ⅛-in. hardboard panels. Groove eight 4-ft. lengths along the edge. Round and notch the ends of the former; leave the others square.

Following the cutting diagrams, cut one of the 4 x 8-ft. panels into 24-in. (actually, 23-⅞-in.) widths. From the other panel, cut the 4 x 4-ft. roof piece and the 6-in. strips to complete the doors and windows. Assemble each wall, using glue and one screw at each corner, and trim the hardboard where necessary to fit. If the perforated panel is used, trim it to size and fit the 1 x 2s around the edges as you did them before.

The front and rear walls are joined to the side walls with screws only, two holes being drilled for them through each vertical member of the side walls. Also, ¼-in. holes are drilled in the top

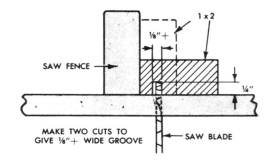

MAKE TWO CUTS TO
GIVE ⅛"+ WIDE GROOVE

framing of the side walls and short dowels are glued in them to hold the curved roof panel. The door and window fill-in panels are next. Trim them to fit flush with the rest, and glue them in the grooved members. Finally, strips of 1 x 2, grooved and slotted to fit over the edges of the fill-in pieces, are installed to add rigidity. Trim them to the openings. It will take at least two persons to spring the roof in place between the dowels in the side walls (note diagram on this).

When finishing, you may use one bright color throughout, or paint the hardboard portions of the walls one color, the wood a second color and the roof a third color. In any event, the easiest way to paint the walls completely is to take the house apart and paint each wall, plus the roof, separately. Whether you plan to use the playhouse outside or inside, all parts should be painted on both sides so they resist moisture and wear. Also, be sure you paint the exposed edges of the hardboard to seal the elements out. When the paint is completely dry, reassemble the playhouse and it's ready for years of enjoyable use by your children.

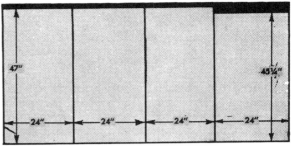

⅛" x 4' x 8' TEMPERED HARDBOARD, 2 REQD.

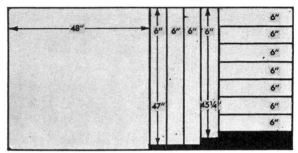

PANEL CUTTING DIAGRAM

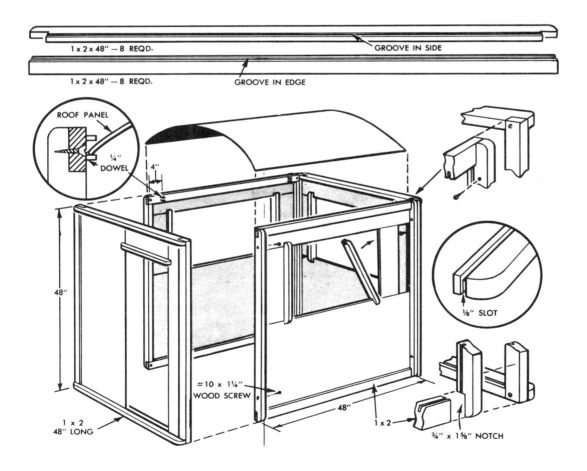

Extra squeeze for your plier wrench

BY WALTER E. BURTON

It transforms your grasp into a ton of gripping power—
or takes a bite as gentle and controlled as a playful pooch

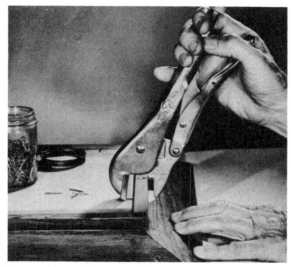

The standard wrench—a straight-jaw 10-incher—
does a better job than a hammer when driving brads
in critical spots. Since the jaw's limit is regulated
by a screw at the end of the handle, all nails will
project the same amount. Note how the padded jaw
protects the frame's finish

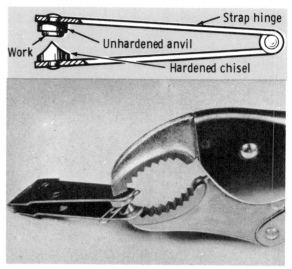

A hinged cutter snips a paper clip into three sizes
of wire staples with a single squeeze of a 12-in.
Lever Jaw wrench (the one shown here has jaws
contoured to grip round stock and offers four points
of contact on nuts). Many wrenches are equipped
with built-in wire cutters

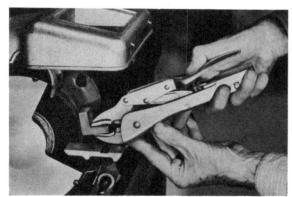

A small-parts handle saves the fingers on such jobs
as grinding. The tool shown here—called a
Lever Wrench—has automatic size-sensing action,
which lets you grip a variety of sizes and shapes
without having to adjust the jaws for each. The
grip is released by spreading the handles

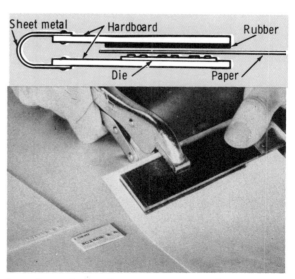

An embossed press for personalized stationery can be
made easily. The die is the nameplate snipped from
a plastic credit card. Adjust the jaws for enough
pressure to emboss the raised letters, but not the
die outline. Then squeeze the nameplate in two
places to gain uniformity

A socket wrench for spots that are too tight to permit the use of a regular handle is what you get when you adjust the jaws to grip a hex socket. A new 5-in. wrench is particularly compact for this purpose, when it is awkward to grip the bolt head directly with the jaws

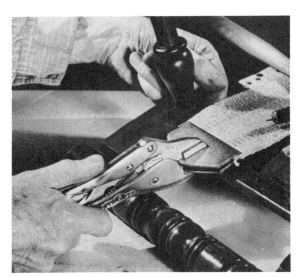

A sheet-metal tool has wide jaws that make it handy for stretching upholstery webbing and fabric or window screening. The contour of this tool often lets you use it as a lever, over a corner or an edge as shown here, to provide the maximum amount of tension while tacking or stapling

continued

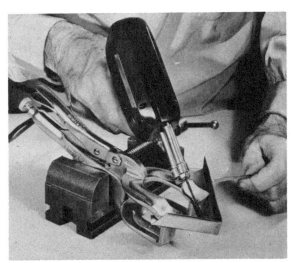

A welding-clamp version has all the features of a standard plier wrench. Its adjustable jaws hold the workpieces in alignment for soldering, and the release lever permits easy removal when the job is done. In the photo above, the clamp is firmly supported in a drill-press vise

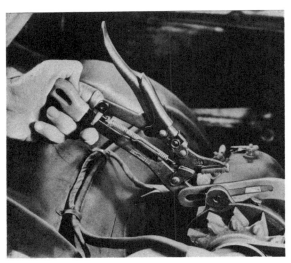

A one-hand version—above, the 910 GripLock—is fine for jobs where you need one free hand, as for holding a flashlight when doing emergency work on the car. When the spring-loaded jaw operator is released, the jaws close on the bolt head. They are locked with a squeeze of the handle

1931

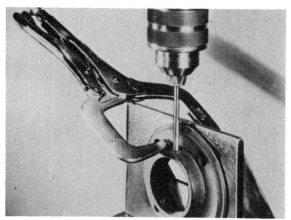

The C-clamp version—Vīse Grip's 11R—has jaws that can be adjusted from zero to 3¾ in., and are shaped to grip objects that other clamps cannot. In the photo above, a floor flange is anchored in order to drill a setscrew hole. The instant-release feature speeds up production work

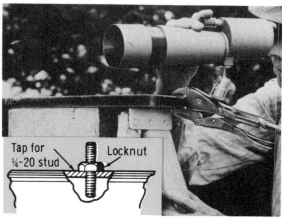

Add a threaded stud to the backbone of a wrench and you've got a versatile clamp support. Above, a clamp is applied to a stepladder to steady a telescope; the ball-and-socket tripod head allows the adjustment. Use this clamp instead of a bulky tripod for a camera, flash or floodlight

added wrench-power, continued

A gentle but firm grip is needed for many chores around the house, such as loosening stubborn caps on tubes of paint or cement. With ordinary pliers, there is the danger of stripping threads or twisting off the neck. This 5-in. wrench has curved jaws and a wire cutter. It can be pocketed easily

Need a nutcracker? A plier wrench makes the best kind. Its jaws can be set to fracture a hickory or other tough nut without crushing the kernel. With the curved jaws shown here, you can also vary the pressure by changing the nut's position. And there is no danger of straining your hand

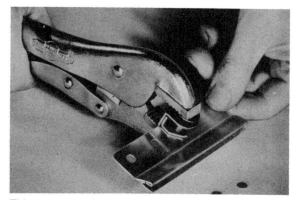

This paper punch will stamp through thin aluminum when you "power" it with a plier wrench. All you do is adjust the jaws to take an uncompressed punch, and a squeeze of the handles gives you a clean hole. The washer between the punch and the lower jaw of the wrench provides ejection space for disks

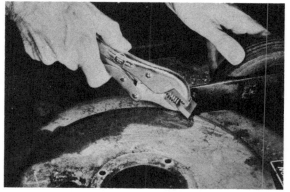

A handle for a scraper—or a cold chisel, or for punch and rivet sets or even campsite cookpans—is yours with a locking-jaw wrench. Above, a piece of tungsten carbide (of the type used for lathe bits) becomes a scraper for removing rust and old paint from a lawnmower housing

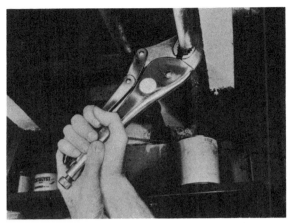

A locking wrench is handy for holding or turning pipe when clearance is limited. The jaws of this 12-in. lever-jaw wrench can be controlled to produce a ratchet action, making it unnecessary to release your grip at the end of a swing. A job like this one requires a wrench with curved jaws

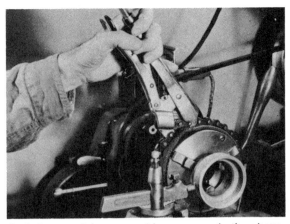

A chain wrench has several bonus uses. In the above photo, it grips (with a pad of belting) a lathe chuck to serve as a lever for a slotting operation. The slot, extending 115 deg. around the sleeve, is made by feeding in the cutoff tool after each forward-and-back swing made by the chuck

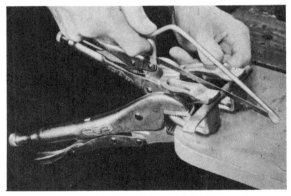

Multiple clamping is best for special jobs, such as the hacksawing setup shown here, or critical filing. Two regular wrenches anchor the welding clamp to a solid surface, for gripping both sides of the cut, limiting vibration and keeping the pieces from falling after the cut is made

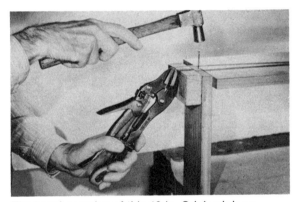

The levering action of this 10-in. GripLock is especially handy for pulling a steel strap taut when you're reinforcing a nailed corner of a box frame. The wood block acts as a fulcrum, and the pre-started nail is driven into the end grain in order to anchor the strap as the wrench is pressed

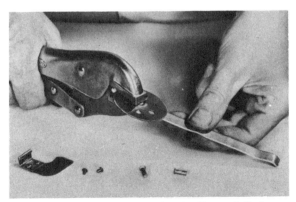

Rivet squeezing is possible with the "ton grip" of larger wrenches. Small, soft rivets can be set with a single squeeze, though the larger, harder ones may require several partial bites, as shown here. The jaws can be easily adjusted to limit the extent of the squeeze to avoid marring

Don't forget the versatility of all types of toggle tools. Using the type of bracket shown above as a template for spotting matching holes in an iron pipe is simple with a chain clamp. It leaves both hands free, and the clamp prevents slipping—something almost no other method can do

Be your own home plumber

BY W. CLYDE LAMMEY

Do-it-yourself plumbing is definitely limited
by your ability and your local code. But there
are some simpler jobs you won't need to
bother your local plumber with when he's busy

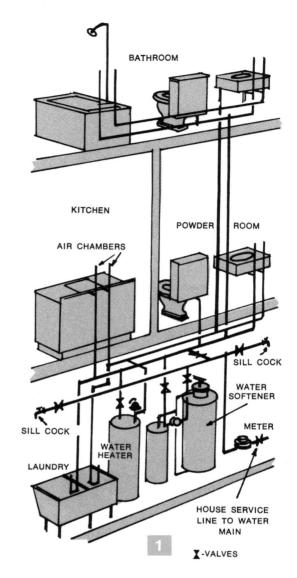

■ IN CASE YOU don't already know it inside out, it won't take you long to get acquainted with the plumbing system in your home.

If your home has a basement, much of the system will be in the open in the basement, beginning at the shutoff valve which is in the house service line between the meter and the water main out in the street. This service line may come up through the floor or in through the basement wall and the valve will be located just inside the wall or a few inches above the floor. Closing this valve shuts off water pressure to all plumbing fixtures in the house.

In common installations there will be a line through the meter rising to a main pipe line across the basement terminating in sill cocks located outside the walls at the front and back of the house. There will be valves in this line just inside the walls so that you can shut off the water to the cocks in freezing weather. There will be drain fittings in these valves; the drain fittings permit you to drain water from that portion of the line between the valves and the sill cocks outside the wall. You open the cocks, then open the drain valves.

From this line you'll see hot and cold-water lines leading to the kitchen sink, the bathroom or bathrooms, the powder room if you have this luxury, also to the softener, water heater and laundry tubs. There will be shutoff valves in these lines so that you can shut off the water to the heater, the softener and also to any part of the system having vertical runs of piping to a second-floor installation such as a bathroom.

Most of this portion of the installation will be

visible at the basement ceiling as the lines will run either between the joists or just below them. The vertical lines are usually run up through inside walls to the fixtures on the first and second floors. If the basement is ceiled, then the horizontal lines, if below the joists, will be housed in soffits. There will be, or should be, access openings in the soffits through which piping and valves can be easily reached.

Fig. 1 shows how the water-supply system is usually arranged in homes with basements. Of course, there will be variations from the arrangement shown. In homes without basements, either crawl-space or concrete-slab type, architects and plumbers strive to locate the plumbing centrally with short branch lines in the walls leading to the fixtures.

The *drainage system,* Fig. 2, is something else. Here, where it's visible, you'll see rough cast-

DATA ON STANDARD WEIGHT WROUGHT IRON AND STEEL PIPE FROM ⅛" TO 2½"; FURNISHED IN RANDOM LENGTHS UP TO 22 FT. (All Dimensions in Inches)						
Nominal Size	Outside Diameter	Inside Diameter	Wall Thickness	No. of Threads Per In.	Length of Effective Threads	Normal Engagement For Tight Fit (W)
⅛	0.405	0.269	0.068	27	.2639	¼
¼	0.540	0.364	0.088	18	.4018	5/16
⅜	0.675	0.493	0.091	18	.4078	⅜
½	0.840	0.622	0.109	14	.5337	7/16
¾	1.050	0.824	0.113	14	.5457	½
1	1.315	1.049	0.133	11½	.6828	9/16
1¼	1.660	1.380	0.140	11½	.7068	9/16
1½	1.900	1.610	0.145	11½	.7235	9/16
2	2.375	2.067	0.154	11½	.7565	⅝
2½	2.875	2.469	0.203	8	1.1375	⅞

3

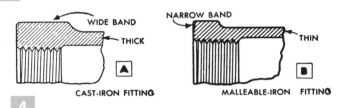

WIDE BAND — THICK — CAST-IRON FITTING **A**

NARROW BAND — THIN — MALLEABLE-IRON FITTING **B**

4

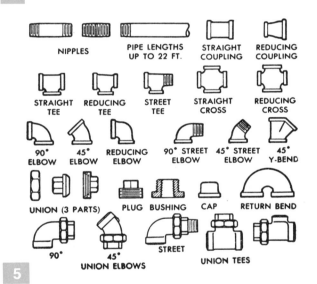

NIPPLES PIPE LENGTHS UP TO 22 FT. STRAIGHT COUPLING REDUCING COUPLING

STRAIGHT TEE REDUCING TEE STREET TEE STRAIGHT CROSS REDUCING CROSS

90° ELBOW 45° ELBOW REDUCING ELBOW 90° STREET ELBOW 45° STREET ELBOW 45° Y-BEND

UNION (3 PARTS) PLUG BUSHING CAP RETURN BEND

90° 45° UNION ELBOWS STREET UNION TEES

5

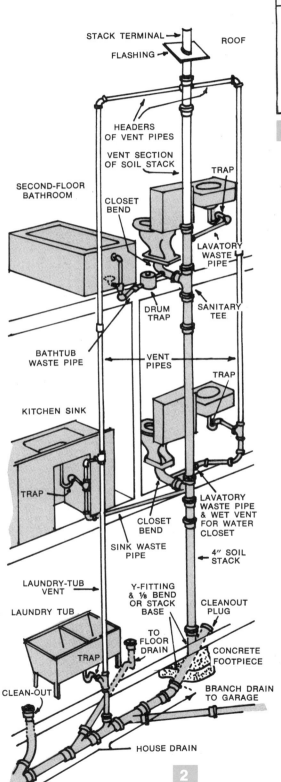

STACK TERMINAL ROOF
FLASHING
HEADERS OF VENT PIPES
VENT SECTION OF SOIL STACK
SECOND-FLOOR BATHROOM
CLOSET BEND
TRAP
LAVATORY WASTE PIPE
DRUM TRAP
SANITARY TEE
BATHTUB WASTE PIPE
VENT PIPES
TRAP
KITCHEN SINK
LAVATORY WASTE PIPE & WET VENT FOR WATER CLOSET
TRAP
CLOSET BEND
SINK WASTE PIPE
4" SOIL STACK
LAUNDRY-TUB VENT
Y-FITTING & ⅛ BEND OR STACK BASE
CLEANOUT PLUG
LAUNDRY TUB
TO FLOOR DRAIN
CONCRETE FOOTPIECE
TRAP
BRANCH DRAIN TO GARAGE
CLEAN-OUT
HOUSE DRAIN

2

DIMENSIONS OF K, L AND M-TYPES COPPER TUBING FROM ⅜" TO 2"							
Nominal Size	Outside Diameter	Inside Diameter			Wall Thickness		
	Types K-L-M	Type K	Type L	Type M	Type K	Type L	Type M
⅜	.500	.402	.430		.049	.035	
½	.625	.527	.545		.049	.040	
⅝	.750	.652	.666		.049	.042	
¾	.875	.745	.785		.065	.045	
1	1.125	.995	1.025		.065	.050	
1¼	1.375	1245	1265	1291	.065	.055	.042
1½	1.625	1481	1505	1527	.072	.060	.049
2	2.125	1959	1985	2009	.083	.070	.058

(All Dimensions in Inches)

6

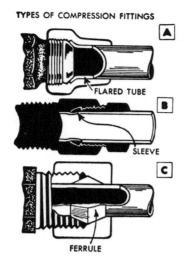

TYPES OF COMPRESSION FITTINGS

A — FLARED TUBE

B — SLEEVE

C — FERRULE

7

COUPLING NUT CAP PLUG

90° ELBOW 90° ELBOW 45° ELBOW

REDUCING TEE REDUCER TEE

10

DRAINAGE FITTING

RECESSED — SURFACES FLUSH

ORDINARY FITTING

RESTRICTING SHOULDER

8

LEAD PIPE FOR VENT AND DRAINAGE LINES			
I.D. (In.)	Wall Thickness (In.)		
1¼	.118	139	171
1½	.138	165	191
2	.142	177	205
2½, 3, 4, 5, 6	.125		250

11

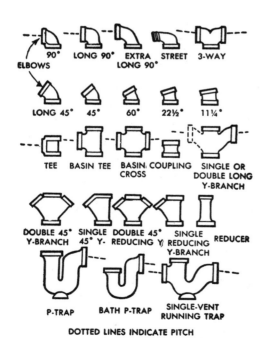

ELBOWS
90° LONG 90° EXTRA LONG 90° STREET 3-WAY

LONG 45° 45° 60° 22½° 11¼°

TEE BASIN TEE BASIN CROSS COUPLING SINGLE OR DOUBLE LONG Y-BRANCH

DOUBLE 45° Y-BRANCH SINGLE 45° Y- DOUBLE 45° REDUCING Y SINGLE REDUCING Y-BRANCH REDUCER

P-TRAP BATH P-TRAP SINGLE-VENT RUNNING TRAP

DOTTED LINES INDICATE PITCH

9

12

CAST-IRON, HUB AND SPIGOT SOIL PIPE

BEAD

BARREL D HUB

C A (SIZE) B E

SPIGOT END

5-FT. LAYING LENGTH

C

DETAIL OF JOINT PACKED WITH OAKUM, HEMP OR ASBESTOS ROPE LEAD GROOVE LEAD CALKING (1" DEEP)

13

1936

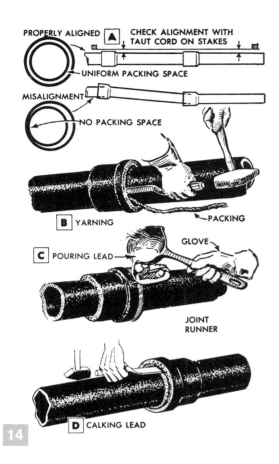

PROPERLY ALIGNED **A** CHECK ALIGNMENT WITH TAUT CORD ON STAKES

UNIFORM PACKING SPACE

MISALIGNMENT

NO PACKING SPACE

B YARNING

C POURING LEAD

GLOVE

JOINT RUNNER

PACKING

D CALKING LEAD

14

iron soil pipe with big, bulgy joints which have been deftly leaded by the plumber and if you look about sharply you'll see a number of openings here and there, each closed with huge brass plugs having square bosses that take a man-sized wrench. The whole arrangement, what you can see of it, is purely utilitarian and definitely unlovely even if painted.

This system is vented to the outside. You will see at least one and maybe two vents sticking from the roof somewhere. Fig. 2 shows how a typical drainage system is commonly vented to one roof vent. Of course, there are variations.

Notice that each fixture is trapped. The water closets form their own traps; the bathtub is fitted with a drum trap and other fixtures with P-traps. Each trap (except the closet trap) retains a portion of the waste, thus preventing sewer gas from entering the house. In many homes most of this system is invisible except perhaps in the basement. Here many home-owners often go to some length to conceal the whole thing by building extra-thick walls, cabinets or storage shelves facing two ways, or maybe just a free-standing screen or rolling wall (or walls) that suit their fancy.

Should you become obsessed with this notion be sure—but be *sure*—you provide access openings enabling you or your plumber to reach all essential elements such as valves and cleanouts, or better still, provide a door or removable panel that exposes the whole installation.

"So," you say, "it's quite simple. I can repair and maintain this whole system and save money."

Oh no, you can't! There are some jobs you're going to have to reserve for your plumber. Reason is you just don't have the equipment to handle the really tough ones, even if you knew how. The stuff and things your plumber brings along for a major repair or replacement job are expensive. It's usually cheaper to hire him.

things you can do

Sure, you can replace faucet washers, even the faucet itself if necessary. All you need are the fixings, an adjustable wrench and the screwdriver every household should have at hand. And you can easily replace the toilet-tank ball or the float or even the valve should it be necessary.

And with the simple, inexpensive cleaner-outers available from your hardware store you can generally dislodge most soapy, greasy deposits that may in time clog the kitchen-sink or lavatory drains or perhaps the house drain. With a more comprehensive kit of tools and using stock sizes and lengths of pipe and fittings you might even make bold to do the plumbing in that new addition you're thinking about building all by yourself. But take care to follow your local plumbing codes and have your work inspected and okayed when it's finished.

But when masses of tree roots sneak into the house drain out somewhere near the curb, or when some obstruction clogs a drain line and refuses to budge or when something else about the system goes blam! for which you have no knowledge, tools or remedy handy, then you're going to need your plumber—but quick!

Properly installed, plumbing is pretty durable. Much of it lasts as long as the house. Major repairs or replacements are relatively rare so maybe you would just as soon figure the odds being mostly in your favor and rely on your plumber when something more than a leaky faucet needs fixing. Watching a craftsman who knows his trade is never uninteresting so perhaps you would like to hang around when your plumber comes in answer to your call, just to see what he does, how he cuts and fits pipe, joins this to that, how he handles his tools and so on.

And if you would like to know more about

TYPES OF HUB AND SPIGOT FITTINGS

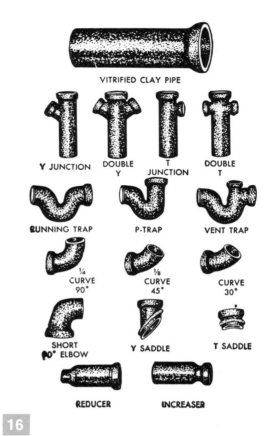

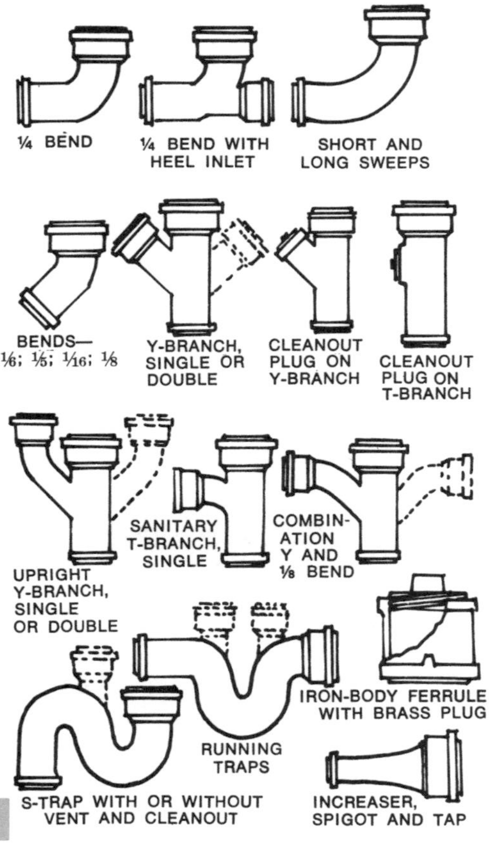

¼ BEND — ¼ BEND WITH HEEL INLET — SHORT AND LONG SWEEPS

BENDS— ⅙; ⅕; 1/16; ⅛ — Y-BRANCH, SINGLE OR DOUBLE — CLEANOUT PLUG ON Y-BRANCH — CLEANOUT PLUG ON T-BRANCH

UPRIGHT Y-BRANCH, SINGLE OR DOUBLE — SANITARY T-BRANCH, SINGLE — COMBINATION Y AND ⅛ BEND

S-TRAP WITH OR WITHOUT VENT AND CLEANOUT — RUNNING TRAPS — IRON-BODY FERRULE WITH BRASS PLUG — INCREASER, SPIGOT AND TAP

15

VITRIFIED CLAY PIPE

Y JUNCTION — DOUBLE Y — T JUNCTION — DOUBLE T

RUNNING TRAP — P-TRAP — VENT TRAP

¼ CURVE 90° — ⅛ CURVE 45° — CURVE 30°

SHORT 90° ELBOW — Y SADDLE — T SADDLE

REDUCER — INCREASER

16

what he may bring along in the way of pipe, fittings and such to do the job, then study Figs. 3 through 21 which detail and name most of the common plumbing fittings, kinds of fittings and piping, including the newer asbestos-cement pipe and bituminous fiber pipe. Fig. 21 shows the methods and procedures in installation and pictures the fasteners and hangers in common use.

After a bit of close study you'll be able to name fittings and other items when you see them (without looking at the book). You'll be pretty sure of yourself when it comes to procedures in joining simple pipe runs. And you may come to know how to handle the common tools of the trade. In that event, you might become your own plumber, take a measure of pride in your skills and do at least *some* of the more advanced jobs all by yourself.

Pipe made from other materials is gradually taking the place of the old reliable cast iron, steel and malleable pipe and fittings. Copper piping is now widely used in home and commercial construction where local codes permit. Many plumbers like plastic pipe because of its ease of han-

dling, cutting and installing and its resistance to damage by freezing. There are three types of plastic pipe—rigid, semirigid and flexible—and some types are suitable for hot-water lines.

There's also concrete pipe, asbestos-cement pipe and a bituminized-fiber pipe, all of which are intended for use as soil pipes. The latter two are rated the most durable. Vitrified-clay pipe comes with an extremely hard, glossy surface that is not affected by acids, alkalies or solvents. It is often used as a flue lining in gas-heating installations as well as in plumbing. It comes in two grades, standard and extra-strength.

Fig. 14, details B, C and D, show how a plumber yarns, leads and caulks a cast-iron pipe joint. Joints in concrete and vitrified-clay pipe are usually sealed with portland-cement mortar. These can be connected to cast-iron soil pipe by use of a special fitting. Asbestos and bituminized pipe are joined with fittings employing rubber rings and machined tapers which make a tight, rootproof and waterproof joint.

See also: bathrooms; drains; faucets; kitchens; septic systems.

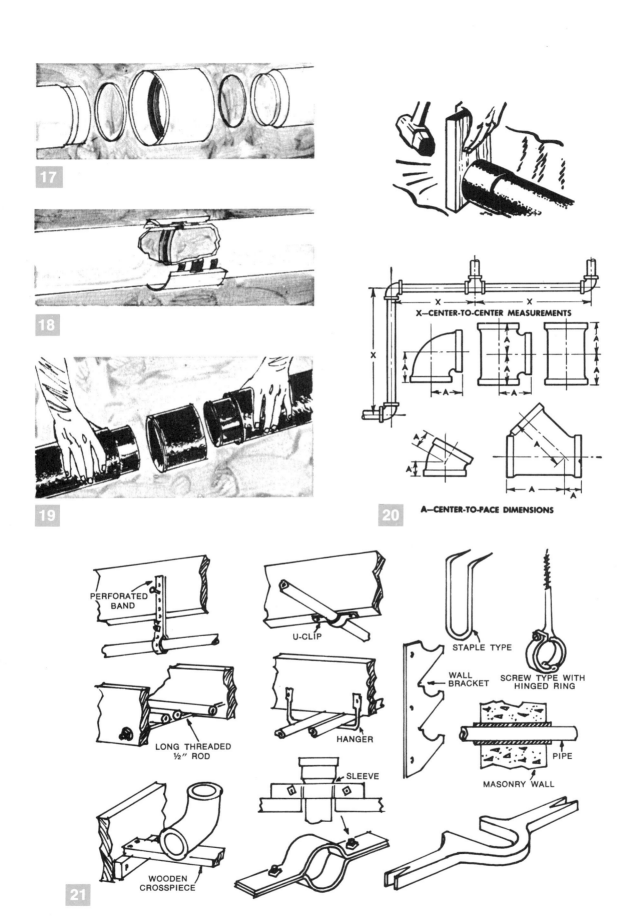

17

18

19

20

X—CENTER-TO-CENTER MEASUREMENTS

A—CENTER-TO-FACE DIMENSIONS

21

PERFORATED BAND

U-CLIP

STAPLE TYPE

SCREW TYPE WITH HINGED RING

WALL BRACKET

LONG THREADED ½″ ROD

HANGER

PIPE

MASONRY WALL

WOODEN CROSSPIECE

SLEEVE

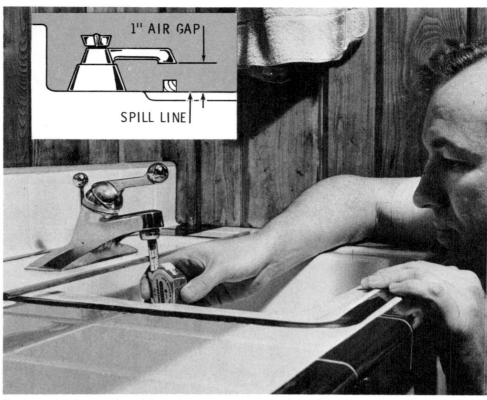

To measure air gap at a sink or lavatory, place a straightedge across the top of the bowl and check the space below the faucet. Minimum safe gap is shown in the drawing

Is your plumbing double-crossing you?

BY RICHARD DAY

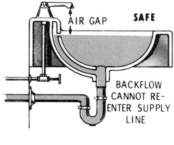

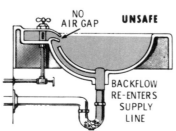

ONE BRIGHT MORNING, a suburbanite on the West Coast was spraying his lawn with an arsenic weed killer from a bottle attached to a sprayer on his garden hose. When he was through, the man disconnected the hose and took a drink of water from the tap. He died of arsenic poisoning within hours.

This man was double-crossed by his home plumbing. His death was caused by what experts call a cross-connection between the potable water inside the house and the arsenic-laced water in the sprayer. A temporary, unnoticed reverse flow drew arsenic into the house piping.

A cross-connection is any arrangement whereby water that is either unfit to drink or of questionable potability can contaminate the household supply.

A coat of yellow paint on all pipes in your home which carry nonpotable boiler or cistern water will remind the plumber not to connect the pipes accidentally to those pipes that carry the household's drinking water

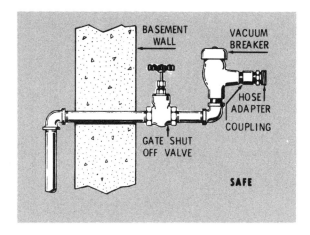

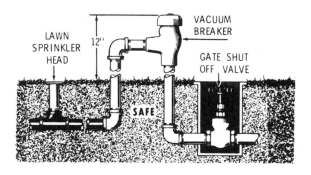

Lawn sprinklers and hose cocks can permit a backflow of water laden with fertilizers, weed killers and other poisons into the house water supply. This danger is easily avoided, however, by installing vacuum breakers. Drawings above show the safe and unsafe way to install underground sprinklers. Top drawing shows typical setup for hose cock. In most cases, breakers are installed on "off" side of the valve

The worst of it is that not one home in a thousand is equipped to prevent what happened to that hapless suburbanite. We Americans have developed a childish faith about our water's purity and we forget that it takes proper control and vigilance to keep our water pure.

Two simultaneous conditions are necessary to contaminate your house water: (1) the existence of a cross-connection at any time there is (2) a backflow of used water toward the potable water system. Backflow can be caused by *back-pressure* on the impure water that forces it into the house system. Or, its cause can be a vacuum in house water lines that draws in contaminated water like soda up a straw. This is call *back-siphonage.*

Back-pressure is not common in residential plumbing; back-siphonage is. It can occur whenever part of the city main has to be shut for repairs. And during a fire, water can be used so rapidly that a vacuum is created in the city mains. Open a faucet and, instead of water coming out, air rushes in. Another cause of back-siphonage

is improper sizing of your house pipes. In that case, turning on a large tap in the lower part of the house can drop the pressure in the risers.

Epidemics of cholera, typhoid fever, gastroenteritis and dysentery all have been traced to cross-connections in home plumbing systems. While the probability of a backflow taking place in a given home at a given time is very small, just one occurrence where contaminated water is present can be a catastrophe for the people

Hooked to a shower head, instead of a lavatory faucet, a shampoo rinse hose is high enough so that its nozzle can't cross-connect with the water in the bathtub. Hose is easy to install

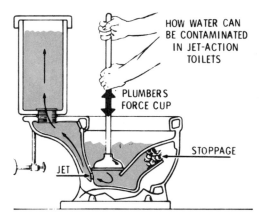

Plumber's friend can be your enemy. Plunging action of the tool can force contaminated water from the clogged bowl of siphon-jet type toilet upward into the flush tank, as the arrows show

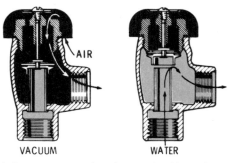

This is how a vacuum breaker works: Normal water pressure (shown at right) holds the plunger tight against the air inlet. Low pressure (shown at left) lets the plunger fall, admitting air

plumbing double-cross, continued

Here is a cutaway view of a toilet tank valve designed to prevent a backflow from the tank. Parts at the left admit air if a vacuum suddenly develops in the water supply line in the house

affected. And, most frightening of all, there is no warning. Sickness or death may be the only indication.

A manual published by the U.S. Public Health Service says that enteric infections caused by cross-connections may occur in almost any city on any day. In Newton, Kans., for a specific example, cross-connections let sewage from 10 families flow into a temporarily closed water main. As soon as water service was restored, an epidemic broke out in which 2500 people went through the miseries of enteric disorders.

The American Standard National Plumbing Code calls for measures that will eliminate *all possibilities* of cross-connections. However, this code is merely a recommendation. Many rural areas have no codes at all. Some cities that do have codes have not applied them to houses built before the dangers of cross-connection were recognized.

Another attack on the problem is to minimize

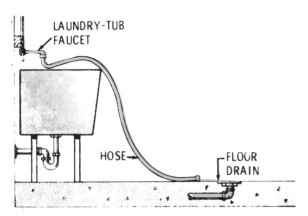

Hoses are a frequent cause of cross-connection. Shown here is how careless use of the hose permits backflow in the pipe to draw dirty water from around the floor drain in the laundry area

All faucets that are connected to cistern water or other nonpotable water supply should be clearly labeled to prevent mixups. And, of course, children should be warned of this water hazard

chances of backflow. In residental plumbing, the most common backflow-preventer is the air gap. An air gap is the distance that a faucet discharges above the highest possible level of water in a bowl, sink or tub. In most cases, this would be the faucet's distance above the bowl's rim. What the gap does is prevent siphon action from drawing water from the tub or sink into the fresh water.

An air gap should generally be twice the diameter of the faucet or pipe opening. Thus, for a lavatory, the tap should discharge at least 1 in. above the rim of the bowl. Air gaps for kitchen sinks and laundry tubs should be at least 1½ in. They should be at least 2 in. for bathtubs.

Where an air gap is not practical, as in sill-cock connections, a useful means of stopping back-siphonage is the *backflow preventer*. A number of types are made. Because each is designed for a particular application, selection and installation of these devices is a job for the plumber.

The most common backflow preventer in house plumbing is a *vacuum breaker*. This patented device has one or more valves that let air enter whenever water pressure drops below atmospheric pressure, breaking up siphonic action inside the pipes.

A vacuum breaker is ordinarily located a minimum of 6 in. above the highest level of water that might be backsiphoned. It is usually positioned on the discharge side of the faucet. Here, it is under pressure only when the faucet is turned on. Plumbers warn that an ordinary check-

valve is not acceptable as a backflow preventer, though there have been many attempts to use check-valves in this way.

Tour your house and grounds right now and look for cross-connections. Measure the air gaps on all your bathroom, kitchen and laundry fixtures to see that they meet the minimums. Many old fixtures have submerged inlets which discharge water below the fixture rim. A clogged drain in such a fixture creates a direct cross-connection between dirty and clean water. A closed faucet offers only partial protection in such situations since bacteria can pass through even the most minute, unobserved leak. So, if you have a fixture with a submerged inlet, replace it.

Check for other locations where a pipe or hose from the house water supply might have its outlet submerged in contaminated water. Inspect washing machines, dishwashers, aspirator sump pumps, float valves, floor-drain trap primers, airconditioning cooling towers and frostproof toilets. Look at outdoor pools, such as swimming pools, fish ponds and lily ponds. Provide air gaps for the water supply pipes at all such spots.

Underground lawn sprinkler systems *must* have vacuum breakers to keep water poisoned with fertilizers, weed killers and insecticides from being drawn into the house supply. The vacuum breaker should be at least 12 in. above the highest sprinkler head. Some municipal codes call for even higher placement of the breaker.

Avoid what one Southern homeowner did. Because his city water pressure wasn't high enough for his underground lawn sprinkler, he put in a booster pump to ram water from a nearby swamp through the sprinkler system.

Unfortunately, he left the sprinkler connected to the house plumbing. Disease-laden swamp water was forced into the fresh-water piping, contaminating his own and the neighborhood water supply for several blocks around. His family and a number of neighbors came down with dysentery. Had the homeowner applied for a permit before installing his pump, city officials would have alerted him to the danger.

check yard hoses

The common yard hose represents a subtle cross-connection that endangers nearly every home. If the nozzle end is submerged in dirty water, a cross-connection is created. In filling a wading pool, watering a tree or drawing a pail of water, a hose end is often submerged.

A length of hose attached to your laundry-tub faucet creates the same condition as a submerged inlet. So does a kitchen-sink rinse hose, if the end is left in the sink. A shampoo rinse attachment slipped over the bathtub or lavatory faucet is a cross-connection whenever the spray head is left in the bowl.

While it is possible to use a hose without creating a cross-connection, people often forget. Therefore, the U.S. Public Health Service says that every faucet to which a hose will be attached should be equipped with a vacuum breaker. Then there's no need to worry about whether you've unhooked a hose after using it.

Another cross-connection exists inside most toilet tanks. To prevent noisy splashing while filling, the toilet-tank water supply tube empties near the bottom of the tank. Thus it is submerged at all times. Because the water in a toilet tank ordinarily is not contaminated, this common cross-connection is often taken lightly. However, in jet action toilets it is possible for tank water to become contaminated when a plumber's force cup is used to unclog a blocked-up bowl. The powerful plunging action in the bowl can force contaminated water back through its jet, up past the tank valve and into the tank. Then if a back-flow from the toilet tank takes place, house drinking water can be contaminated.

Because there are a lot of "ifs" to toilet-tank cross-connections, many plumbers think they represent a relatively minor danger. For that reason, not all fixture manufacturers have made their toilet tanks fail-safe. Public health authorities advise that tanks should have antisiphon ballcock water supply valves. Part of this device sticks up out of the tank water and contains ports for air to enter in case of back-siphonage.

The new low-tank toilets all should be equipped with vacuum-breaker water supply valves. Their integral water storage tanks are partly below the bowl's rim. In event of a bowl stoppage, contaminated water can flow by gravity from the full bowl into the near-empty tank.

some need special protection

Homes with water or steam boilers need special cross-connection protection. Otherwise boiler chemicals can be back-siphoned through the boiler intake pipe into the house plumbing. Usually the installation of a double-check double-gate valve type of backflow-preventer at the boiler water intake does the job. This unit has multiple drain cocks for periodic tests of its effectiveness.

Homes using nonpotable cistern water at some faucets have special cross-connection problems. Separate water systems containing pure and impure water should never be piped into each other, even with a valve between. Valves too often leak or are left open by mistake. Neither should impure cistern water and potable water be piped into a combination mixer faucet. Instead, the two water systems should have separate faucets.

A faucet serving nonpotable water should be clearly labeled to prevent accidentally drinking from it. Also, pipes carrying nonpotable water should be painted yellow to prevent accidental connection to fresh-water pipes.

Owners of farm homes should look for cross-connections between house plumbing and watering tanks, cleaning tanks, cooling tanks, slop tubs, livestock watering systems, water storage tanks and auxiliary nonpotable water pumping systems.

If your home plumbing inspection tour turns up anything that looks like a cross-connection, call a plumber. Have him check it and recommend corrective measures. While the danger from some cross-connections may seem remote, the possibility is still there. As the U.S. Public Health Service says, *any* chance with your family's health or your community's health is too much to take. Before you realize what's happened, it may be too late.

To conceal the cord from a wall-mounted clock, drill a ⅜-in. hole about 2 in. below the support hanger and drop a length of furnace chain down inside the wall. Remove a knockout from the outlet box, catch the end of the chain with a paper-clip hook, and then use it to lead the cord through a hole drilled in the cover plate and up inside the wall to the hole. (Lamp cords inside walls are not approved by some electrical codes. Check your local code.)

Next time your wife asks you to hold a skein of knitting yarn while she rolls it in a ball, show her how a couple of clip-type clothespins and a wastebasket will do nicely in your sudden absence. All she need do is clip the pins to the rim of the basket, spacing them to suit the length of the skein, and loop the latter around the upright pins. This temporary arrangement is a good substitute for your outstretched arms.

Frozen sink drains in vacation cabins and second homes can be prevented by soldering a pet cock to the trap. When closing the premises merely drain the trap, close the pet cock and the sink will be ready for use. If sewer gas is a problem, pour a pint of kerosene or antifreeze into the trap after draining.

Painting a picture frame always brings up the problem of finding a place to hold the frame while making those last few strokes with the brush. The next time you finish a frame, try tacking a thin strip such as wood lath across the back. You'll find that the whole job will go faster. When the frame is dry the strip can be removed easily.

1945

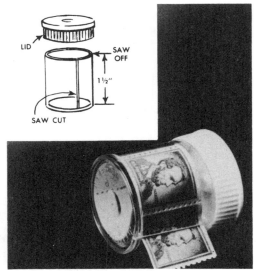

Postage-stamp holders can easily be made from discarded plastic pill containers. Choose a pill container about 1⅜ in. in diameter and saw it off to a height of about 1½ in. Using a thin-bladed fine-toothed hacksaw, cut a slot the length of the container. Smooth the rough edges with a knife. Then roll the stamps up, insert them in the bottle with the end sticking out through the slot, and snap the lid back on the container.

Two-o'clock feedings will be a lot easier if you fill a Thermos with boiling water before retiring. Just a brief trip to the refrigerator to pick up the bottle and you can begin changing the baby while the bottle is warming in a container of hot water nearby. You can empty the container in the morning and return it to the nightstand for use the next night. Eliminating the time it takes to heat the water makes this late-night trip much shorter.

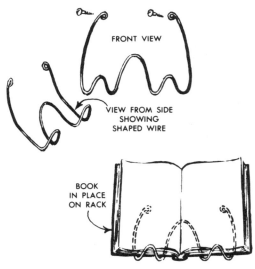

Is your alarm clock broken? You have a very accurate emergency alarm clock right in your kitchen if the stove has an automatic time outlet. Plug a table radio into this outlet, tune it to your favorite station and set the volume so that it can be heard in your bedroom. Finally set the automatic timer for the time you wish to arise. Make sure the station that you tune to will be broadcasting by the time you want to get up.

This kitchen book rack which will hold a recipe book open to the right page is easy to make from a wire coat hanger. Straighten the hanger and cut it to a length of about 31 in. Bend a small loop in each end with pliers, and then shape it as shown above. Mount the rack on a wall or inside a cupboard door. This rack prevents the pages of your wife's favorite cookbooks from being ruined by sticky fingers while baking.

The nail size is determined by the thickness of the plywood. Used with glue, the nails shown will produce strong joints. For a heavier nail, use casing nails

All about plywood

BY RICHARD NUNN

Here's what you need to know to purchase it, work with it in your shop and finish it

PLYWOOD, IN BIG LAMINATED sheets that nearly every lumberyard in the nation sells, is one of the most versatile materials on the market today. With it you can build houses, boats, airplanes, cabinets, furniture and toys. Added to this versatility is the material's easy workability. And it is relatively inexpensive.

Historically, plywood dates back to 1500 years before Christ. Egyptian artisans fashioned the first veneered furniture, and other ancient peoples advanced the art of veneering—and making plywood. With the development of tough adhesives and new manufacturing techniques, plywood has become one of the world's most standard and staple building products.

There are two basic types of plywood: hardwood-faced and softwood-faced. You probably will work mostly with softwood-faced plywood, although many hardwood-faced plywoods are available in veneers ranging from ash to zebrawood.

Hardwood-faced plywood is graded differently than the softwood products. Custom grade (No. 1) is free of knots, patches and plugs. Good grade (No. 2) has a tight, smoothly cut veneer; the joints are evenly matched so the grain runs true. Sound grade (No. 3) doesn't have open defects; the veneer may not be matched, and it might have mineral streaks and stains. Utility grade (No. 4) has discolorations. Reject grade (No. 5) can have knotholes up to 2-in. in diameter and ½ in. splits. (This information has been oversimplified.) Most any grade combination of face and back veneers in the standard grades can be purchased. The combinations include 1-1, 1-4, 1-2, 1-3, 2-4 and 2-3.

The hardwood-faced panels come in three types of bonds: waterproof, water-resistant and dry. The use, of course, determines which type to specify: waterproof for exterior; water-resistant where the material won't be constantly ex-

Use flathead wood screws where the nails will not provide adequate holding power. If possible, use glue also. Use longer screws when the work permits

The good face of the plywood should be up when sawing with a radial or table saw. Use a sharp combination blade or a fine-tooth blade without much set

posed to the elements; and dry bond where the panels won't be exposed to water, dampness or high humidity.

The panels are made with three different types of cores: veneer, lumber and particleboard. Veneer cores have a series of laminated veneers, alternating at right angles to each other. Lumber core also has a series of laminated veneers, but the center core is solid wood strips that are edge-glued together. This material is used basically for furniture, built-ins, etc. Particleboard cores are made up of resin-coated wood particles with top layers of hardwood veneer. The panels are lightweight and can be worked with regular hand and power tools.

Most of the plywood used in this country for light construction is termed "softwood plywood." It is classified by species, type and grade. For example, Group 1 in the classification of species includes Douglas fir, western larch, southern pine, loblolly and longleaf pine. Group 2 includes Douglas fir, western hemlock, Sitka spruce. There are some 30 different species of woods which are classified into four groups in the Product Standard PS 1-66.

The panels are manufactured in two types. Exterior type has a 100-percent waterproof glue while interior type has a highly moisture-resistant glue. The veneers in the backs and inner plys of the exterior type are a higher grade than those of the interior type. Exterior grade panels may be used for boats, farm structures, siding and other applications where the material will be exposed

to constant wetting, drying, soaking or other moisture conditions, including those involving constant high humidity. Interior grade plywood is recommended for use where the material will not be exposed to moisture or continuing high humidity, such as paneling, indoor furniture, wall sheathing, roof decks and other structural applications.

Plywood produced by mills belonging to the American Plywood Association is in strict accordance with government standards. APA has registered certain grade-trademarks which are used by the member-manufacturers. Within each type there is a variety of appearance, generally determined by the grade of veneer used on the face and back of the panel. The grades are N, A, B, C, C-plugged and D.

N-grade is a special order "natural finish" veneer. It is select all heartwood or all sapwood. It is free of open defects, but allows some repairs.

A-grade is smooth and paintable. Neatly made repairs in the veneer are permissible. The panels may be used for a natural finish in less demanding applications.

B-grade has a solid surface veneer. Circular repair plugs and tight knots are permitted.

C-grade has knotholes up to 1-in. Occasional knotholes ½ in. larger are permitted providing the total width of all knots and knotholes within a specified section doesn't exceed certain limits. Limited splits are permitted; minimum veneer is permitted in exterior-type plywood.

With a portable power saw, turn the good face down. Scraps of lumber tacked to the sawhorses let you saw right through it without damaging the horse

To hide edges of the panels, a thin strip of real wood edge-banding is available. The strips are coated with pressure-sensitive adhesive; simply peel, stick

C-plugged has improved C-veneer with splits limited to ⅛ in. in width and knotholes and borer holes limited to ¼ x ½ in.

D-grade permits knots and knotholes to 2½ in. in width and ½ in. larger under certain specified limits. Limited splits are permitted.

interior grade use-guide

What grade and type of plywood you buy depends, of course, on the project at hand. Below is a guide to interior appearance grades:

A-A INT-DFPA: Both faces are the highest standard veneer grade for use where both sides will show: built-ins, cabinets, furniture, partitions, etc. The most common thicknesses are: ¼ in., ⅜ in., ½ in., ⅝ in., ¾ in. and 1 in. The veneer grade is A face, A back and D-grade inner plys.

A-B INT-DFPA: This panel is similar to A-A, but it is used where the appearance of one side is less important, and two smooth solid surfaces are desirable. Thicknesses are the same.

A-D INT-DFPA: Used for built-ins, paneling, shelving, partitions, etc., where only one side will show. Thicknesses are standard, with D inner plys.

B-B INT-DFPA: An interior utility panel for use as partitions, utility built-ins, mounting boards, etc. Both sides are smooth and may be painted. Thicknesses are standard, with D inner plys.

B-D INT-DFPA: For use where one smooth side is needed. Shelving, sides and backs for built-ins, economy cabinet work, slip sheets, separator boards and bins. Standard thickness; inner plys, D.

DECORATIVE PANELS: This material is rough sawn, brushed, grooved, striated or embossed on one side. Use it for accent walls, paneling, counter fronts and where wood with various surface textures is desired. The most common thicknesses are ⁵⁄₁₆ in., ⅜ in., and ½ in. Veneer grade is C or better face, plys, D back and D inner.

PLYRON: These panels have a hardboard face and back and are used for built-ins, cabinet doors, countertops, worktables and furniture. The faces may be tempered, untempered, smooth or screened hardboard. The most common thicknesses are ½ in., ⅝ in. and ¾ in., with C and D inner plys.

N-N INT-DFPA: A natural finish cabinet-quality panel, designed to be used where both sides will show. Both sides are select all heartwood or all sapwood veneer. Typical uses are for cabinet doors, built-ins and furniture having a natural finish. The panels are usually a special order item. In thicknesses of ¾ in. only with C inner plys.

N-A and N-B INT-DFPA: This is similar to the grade listed above, but it permits an A or B-grade veneer on the backside. The panel is designed for economy when building cabinet doors, built-ins, furniture. It is a special-order item in ¾-in. thickness only with C inner plys.

N-D INT-DFPA: One side is select all heart-

1949

Where nails must be very close to the edge, predrill the nail holes. The drill you use should be slightly smaller in diameter than the nails you'll use

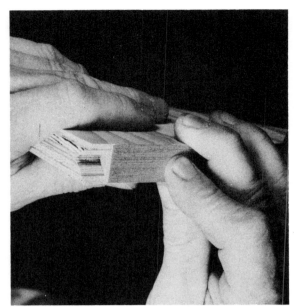

Another edge treatment is achieved by cutting a V-groove in the edge of the material and inserting a matching wood strip. However, this takes skill

all about plywood, continued

Always apply clamps with the full-jaw length in contact with the wood. When the jaws are not parallel, as shown at the right, the pressure is applied to only part of the joint, making it weak

wood or all sapwood veneer. Use it for interior paneling that will have a natural finish. Usually a special order item in ¼-in. thickness only with D inner plys.

UNDERLAYMENT INT-DFPA: For underlayment or combination subfloor-underlayment under resilient floor coverings. Ply beneath the face is C or better veneer; it is sanded or touch sanded as specified. Most common thicknesses: ¼, ⅜, ½, ⅝ and ¾ in.

2-4-1 INT-DFPA: A combination subfloor-underlayment panel for use with supports on 4-ft. centers. The panels provide a good base for direct application of resilient flooring. Available square-edged or tongue-and-grooved two or four sides as specified. Thickness: 1⅛ in. only; D back and other inner plys.

A-A EXT-DFPA: Designed for exposed applications where both sides will show: fences, windscreens, exterior cabinets and built-ins, boats, etc. The most common thicknesses are: ¼, ⅜, ½, ⅝, ¾ and 1 in. Panels have an A face and back with C inner plys.

A-B EXT-DFPA: Similar uses to A-A EXT, but where the appearance of one side is less important. The thicknesses are the same with C inner plys.

MDO EXT-DFPA: A medium-density overlaid plywood panel with opaque resin-impregnated fiber overlay, heat-fused to one or both panel faces. It provides an ideal base for paint.

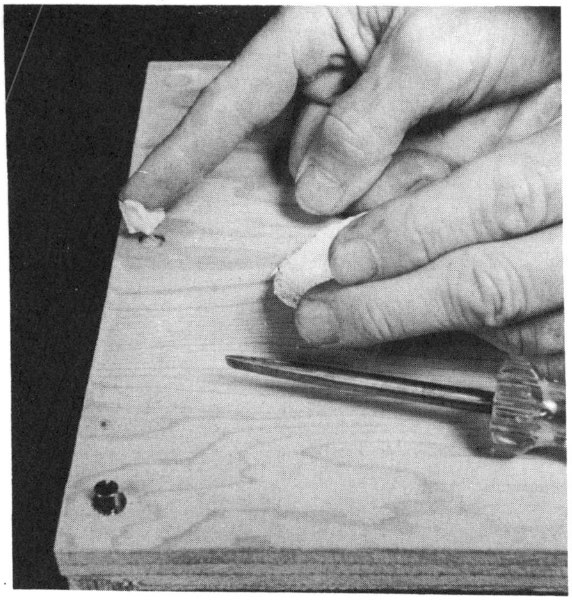

When screws or nails are countersunk, fill the holes with wood plastic or water-mixed wood putty. Sand the surface level when dry. Prime before finishing

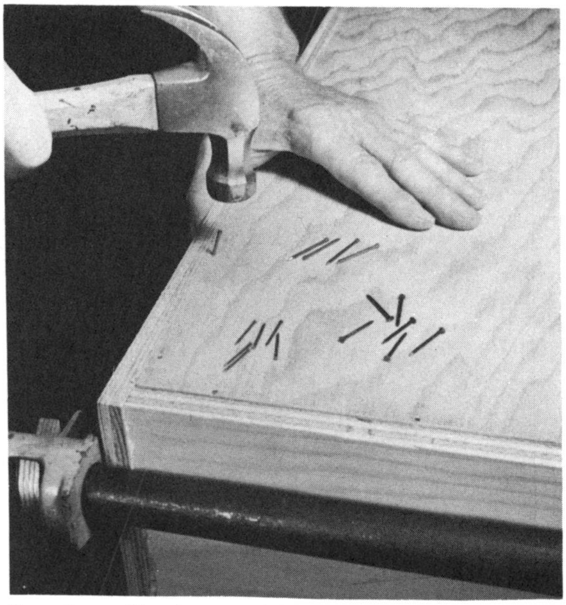

If you're nailing into a rabbet, such as a cabinet back, drive the nails at a slight angle. Brads or finish nails should be used for the best results

Uses include siding, soffits, windscreens, exterior painted cabinet work, etc. Thicknesses: 5⁄16, ⅜, ½, ⅝, ¾ and 1 in. Veneer grade is B face, B or C back, C or C-plugged inner plys.

TEXTURE 1–11: The unsanded panels have parallel grooves ¼ in. deep, ⅜ in. wide on 2-in. or 4-in. centers. The edges are shiplapped for a continuous visual pattern. Uses include siding, accent paneling, fences, etc. It is available in 8 and 10-ft. lengths and sanded or with MD overlay. Thicknesses: ⅝ in. only; C or better face, C back and inner plys.

303 SPECIALTY SIDING EXT-DFPA: The grade covers proprietary plywood products for siding, fencing, soffits, windscreens and other exterior applications or interior panels. The panels have special surface treatments which include rough-sawn, striated and brushed, and may be V-grooved, channel-grooved, etc. It is available in redwood, cedar, hemlock, Douglas fir, lauan and other woods. The most common thicknesses are ⅜, ½ and ⅝ in. The veneer grade is B or better face, C back and plys.

PLYRPN EXT-DFPA: The panels are surfaced on both sides with tempered hardboard with smooth or screened surfaces. Thicknesses are ½, ⅝ and ¾ in. The panels have C inner plys.

MARINE EXT-DFPA and SPECIAL EXTERIOR DFPA: Marine-grade panels are made only with Douglas fir or western larch, and a special solid joined core construction. The panels are subject to special limitations on core gaps and the number of face repairs. Use them for boat hulls. The panels are also available with overlaid faces. Exterior is a premium panel similar to the marine grade but permits any species covered under PS 1–66. The most common thicknesses are ¼, ⅜, ½, ⅝, ¾ and 1 in. The veneer grade has an A or B face and back with B inner plys.

C-C PLUGGED EXT-DFPA: For exterior underlayment, these panels are also ideal for tile backing where a permanently waterproof material is needed. The panels are sanded or touch sanded as specified. The most common thicknesses are ¼, ⅜, ½, ⅝, ¾ and ⅞ in. The veneer grade is C (plugged) face, C back and inner plys.

The types and grades mentioned above are available in 4 x 8-ft. panel. However, other lengths and widths are manufactured. Generally, larger sizes can be ordered by your lumber dealer.

Many lumber dealers have "plywood bins" in which random-size pieces and trimmings are available. Many dealers also will cut a panel for you in multiples of 2 ft. When buying plywood, it is often to your advantage to preplan the project at hand so the amount of material needed can be purchased at one time. Costs can be cut with quantity, and any irregular sizes can be picked out of the plywood bins—another saving.

Plywood panels are easy to work with, al-

Laminated-plastic surfacing materials can be used for edges of tables. Use contact cement to stick on the laminated plastic. Coat the edge and material

though there are several tips that will make the job even easier:

1. To prevent waste, lay out the panel for cutting. If there will be many pieces cut from a single panel, sketch the arrangement on a piece of paper before you transfer it to the panel as a cutting pattern. Allow for the saw kerf between the pieces. Have the grain of the panel running the long way of the piece, if possible.

2. If you use a handsaw, cut the panel with the best face up. Use a saw with 10 to 15 points to the inch and support the panel on sawhorses so it won't sag. Always use a sharp saw.

3. For power sawing on a table saw, cut with the good face of the panel up. Use a sharp combination blade or fine-tooth blade without too much set. The blade should be set so it protrudes above the panel about the height of the teeth.

4. With a portable power saw, place the good face of the panel down.

5. When planing edges, work from both ends of the edge toward the center of the panel. This will prevent splitting out the plys at the end of the cut. Always use a plane with a sharp blade and set it to take a fine shaving. Work slowly.

6. Since plywood is sanded smooth at the time it is made, sanding it before a sealer or prime coat of finish should be confined to the edges. After the surface is sealed, however, you may sand in the direction of the grain only.

7. It is difficult to nail or screw into the edges of veneer-core plywood. Plan your work so you can avoid these problems.

Plywood panels can be bent to certain minimum radii depending, of course, on the thickness of the panel. In some applications you may have to bend two thin panels to build up a particular thickness. For example, ¾-in. panels can be bent only in a circle with a 10-ft. radius, while ⅜-in. panels can be bent to a radius of 36 in. Two layers of the ⅜-in. material will produce a much sharper bend and yet will give you the same effect as a ¾-in. panel.

finishing plywood

Fir plywood has a "wild grain" that must be "tamed" in finishing it. This reduces the contrast between the hard and soft growth in the tree. The American Plywood Association recommends the following steps (simplified) in obtaining a light-stain glaze. Here are the procedures:

1. If you want to whiten the panel, apply a coat of interior white undercoat thinned with an equal amount of turpentine. This may be wiped with a rag for more grain "show through."

2. Seal the wood. Apply one coat of thinned white shellac or clear resin sealer.

3. If you want to color the panel, apply a color coat of thinned undercoat or enamel, or color-in-oil. Light stains may also be used. The color coat is wiped to the proper tone.

4. To make a wearing surface, apply a coat of flat varnish.

5. When using conventional stain, first apply a clear resin sealer or thinned white shellac to subdue the contrast.

6. To prepare plywood panels for wallpapering, fill all the joints and prime the panels with thinned, flat-white paint. Next, coat the surface with wheat-flour paste combined with a glue size. Then apply a smooth wall liner or felt. Apply the wallpaper over this liner.

7. For enameled walls, first apply a painter's canvas or unbleached muslin, following the steps outlined above. Then apply a coat of glue size, and finish with the paper of your choice.

8. Conventional paint finishes are possible if high-grade paints are used. To be on the safe side, first apply a clear resin sealer, shellac or flat-white paint, followed by a prime coat and finished coat.

9. In exterior finishing, the prime coat is most important. It should be a high-grade primer thinned with a pint of raw linseed oil per gallon of paint. Over this apply the second and third coats. All edges should be well sealed.

See also: drywall; hardboard; paneling, hardboard; paneling, plywood; paneling, wood; walls.

Pole-lamp table at your elbow

BY LEN SAMUELS

IF YOUR POLE LAMP lacks a table, you're usually stuck. Such tables normally fit between pole sections designed to accept them. But if you have a lathe, you can make a fine hardwood table to fit any pole lamp.

Cut a 6-ft. length ¾ x 5-in. walnut into 18-in. lengths. Then edge-dowel and glue them together. Cut an 18-in. disk and save the corner scraps for brackets.

Attach this disk to a faceplate and mount it on the outboard end of your lathe headstock. Run the lathe at slow speed, true up the disk and bevel its edge. Then drill a hole in the center for a snug fit on the pole, approximately 1½ in. in diameter. Sand it glassy smooth.

With the scrap pieces stacked, bandsaw them to the pattern shown. Drill a No. 8 hole in each bracket 1½ in. in from the end of the top leg and perpendicular to the curved face, then countersink flush. Clamp opposite brackets together and drill ¼-in. holes through from one curved edge to the other. Note that the pairs of holes do not line up since the bolts used must bypass each other in the pole. These are 3½ and 4-in. F.H. brass stovebolts. For such sizes, see your marine hardware dealer. Countersink one end of each bolt hole so that the lower edge of the screwhead will be flush. At the opposite ends, counterbore recesses to wedge the nuts in the holes.

Wrap a piece of dowel or pipe the same diameter as the pole with sandpaper and form a concave groove in the edges of the longer legs of each bracket.

With the dowel positioned between the brackets so it falls short of the bolt holes and passes through the pole hole, glue and screw the brackets to the underside of the disk. Use the bolts to insure that the brackets are lined up, and turn the bracket assembly so that it covers the holes made in attaching the faceplate.

To mount the table on the lamp, separate the pole sections and slip off the wire nuts to separate the wiring. Slide the table down to armchair height and drill through the pole via the bolt holes, taking care not to catch the wires inside. Finally, bolt on the table.

See also: electrical wiring; lamps; lighting; shelves; tables.

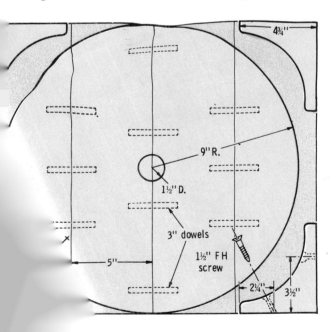

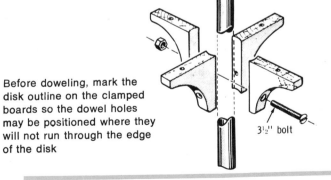

Before doweling, mark the disk outline on the clamped boards so the dowel holes may be positioned where they will not run through the edge of the disk

3½" bolt

4¾"

9" R.

1½" D.

3" dowels

1½" FH screw

5"

2¼"

3½"

1953

Fun afloat
on this
platform boat

BY ART MIKESELL

■ START WITH THIS easy-to-build pontoon platform and you'll have no trouble turning out a customized boat exactly suited to your needs. It's a big, roomy craft offering plenty of space for installing all the features you'd like to see in a boat.

Of course, no pontoon boat is designed for towing skiers or running in really rough water, so don't try to turn it into an SK or deep-V.

When screws or nails are countersunk, fill the holes with wood plastic or water-mixed wood putty. Sand the surface level when dry. Prime before finishing

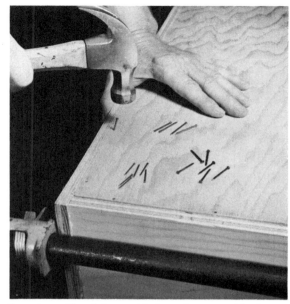

If you're nailing into a rabbet, such as a cabinet back, drive the nails at a slight angle. Brads or finish nails should be used for the best results

Uses include siding, soffits, windscreens, exterior painted cabinet work, etc. Thicknesses: ⁵⁄₁₆, ⅜, ½, ⅝, ¾ and 1 in. Veneer grade is B face, B or C back, C or C-plugged inner plys.

TEXTURE 1–11: The unsanded panels have parallel grooves ¼ in. deep, ⅜ in. wide on 2-in. or 4-in. centers. The edges are shiplapped for a continuous visual pattern. Uses include siding, accent paneling, fences, etc. It is available in 8 and 10-ft. lengths and sanded or with MD overlay. Thicknesses: ⅝ in. only; C or better face, C back and inner plys.

303 SPECIALTY SIDING EXT-DFPA: The grade covers proprietary plywood products for siding, fencing, soffits, windscreens and other exterior applications or interior panels. The panels have special surface treatments which include rough-sawn, striated and brushed, and may be V-grooved, channel-grooved, etc. It is available in redwood, cedar, hemlock, Douglas fir, lauan and other woods. The most common thicknesses are ⅜, ½ and ⅝ in. The veneer grade is B or better face, C back and plys.

PLYRPN EXT-DFPA: The panels are surfaced on both sides with tempered hardboard with smooth or screened surfaces. Thicknesses are ½, ⅝ and ¾ in. The panels have C inner plys.

MARINE EXT-DFPA and SPECIAL EXTERIOR DFPA: Marine-grade panels are made only with Douglas fir or western larch, and a special solid joined core construction. The panels

are subject to special limitations on core gaps and the number of face repairs. Use them for boat hulls. The panels are also available with overlaid faces. Exterior is a premium panel similar to the marine grade but permits any species covered under PS 1–66. The most common thicknesses are ¼, ⅜, ½, ⅝, ¾ and 1 in. The veneer grade has an A or B face and back with B inner plys.

C-C PLUGGED EXT-DFPA: For exterior underlayment, these panels are also ideal for tile backing where a permanently waterproof material is needed. The panels are sanded or touch sanded as specified. The most common thicknesses are ¼, ⅜, ½, ⅝, ¾ and ⅞ in. The veneer grade is C (plugged) face, C back and inner plys.

The types and grades mentioned above are available in 4 x 8-ft. panel. However, other lengths and widths are manufactured. Generally, larger sizes can be ordered by your lumber dealer.

Many lumber dealers have "plywood bins" in which random-size pieces and trimmings are available. Many dealers also will cut a panel for you in multiples of 2 ft. When buying plywood, it is often to your advantage to preplan the project at hand so the amount of material needed can be purchased at one time. Costs can be cut with quantity, and any irregular sizes can be picked out of the plywood bins—another saving.

Plywood panels are easy to work with, al-

Laminated-plastic surfacing materials can be used for edges of tables. Use contact cement to stick on the laminated plastic. Coat the edge and material

though there are several tips that will make the job even easier:

1. To prevent waste, lay out the panel for cutting. If there will be many pieces cut from a single panel, sketch the arrangement on a piece of paper before you transfer it to the panel as a cutting pattern. Allow for the saw kerf between the pieces. Have the grain of the panel running the long way of the piece, if possible.

2. If you use a handsaw, cut the panel with the best face up. Use a saw with 10 to 15 points to the inch and support the panel on sawhorses so it won't sag. Always use a sharp saw.

3. For power sawing on a table saw, cut with the good face of the panel up. Use a sharp combination blade or fine-tooth blade without too much set. The blade should be set so it protrudes above the panel about the height of the teeth.

4. With a portable power saw, place the good face of the panel down.

5. When planing edges, work from both ends of the edge toward the center of the panel. This will prevent splitting out the plys at the end of the cut. Always use a plane with a sharp blade and set it to take a fine shaving. Work slowly.

6. Since plywood is sanded smooth at the time it is made, sanding it before a sealer or prime coat of finish should be confined to the edges. After the surface is sealed, however, you may sand in the direction of the grain only.

7. It is difficult to nail or screw into the edges of veneer-core plywood. Plan your work so you can avoid these problems.

Plywood panels can be bent to certain minimum radii depending, of course, on the thickness of the panel. In some applications you may have to bend two thin panels to build up a particular thickness. For example, ¾-in. panels can be bent only in a circle with a 10-ft. radius, while ⅜-in. panels can be bent to a radius of 36 in. Two layers of the ⅜-in. material will produce a much sharper bend and yet will give you the same effect as a ¾-in. panel.

finishing plywood

Fir plywood has a "wild grain" that must be "tamed" in finishing it. This reduces the contrast between the hard and soft growth in the tree. The American Plywood Association recommends the following steps (simplified) in obtaining a light-stain glaze. Here are the procedures:

1. If you want to whiten the panel, apply a coat of interior white undercoat thinned with an equal amount of turpentine. This may be wiped with a rag for more grain "show through."

2. Seal the wood. Apply one coat of thinned white shellac or clear resin sealer.

3. If you want to color the panel, apply a color coat of thinned undercoat or enamel, or color-in-oil. Light stains may also be used. The color coat is wiped to the proper tone.

4. To make a wearing surface, apply a coat of flat varnish.

5. When using conventional stain, first apply a clear resin sealer or thinned white shellac to subdue the contrast.

6. To prepare plywood panels for wallpapering, fill all the joints and prime the panels with thinned, flat-white paint. Next, coat the surface with wheat-flour paste combined with a glue size. Then apply a smooth wall liner or felt. Apply the wallpaper over this liner.

7. For enameled walls, first apply a painter's canvas or unbleached muslin, following the steps outlined above. Then apply a coat of glue size, and finish with the paper of your choice.

8. Conventional paint finishes are possible if high-grade paints are used. To be on the safe side, first apply a clear resin sealer, shellac or flat-white paint, followed by a prime coat and finished coat.

9. In exterior finishing, the prime coat is most important. It should be a high-grade primer thinned with a pint of raw linseed oil per gallon of paint. Over this apply the second and third coats. All edges should be well sealed.

See also: drywall; hardboard; paneling, hardboard; paneling, plywood; paneling, wood; walls.

Pole-lamp table
at your elbow

BY LEN SAMUELS

IF YOUR POLE LAMP lacks a table, you're usually stuck. Such tables normally fit between pole sections designed to accept them. But if you have a lathe, you can make a fine hardwood table to fit any pole lamp.

Cut a 6-ft. length ¾ x 5-in. walnut into 18-in. lengths. Then edge-dowel and glue them together. Cut an 18-in. disk and save the corner scraps for brackets.

Attach this disk to a faceplate and mount it on the outboard end of your lathe headstock. Run the lathe at slow speed, true up the disk and bevel its edge. Then drill a hole in the center for a snug fit on the pole, approximately 1½ in. in diameter. Sand it glassy smooth.

With the scrap pieces stacked, bandsaw them to the pattern shown. Drill a No. 8 hole in each bracket 1½ in. from the end of the top leg and perpendicular to the curved face, then countersink flush. Clamp opposite brackets together and drill ¼-in. holes through from one

curved edge to the other. Note that the pairs of holes do not line up since the bolts used must bypass each other in the pole. These are 3½ and 4-in. F.H. brass stovebolts. For such sizes, see your marine hardware dealer. Countersink one end of each bolt hole so that the lower edge of the screwhead will be flush. At the opposite ends, counterbore recesses to wedge the nuts in the holes.

Wrap a piece of dowel or pipe the same diameter as the pole with sandpaper and form a concave groove in the edges of the longer legs of each bracket.

With the dowel positioned between the brackets so it falls short of the bolt holes and passes through the pole hole, glue and screw the brackets to the underside of the disk. Use the bolts to insure that the brackets are lined up, and turn the bracket assembly so that it covers the holes made in attaching the faceplate.

To mount the table on the lamp, separate the pole sections and slip off the wire nuts to separate the wiring. Slide the table down to armchair height and drill through the pole via the bolt holes, taking care not to catch the wires inside. Finally, bolt on the table.

See also: electrical wiring; lamps; lighting; shelves; tables.

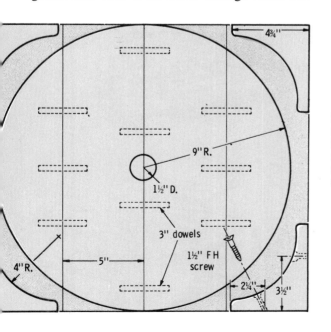

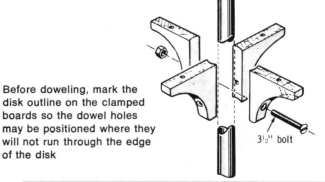

Before doweling, mark the disk outline on the clamped boards so the dowel holes may be positioned where they will not run through the edge of the disk

3½" bolt

pole shelves: see shelves
polisher, floor: see floor polisher
polisher-grinder: see gemstones
polishing marble: see marble
polishing machines: see tumbling machines

Fun afloat
on this
platform boat

BY ART MIKESELL

(Actually, this one plugs along at a stately 8 mph or so.) But outside of these limitations, this type of hull is one of the most practical choices for general use on small lakes and rivers.

Turn it into a floating picnic pavilion, with seats, table and storage space for coolers and hampers. Or, a powered fishing dock with live bait and catch wells, underdeck rod storage, fish finder and anything else necessary. Or, even a deluxe swimming station complete with diving tower, swimming slide and colorful dressing tents.

If you want to trailer the boat, you'll have to alter the dimensions of the pontoons. While the width falls within that permitted by regulation, the spacing between pontoons (48 in.) is too narrow to fit on a pontoon trailer, most of which require from 50 to 54 in. The 4-ft. spacing was decided upon to take advantage of stock plywood panel size and economize on materials.

By building the pontoons slightly narrower and widening the tunnel, the boat can be tailored to fit any pontoon trailer. Since it normally draws only about 4 in., the slight increase in draft caused by narrowing the pontoons shouldn't cause any problems.

General specifications. Douglas fir is satisfactory for the framing, so long as it's first grade and free of knots and shakes. For a slightly stronger boat, use white oak, Philippine mahogany or Sitka spruce. Likewise, exterior-grade plywood is satisfactory in all cases, though marine-grade will result in a stronger construction. You also have some leeway in choosing the quality plywood to be used at different locations. For example, AC panels could be used for decking with the C face down.

All joints should be glued, as well as screwed or nailed. If you plan to fiberglass the hull, a hard-setting glue (resorcinol or urea-resin type) should be used. If not, however, select a mastic or flexible, water-type glue for all underwater junctions.

All fastenings should be either of bronze or hot-dipped galvanized iron. The latter are quite adequate here, and are less expensive. Incidentally, all nails should be the annular-ring type.

Review the plans and text carefully before you begin construction.

Building bulkheads. The three building bulkheads each consist of two ¼-in. plywood bulkheads framed with 1 x 2 stock and fastened to a 2 x 6 beam. As shown in the photos, lightening holes may be cut in each of the bulkheads to reduce the weight of the boat. Limbers (drainage holes) should be cut adjacent to the keel notch to allow any bilge water to drain aft where it can be removed through drain plugs installed in the transom or pumped out, gaining access

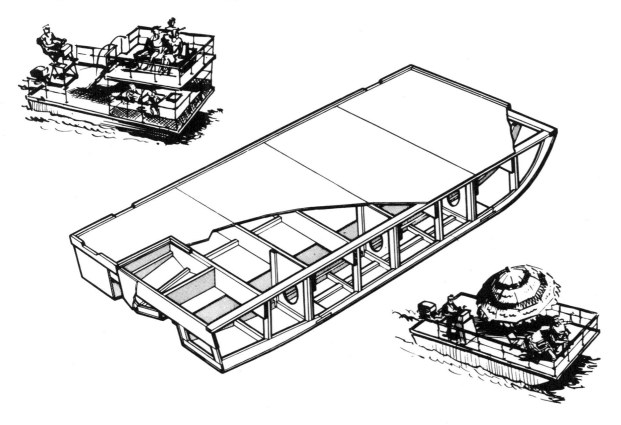

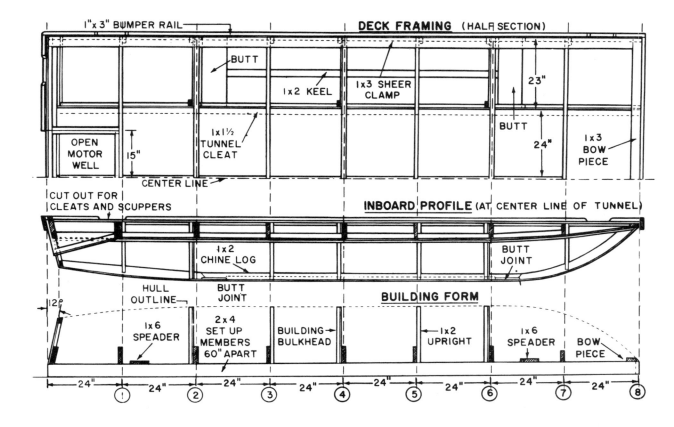

DECK FRAMING (HALF SECTION)

1"x 3" BUMPER RAIL

BUTT

1x2 KEEL

1x3 SHEER CLAMP

23"

BUTT

1x1½ TUNNEL CLEAT

OPEN MOTOR WELL

15"

24"

1x3 BOW PIECE

CENTER LINE

CUT OUT FOR CLEATS AND SCUPPERS

INBOARD PROFILE (AT CENTER LINE OF TUNNEL)

1x2 CHINE LOG

BUTT JOINT

HULL OUTLINE

BUTT JOINT

BUILDING FORM

12°

1x6 SPEADER

2x4 SET UP MEMBERS 60" APART

BUILDING BULKHEAD

1x2 UPRIGHT

1x6 SPEADER

BOW PIECE

24" 24" 24" 24" 24" 24" 24" 24"

① ② ③ ④ ⑤ ⑥ ⑦ ⑧

boat, continued

through small hatches set flush with the deck near the transom.

Note that two types of bulkheads may be used at bulkhead No. 4, depending on whether the side planking is a continuous 16-ft. panel (usually available only on special order) or two butt-joined, 8-ft. panels. If the planking is butt-joined, you'll have to make allowance in the bulkheads for the thickness of the ⅜-in. butt blocks that will mate to the side of the bulkhead and extend 8 in. on either side of the joint.

Beams. At stations 1, 3, 5 and 7, use 1 x 6 beams with uprights at their outer extremities in place of full bulkheads. Note that the beam at No. 7 must be trimmed and bevelled to mate with the ¼-in. plywood tunnel planking.

The building form is just two 2 x 4 setup rails on which the basic framing pieces are mounted

Plywood bulkheads mounted on the 2 x 6 beams make up three building bulkheads spaced 4 ft. apart

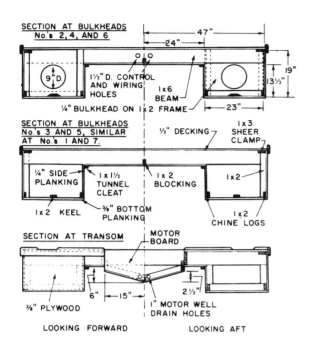

SECTION AT BULKHEADS
No.'s 2, 4, AND 6

47"
24"
9" D.
1½" D. CONTROL
AND WIRING
HOLES
1x6
BEAM
19"
13½"
23"
¼" BULKHEAD ON 1x2 FRAME

SECTION AT BULKHEADS
No's 3 AND 5, SIMILAR
AT No's 1 AND 7.

½" DECKING
1x3
SHEER
CLAMP
¼" SIDE
PLANKING
1x1½
TUNNEL
CLEAT
1x2
BLOCKING
1x2
1x2 KEEL
⅜" BOTTOM
PLANKING
1x2
CHINE LOGS

SECTION AT TRANSOM
MOTOR
BOARD
⅜" PLYWOOD
6"
15"
2½"
1" MOTOR WELL
DRAIN HOLES

LOOKING FORWARD   LOOKING AFT

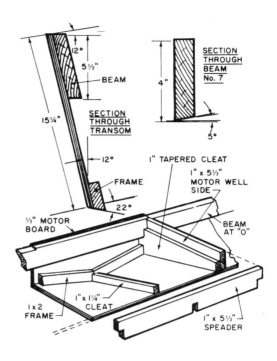

12°
5½"
BEAM
SECTION
THROUGH
BEAM
No. 7
4"
15¼"
12°
SECTION
THROUGH
TRANSOM
5°
FRAME
1" TAPERED CLEAT
1" x 5½"
MOTOR WELL
SIDE
22°
½" MOTOR
BOARD
BEAM
AT "O"
1x2
FRAME
1" x 1¼"
CLEAT
1" x 5½"
SPEADER

The uprights at Nos. 1 and 7 may be left long and cut to size later during assembly of the side planking, or may be left out temporarily and installed after the planking is in place.

Cut notches in the beams for the sheer clamp and in the uprights for the chine log.

Transom. The transom is constructed in much the same way as the bulkheads. It's framed on the inside surface, with notches for the sheer clamp and chine log in the frame only and not extending through the plywood transom. Since the transom is set at an angle of 12 deg., the beam that connects the two bulkheads should be beveled 12 deg. where it must mate with the tunnel and deck planking.

Building form. The hull is intended to be constructed bottom-side-up on a building form consisting of two 2 x 4 setup members spaced

Chine-log joints fall under joints in bottom planking and must be notched for ⅜-in. butt plates

Stem curve is a 4-ft., 6-in. radius which may be cut from 1 x 6 stock or laminated from ½-in. plywood

1957

All four pieces of side planking have the same curve; make one and use it as a pattern

Mount side planking; then sand edges flush with framing to mate bottom planking tightly

Begin nailing forward section of bottom planking at aft ends; work down the curve of stem

Mount ½-in.-plywood motor board on the outside of the transom; it goes on last

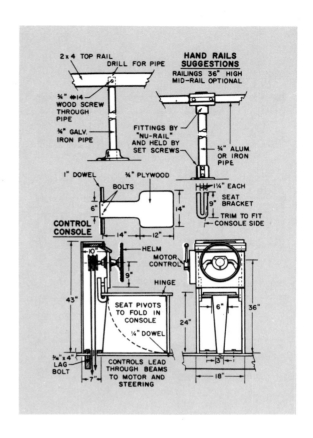

boat, continued

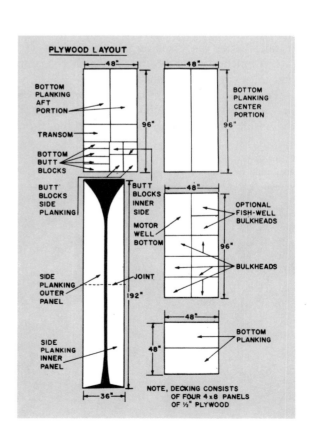

5 ft. apart. These may be fastened directly to the floor or raised to a more convenient working level by mounting them on saw horses, as shown in the photos. In any case, they should be level lengthwise and athwartships, and held securely in position to prevent movement.

The bulkheads and beams are mounted on this form, spaced as shown and centered horizontally. The transom must be accurately spaced from the No. 2 frame on the hull center line and braced at an angle of 12 deg. The 1 x 3 bow piece should also be positioned on the form, as shown in the building-form drawing. Fasten all these framing members securely to the form and to one another to prevent movement during construction, since it's imperative that they remain vertical, accurately centered and properly spaced.

Avoid moving the form during construction. If you do so accidentally, however, return the structure before you continue.

Sheer clamps and stiffening. The 1 x 3 sheer clamps fit into notches at each of the beams and butt to the bow piece. Fasten with two 1½-in. No. 8 screws at each joint.

To stiffen the structure, notch a length of 1 x 2 vertically into the bottom of beams No. 1 through 7 along the center line. Secure it in place with 1½-in. No. 8 screws driven angularly into the beams.

Motor-well frame. In building the prototype, a width of 24 in. between longitudinals was used. While this is adequate for many small motors, the spacing was extended to 30 in. on the plans to accept larger motors and to provide more room for hooking up the steering and remote-control cables. The 1 x 6 longitudinals extend from the transom to beam No. 1, with 1 x 6 blocking on the beam acting as a spreader.

The motor well itself is in the shape of a V when viewed from the stern. Two cleats cut from 1-in. stock extend 1½ in. below the tunnel planking at the transom and must be tapered to be flush with the tunnel planking at No. 1. Fasten these cleats to the longitudinals with 1½-in. No. 8 screws.

The motor board can be cut from ½-in. plywood (not included in the materials list) or laminated from ¼-in. plywood. Add 1 x 2 blocking along the bottom edges for attaching the bottom planking, then mount the motor board on the beam and install the center bottom cleat which runs from the transom board to the beam at No. 1. Fair this framing but don't install the plywood planking until after the tunnel has been planked.

After finishing the motor-well, sand and fiberglass the bottom to avoid turning the hull again later. Dynel was used to finish the prototype

Then flip the hull and apply the decking which consists of four panels of ½-in. plywood. Fair all upper surfaces before installing it

Tunnel planking. To provide a flush mating surface for the tunnel planking, bevel the bow piece and any beams which might require it. Two 4 x 8-ft. panels of ¼-in. plywood are used to plank the main part of the tunnel. The motor-well area is also planked with ¼-in. plywood, cut to fit. Coat the mating surfaces of the frame with glue and fasten the planking in place by driving 1-in. nails 3 in. apart around the edges of the panels and 6 in. apart along the other framing members.

Side planking and chine logs. If you wish, the chine logs and stem may be preassembled to the inner and outer side planking before these pieces of plywood are secured to the frames. To do this, lay out the stem curve at one end and spring a batten between stations 0 and 2 to determine the curve at the stern end. Once you have laid out both curves on a side panel, use this as a

On the prototype, the rails and top bows were made from aluminum assembled with NuRail fittings

MATERIALS LIST

LUMBER

No. Reqd.	Size*	Use
4	1 x 6—4'	Stem
2	1 x 2—8'	Keel
4	1 x 2—10'	Chine log
4	1 x 3—4'	Sawn chine from Nos. 0 to 2
2	1 x 3—16'	Sheer clamp
2	1 x 1½—16'	Tunnel cleat
1	1 x 2—12'	Vertical blocking for tunnel
4	1 x 6—8'	Athwartship beams (Nos. 1, 3, 5, 7)
3	2 x 6—8'	Bulkhead beams (Nos. 2, 4, 6)
1	1 x 3—8'	Bow piece
1	2 x 8—8'	Transom beam (thickness may vary with motor)
3	1 x 3—16'	Bumper rail
8	1 x 2—19'	Side uprights (Nos. 1, 3, 5, 7)
3	1 x 2—12'	Bulkhead frames

* All sizes above are nominal, or "lumberyard size," rather than actual size. Dimensions allow for cutting to length.

PLYWOOD

2	¼" x 3' x 16'	Side planking
1	⅜" x 4' x 8'	Bottom planking (center portion)
1	⅜" x 4' x 8'	Bottom planking (forward portion)
1	⅜" x 4' x 8'	Bottom planking (aft portion, misc.)
2	¼" x 4' x 8'	Tunnel planking
1	¼" x 4' x 8'	Bulkheads
4	½" x 4' x 8'	Deck

FASTENINGS

Nails: annular-thread, bronze or Monel
3½ lbs.   1" No. 12
2½ lbs.   1¼" No. 12
FH Screws: hot-dipped, galvanized or bronze
1 gross   1½" No. 8

GLUE

Plastic resin (5 lbs.) or resorcinol (1 gal.)

boat, continued

template to cut the stern and bow members. Since the contours are identical, you may saw all of these at the same time.

Fasten the stem at the bow piece and uprights with 1½-in. No. 8 screws. Along the sheer, fasten the side planking with 1-in. nails spaced 3 in. apart. At the transom, use the same size nails spaced 2 in. apart. While you don't have to fasten the side planking at each bulkhead, it's desirable to secure the inside runner planking at bulkheads where it makes a junction with the tunnel planking.

Tunnel cleats. The 1 x 2 tunnel cleats cover the junction between the side and tunnel planking and are on the outside of the hull. If possible, fasten these from the inside, driving 1-in. nails from the underside of the tunnel planking and from the inside of the runner planking, spacing them 3 in. apart. Use 1½-in. No. 8 screws to attach to each beam.

Keel. The 1 x 2 keel is notched into the bulkheads and extends between the two butt blocks used to reinforce the joints in the bottom plank-

FASTENING SCHEDULE

Item	Size	Type	Spacing or No.
Frame to bulkheads	1"		
Beams to bulkheads and transom	1"	Nails	3" apart
Beams to uprights	1½" No. 8	Nails	3" apart
Side planking to chine logs and stems	1"	Screws	2 ea. joint
Chine logs to bulkhead and transom frame	1½" No. 8	Nails	2" apart
Sheer clamp to beams	1½" No. 8	Screws	1 ea.
Bow piece to stem	1½" No. 8	Screws	1 ea. joint
Keel to bulkheads	1½" No. 8	Screws	2 ea. joint
Tunnel vertical blocking to beams	1½" No. 8	Screws	1 ea. joint
Side planking to sheer	1"	Screws	1 ea. joint
Bottom planking at outer edges	1¼"	Nails	3" apart
Bottom planking along keel	1¼"	Nails	3" apart
Tunnel and side planking at tunnel cleat	1"	Nails	6" apart
Decking at outer edges	1¼"	Nails	3" apart
Decking at inner edges	1¼"	Nails	4" apart
Bumper rail to hull	1½" No. 8	Screws	6" apart

ing. Secure to each bulkhead with 1½-in. No. 8 screws.

Bottom planking. The entire bottom runner surface must be faired for the bottom planking. If the chine has been fitted to the side planking carefully, little, if any, fairing should be required along this area. The bow piece will have to be beveled to accommodate the bottom planking, however.

In the forward section, the grain of the ⅜-in. plywood bottom planking runs athwartship, extending the width of a 4-ft. sheet to butt-join just forward of station No. 6 with the main bottom planking where the grain runs lengthwise. This 8-ft. main section of bottom planking runs aft to where it butt-joins with the stern portion of the planking. Make the butt blocks from ⅜-in. plywood a minimum of 8 in. wide, fastening them with two rows of ¾-in. No. 8 screws spaced 2 in. apart on either side of the joint. Fasten the bottom planking with 1¼-in. nails spaced 3 in. apart along the outer edges and 6 in. apart along the keel.

Motor-well area. The bottom of the motor well is made up of two pieces of ¼-in. plywood, one on either side of the center line. Fasten these in place with 1-in. nails as you did the tunnel planking, after coating the frame surfaces liberally with glue.

At this point, the hull is ready to be turned right side up. To avoid turning the boat once again to finish it, however, take time out to sand and finish the bottom before you continue construction. (The prototype was covered with Dynel reinforced with resin, a process similar to fiberglassing but considerably easier because of the stretchable nature of the fabric.)

Since the hull could be wracked at this stage, block it at bulkheads Nos. 2 and 6 and level it both lengthwise and athwartships. This makes sure it will remain level.

Decking. The decking consists of four panels of ½-in. plywood laid athwartships. Before installing it, fair all upper surfaces so it will lie flat on the framing and coat all mating areas with glue. Then fasten it in place with 1¼-in. nails spaced 4 in. apart along outer edges and 6 in. apart along inner framing members.

Before nailing the decking in place, however, decide where you wish to locate the control console and drill the necessary lead holes in the beams for steering and control cables. Also, any special storage ideas for utilizing space in the pontoons or wing deck should be considered at this time.

For instance, if you wish to locate fuel tanks and battery in the pontoons, it's easier to install plywood mounting plates and hold-down straps before the decking is in place. Hatches and provisions for ventilation can be taken care of afterward. The same goes for live bait or catch wells in the pontoons, or a rod storage rack in the wing deck. You might even consider filling this wing section with planks of Styrofoam, which would provide an extra 1000 lbs. of reserve buoyancy.

Bumper rail. The 1 x 3 bumper rail extends around the deck and projects 1 in. above the surface. Fasten it with 1½-in. No. 8 screws spaced 6 in. apart and countersunk so that they can be concealed with wood plugs.

Control console. Actually, the shape and location of the control console as detailed here is entirely optional. Any shape console may be used and it could just as well be mounted almost anywhere along the center line of the boat. It's up to you.

As shown in the plan, the console features a swing-out seat with a folding leg. The seat is hinged to the leg, and the leg is equipped with a ¼-in. dowel which fits into a hole drilled in the deck. Controls are mounted on the side, and control cables and steering lines are led beneath the deck back to the motor area.

Painting. If you fiberglass the deck, be sure to select paint compatible with the resin used. If you omit this, give the plywood a couple of coats of paint to hide the grain.

Sand between coats and finish off with a good nonskid deck paint.

Incidentally, if the boat is to be left in the water, all interior surfaces should be coated with a rot preventative ("Cuprinol" or similar) before the decking is applied. You may wish to consider this even though you plan to store the boat on a trailer during the season rather than leaving it in the water.

All areas to be left natural should be filled, stained and given three to five coats of good marine varnish, sanding between coats.

Fittings. Lights, cleats and other fittings are matters of personal taste, so long as they satisfy regulations in your area. As shown in the photograph at the beginning of this article, the prototype was outfitted with DIY aluminum railings assembled with NuRail fittings, and a canvas top stretched over aluminum bows. Such features are purely optional.

See also: boat camping; boats, buying; boats, used; floats and docks; pram; riverboat.

Flip-top table for all kinds of fun

BY JOHN JEFCHAK

What does your family want to do in the game room?
Play table tennis? Shoot billiards? Set up an HO-gauge
model railroad? Whatever they vote for, this
versatile table will let them do it. Best
of all, you can build it for about twenty
percent of the cost of a ready-made table

■ HERE'S A CONVERTIBLE FUN TABLE that the whole family will enjoy the year around.

Basically it's a home-size pool table with an extra two-faced top which lets you enjoy table tennis or HO-ga. railroading on the same table by merely flipping over the piggyback top. For pool, you simply lift off the extra top and lean it against the wall.

Roomy compartments in the base of the table provide a convenient place to store rolling stock, the scenic mountain and other lift-off props of the model track layout, and the table-tennis equipment; there's also room to spare for other games and playroom toys. The whole thing rolls

about on casters and is designed to dismantle in easy-to-handle sections.

A logical beginning is to construct the pool-table top first and Fig. 1 shows the basic assembly at a glance. Begin with the side rails, using ¾ x 8-in. solid stock (or plywood if you prefer). Hardwood is best.

Rip the rails to a width of 7½ in. The sides measure 92 in. long, while the ends are 48 in. in length. Cut a rabbet ¼ x ½ in. along the outer edge of each board, with the remaining tongue, or tenon, considered as being on the inside. This is accomplished with two passes on the table saw. Next, cut a ⅜ x ¾-in. dado on the inside, at a point 2¼ in. down from the top of the tongue. Use either a standard saw blade or, preferably, a dado head, which will cut the groove in one pass. Mark out the ball-return opening on one end rail, Fig. 12. Cut out, using a portable electric saber saw or a key-hole saw (if done by hand), and smooth and round off all edges. Cut a 45-deg. miter at each end of each piece, 8 miters in all. Take care to retain a small flat edge, about ¹⁄₃₂ in., on the ends of the miters in order to maintain the true dimensions. Now cut

a groove ¼ x ⅜ in. across each mitered surface, ⅛ in. in from the inside corner, to receive a ¼ x ⅝ x 8-in. plywood spline, Fig. 4.

Cut 24 triangular clamp blocks from ¾-in. stock. Using a water-soluble hide glue, place three blocks equally spaced, at each end, about ⅛ in. from the mitered edge. Make certain that corresponding clamp blocks are in line in order to receive the clamps for permanent clamping and for trial fitting. Prime the mitered edges with a thinned mixture of plastic-resin glue to insure a good bond. Allow to dry thoroughly. Then apply glue to the spline and both mitered edges and clamp together, using an equal pressure on

flip-top table for fun, continued

The HO-gauge layout, as you can see, is large enough to satisfy even advanced HO fans. There's room for even more model-railroad equipment than you see here. Rolling stock and scenery store in the base cabinet

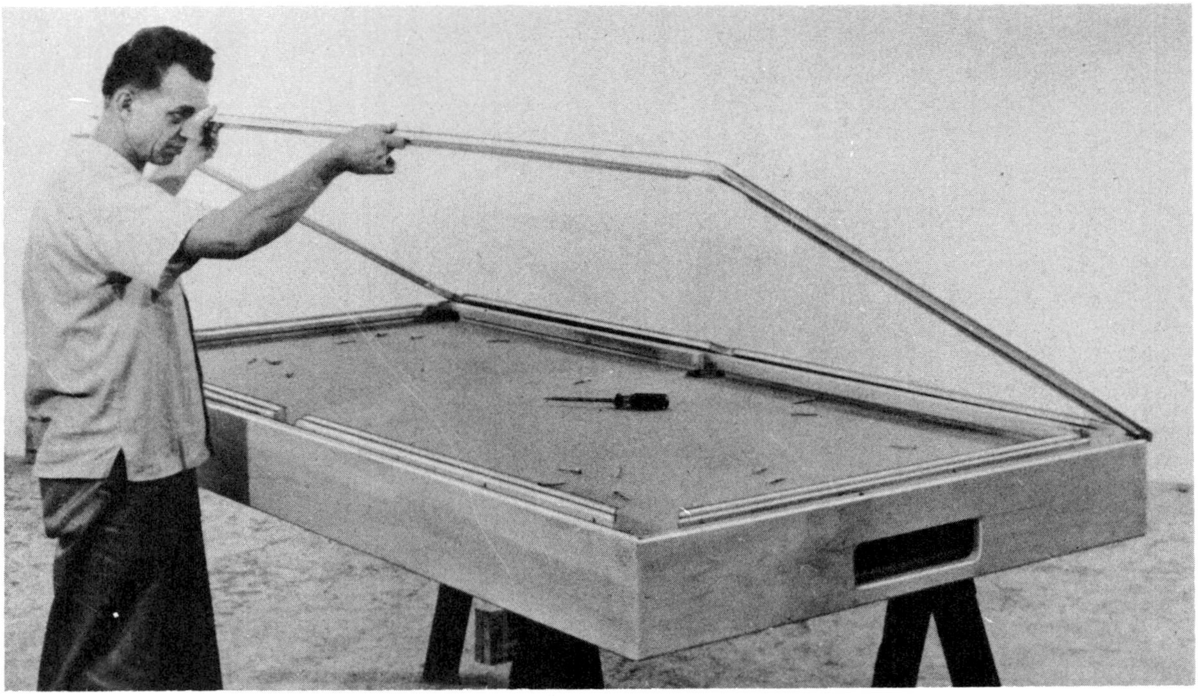

Here the top is completely framed with the playing board in place and the mitered top rail being tried for fit

all clamp blocks. It takes 12 clamps to complete the 4 corners at one time.

Check for squareness before the glue sets, since it is essential that all four corners be joined at 90 deg. Use a framing square in each corner, then hold in position with diagonal strips. Use a wood chisel to remove excess glue down to the glue line of each joint. Remove any glue residue from the wood with a damp cloth. Allow glue to set for at least 24 hrs., then carefully trim off the clamping blocks with a wood chisel and trim the splines off flush at each end.

Cut out two pieces of plywood ¾ x 5¼ x 86¼ in. These are the side walls for the ball-return tunnels running lengthwise, Fig. 1. Cut out two pieces ¾ x 5¼ x 36½ in. to serve as side walls for the ends, one of which blocks off an unused space at the end opposite the ball-return opening. The bottom piece for this unused space measures ¾ x 4¼ x 36½ in. There is a rise in the bottoms of the side tunnels of ⅝ in. from one end to the other lengthwise, Fig. 2. The ends therefore require an angle cut of approximately 1 deg. Allow at least ¼ in. for fitting and trimming. The tunnel bottom at the ball opening is made from solid stock, measuring ¾ x 4¼ x 46½ in., Fig. 3. A groove with a 1⅛-in. radius runs down the center for the entire length and is cut out on the table saw by passing the work repeatedly across the saw table at an angle as in Fig. 10. This is done by raising the blade slightly with each pass of the work. The piece is curved by forcing down the center ½ in. below the ends which rest on two ½ x ¾ x 5-in. supporting blocks, glued and nailed to the side rails, Fig. 1. Ends of the grooved piece are cut at approximately 1½ deg. on the table saw. The length is approximately 1/32 in. longer than the dimension of 46½ in. between the side rails.

Cut out parts for the bed shelf, two pieces ¾ x 1¾ x 91¼ in. for the sides and two pieces ¾ x 1¾ x 43¾ in. for the ends. Apply glue and insert into the ⅜ x ¾-in. dadoes in the rails, the long pieces first, followed by the short ones. Mark off the ⅝-in. incline with a pencil on the inside of the side rails, ½ in. at the ball-opening end, and 1⅛ in. at the other end, Fig. 2. Likewise mark off the same incline on the two side walls of the tunnel returns. Now glue and nail the bottoms to the sides, placing glue liberally on the edges that come into contact with the side walls. Follow the guide lines and clamp into position.

Check for squareness. The bottom edges of the side rails and the sides of the ball-return tunnel should be flush, Fig. 3. Follow the same procedure at the end opposite the ball opening. Glue in place the remaining tunnel end wall (ball opening end) and hold in place with several nails driven in at the top edges. When glue in these joints has set, spread glue on the edges of the

flip-top table for fun, continued

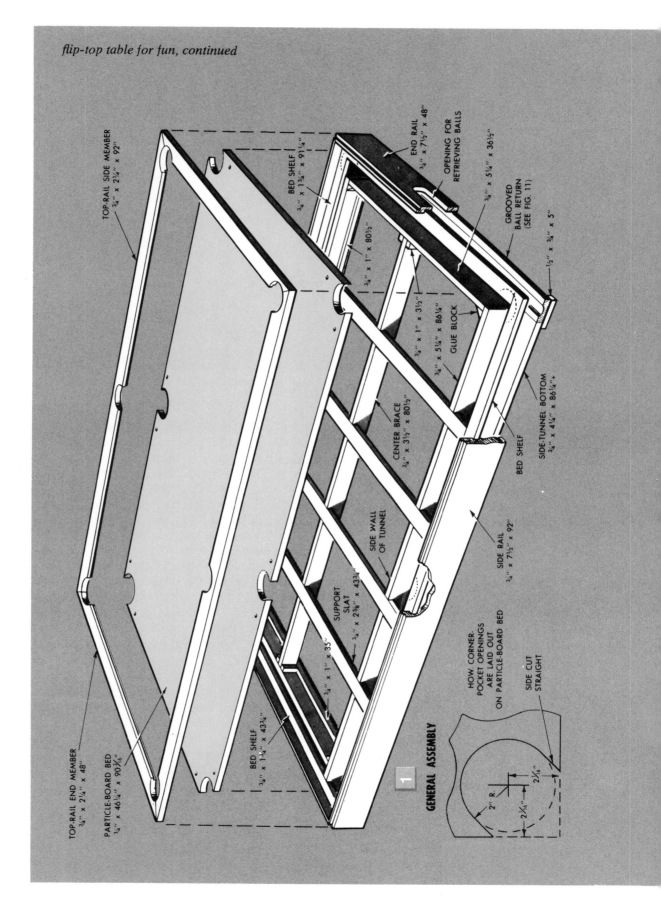

TOP-RAIL SIDE MEMBER
¾" x 2¼" x 92"

BED SHELF
¾" x 1¾" x 91¼"

END RAIL
¾" x 7½" x 48"

OPENING FOR
RETRIEVING BALLS

¾" x 5¼" x 36½"

GROOVED
BALL RETURN
(SEE FIG. 11)

½" x ¾" x 5"

¾" x 1" x 80½"

¾" x 1" x 3½"

¾" x 5¼" x 86¼"

GLUE BLOCK

SIDE-TUNNEL BOTTOM
¾" x 4¼" x 86¼"+

BED SHELF

CENTER BRACE
¾" x 3½" x 80½"

SIDE WALL
OF TUNNEL

SUPPORT
SLAT
¾" x 2⅝" x 43¾"

SIDE RAIL
¾" x 7½" x 92"

¾" x 1" x 35"

BED SHELF
¾" x 1¾" x 43¾"

TOP-RAIL END MEMBER
¾" x 2¼" x 48"

PARTICLE-BOARD BED
¾" x 46¼" x 90⅜"

HOW CORNER-
POCKET OPENINGS
ARE LAID OUT
ON PARTICLE-BOARD BED

SIDE CUT
STRAIGHT

GENERAL ASSEMBLY

2"R

2½₁₆

2½₁₆

1

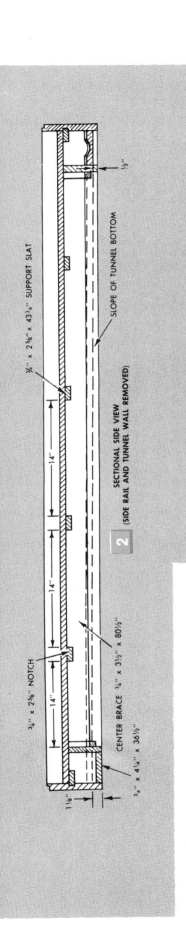

¾" x 2⅝" x 43¾" SUPPORT SLAT

SLOPE OF TUNNEL BOTTOM

½"

SECTIONAL SIDE VIEW
(SIDE RAIL AND TUNNEL WALL REMOVED)

CENTER BRACE ¾" x 3½" x 80½"

14"

14"

14"

¾" x 2⅝" NOTCH

1⅛"

¾" x 4¼" x 36½"

2

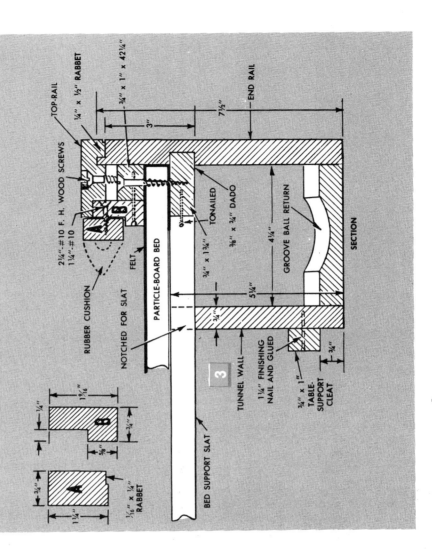

TOP-RAIL

¼" x ½" RABBET

¾" x 1" x 42¼"

END RAIL

3"

7½"

2¼"-#10 F. H. WOOD SCREWS
1¼"-#10

A B

RUBBER CUSHION

FELT

NOTCHED FOR SLAT

PARTICLE-BOARD BED

TONAILED

⅜" x ¾" DADO

GROOVE BALL RETURN

4¼"

SECTION

¾" x 1¾"

5¼"

¾"

TUNNEL WALL

1¼" FINISHING
NAIL AND GLUED

¾" x 1"
TABLE-
SUPPORT
CLEAT

¾"

BED SUPPORT SLAT

3

1⅝"

¼"

B

¾"

⅝"

¾"

A

1¼"

1/16" x ¼"
RABBET

grooved ball-return bottom, force into position and nail from both sides. Set exposed nails on the side rail and putty over.

Mark off ¾ in. from the lower edge on the inside of the tunnel walls and nail and glue ¾ x 1 x 80½-in. cleats above this line along the sides and ¾ x 1 x 35-in. cleats along the ends, Fig. 3. These cleats support and register the pool-table-top on the storage base. Lay out and cut a center brace ¾ x 3½ x 80½ in. which serves as the center support underneath the particle-board bed. Cut ¾ x 2⅝-in. notches in it, spacing them 14 in. apart. Next cut four pieces ¾ x 2⅝ x 43¾ in. These serve as support slats for the bed, Fig. 1. Since these butt against the shelf members, ¾ x 2⅝-in. notches also must be cut in the tunnel side walls to receive the slats, using a miter or back saw and chisel to cut the notches. Apply glue generously in the notches and to the ends of the slats, and nail into place. Toenail the ends of the support slats to the support shelf. Nail

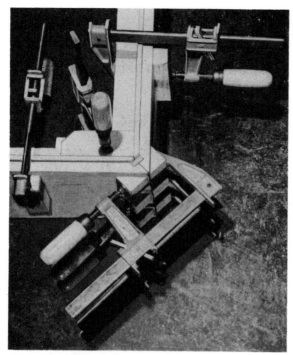

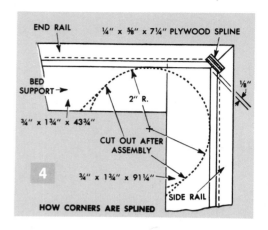

How corners are splined

The mitered and splined corners of the side rails are glue-blocked and clamped. Note that three clamps and six blocks are used per corner. Note also the spline detail and refer to Figs. 4, 6 and 8

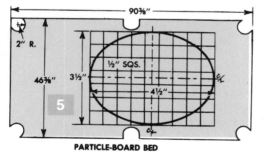

PARTICLE-BOARD BED

¾ x 1½ x 3½-in. corner blocks on each side of the center support at the ends, Fig. 1.

Lay out the ¾-in. particle-board playing bed, following Fig. 5. The detail below Fig. 1 shows how to scribe the corner pockets; a pattern is made for the elliptical side pockets. Cut out the pockets, using either a portable saber saw or a coping saw. Now place the bed on the 1⅜-in.-wide shelf and check the fit. There should be at least ⅟₁₆ in. clearance equally around the edge. Plane down to fit, reducing the given dimension of 46⅜ x 90⅜ in. to 46¼ x 90¼ in. should the thickness of the cloth, or felt, used require additional clearance. As soon as the bed is properly fitted, drill holes to receive the 12 hold-down screws, each being placed 2½ in. back from the pocket holes. Countersink the heads for 1¼ in. No. 10 flathead wood screws. With the bed in place trace the outline of the pockets on the bed-support rails. Fig. 4 shows how a compass is used to strike a 2-in. radius at the corner pock-

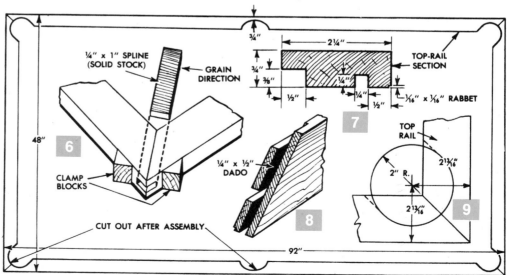

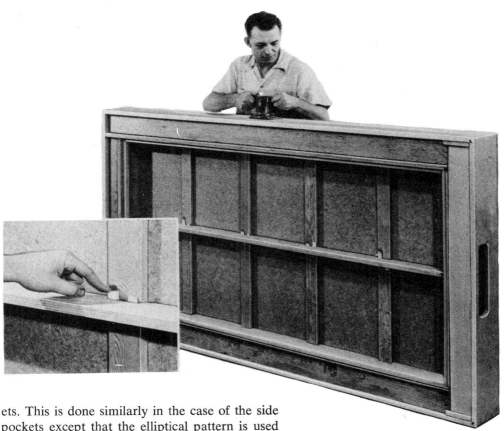

ets. This is done similarly in the case of the side pockets except that the elliptical pattern is used to mark the outline instead of a compass. A keyhole saw is used to cut out the pocket openings.

Next comes the top rail, Figs. 6 through 9. Like the side rails of the table, the top-rail members are mitered like a picture frame and grooved for a spline as shown in Fig. 6. This is done first, after which the members are rabbeted and dadoed on the underside as in the sectional detail in Fig. 7. Note the ¹⁄₁₆ x ¹⁄₁₆-in. rabbet that is made along the outer edge. This serves as a parting line at the joint so there is no chance of chipping the finish when it is necessary to lift off the top rail at a future date. Clamping blocks are glued temporarily on each side of the mitered joints as before, Fig. 6, and splines are cut from solid stock with the grain running crosswise. Now you can glue and clamp the joints. Pocket

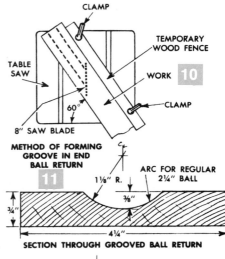

CLAMP

TEMPORARY WOOD FENCE

TABLE SAW

WORK **10**

CLAMP

60°

8" SAW BLADE

METHOD OF FORMING GROOVE IN END BALL RETURN

11

1⅛" R.

ARC FOR REGULAR 2¼" BALL

⅜"

¾"

4¼"

SECTION THROUGH GROOVED BALL RETURN

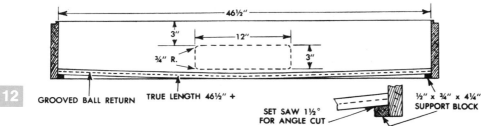

46½"

3"

12"

3"

¾" R.

12 GROOVED BALL RETURN TRUE LENGTH 46½" +

SET SAW 1½° FOR ANGLE CUT

½" x ¾" x 4¼" SUPPORT BLOCK

openings in the rail itself are laid out and cut after the glue is dry, the corner pockets being scribed as in Fig. 9. When placed over the tongue, or tenon, on the side-wall members, the rail should come flush with the outside surfaces.

The next step is making and installing the filler blocks which rough-in the side and end pockets. Figs. 13, 14, 16 and 17 give the sizes of these blocks and show where they fit into the assembly. Note that the side-pocket filler blocks fit flush into the side-pocket openings already cut in the particle-board bed, Figs. 13 and 14, but that the corner-pocket fillers are fitted and glued in the open corners above the bed shelves, Fig. 17, the right-hand detail. The corner fillers are made by sandwiching and gluing three pieces of ¾-in. stock, then squaring to the overall size given and bandsawing to a 2-in. radius as in Fig. 16.

Coming up next are the fillets, Fig. 19. The fillets for the head-corner pockets (those at the end of the table opposite the ball-return opening) are shaped as in the upper detail in Fig. 19. These serve to give the balls that drop into the head pockets the initial start along the tunnels

and into the return at the opposite end of the table. Now note the corner fillets in Fig. 19. The part A, Fig. 19, serves as a deflector for balls coming down the long side tunnels from the head and side pockets, and must be made right and left–hand. The whole assembly, including the fillets and deflectors, prevents balls from lodging in the corners. These parts are glued in place. Now the bottoms of the ball returns are covered with flexible countertop material. This material, which dampens the sound of the rolling ball, is cemented in place with contact cement and it's important to make sure that it takes the curvature of the round-bottom groove in the ball return.

At this stage you can cover the particle-board bed with felt, or billiard cloth. You should position the bed beforehand and fasten it temporarily to the shelf members with one screw on each side of each pocket. Once done it is removed. Cut the cloth about 2 in. larger each way than the overall size of the bed. Position the felt, bring it over the edges of the bed and begin tacking, following the tacking sequence in Fig. 21. It's important that this be followed in detail and

Balls in play that drop into side and corner pockets are automatically returned to the ball-return opening in the end rail, pictured above and at the left. Balls are easily reached through opening

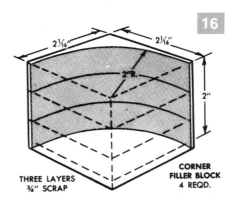

16

THREE LAYERS ¾" SCRAP

2¹⁄₁₆"   2¹⁄₁₆"   2"

CORNER FILLER BLOCK 4 REQD.

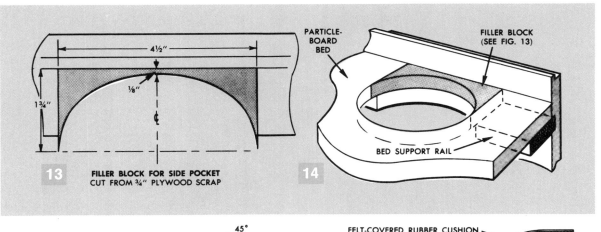

13 FILLER BLOCK FOR SIDE POCKET
CUT FROM ¾" PLYWOOD SCRAP

4½"

1¾"

⅛"

¢

PARTICLE-
BOARD
BED

FILLER BLOCK
(SEE FIG. 13)

BED SUPPORT RAIL

14

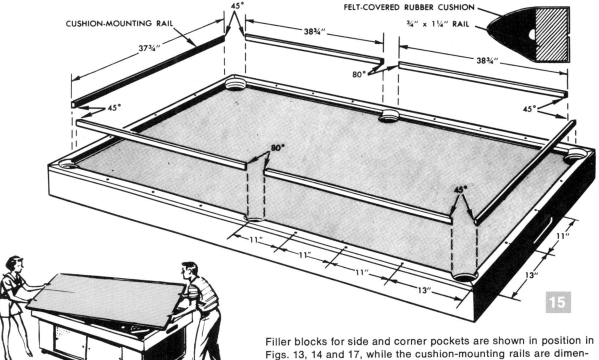

CUSHION-MOUNTING RAIL

FELT-COVERED RUBBER CUSHION

45°

38¾"

¾" x 1¼" RAIL

37¾"

38¾"

80°

45°

45°

80°

45°

11"

11"

11"

13"

11"

13"

15

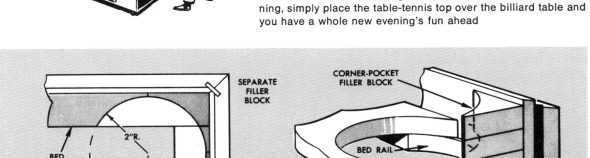

Filler blocks for side and corner pockets are shown in position in Figs. 13, 14 and 17, while the cushion-mounting rails are dimensioned above and also in Fig. 3. If you tire of billiards some evening, simply place the table-tennis top over the billiard table and you have a whole new evening's fun ahead

SEPARATE
FILLER
BLOCK

CORNER-POCKET
FILLER BLOCK

2"R.

2⅛"

BED RAIL

BED
SUPPORT
RAILS

PARTICLE-
BOARD BED

17

CUT OUT WITH KEYHOLE SAW

BED RAIL

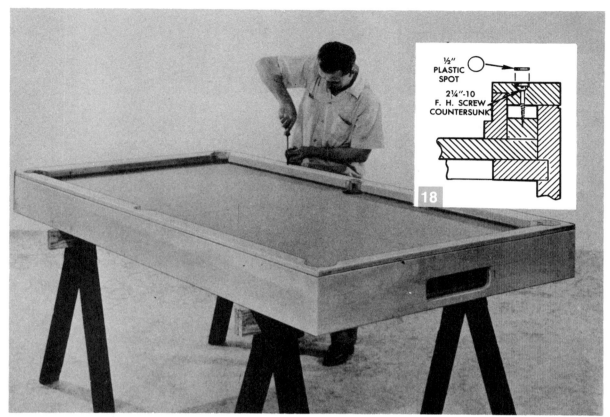

½"
PLASTIC
SPOT

2¼"-10
F. H. SCREW
COUNTERSUNK

18

A trial assembly of the several parts of the table is pictured above. For a sectional view of the complete assembly, see Fig. 3. Fig. 18 shows a cross section of the side of the table

that the tension on the felt be just sufficient to remove all wrinkles. Tension should be kept uniform in two directions. When the tacking sequence in Fig. 21 has been completed, work the ball openings as in Fig. 24, making the initial end-pocket cuts as in Fig. 23.

Set the felted bed aside and install the ball-

The corner and side-pocket liners are made from No. 2½ tin cans, lined with a flexible countertop material which is cemented in position

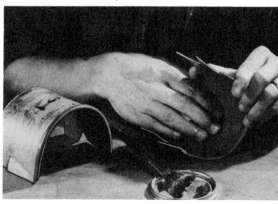

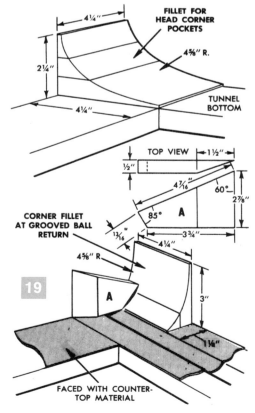

FILLET FOR
HEAD CORNER
POCKETS

4⅝" R.

4¼"

2¼"

4¼"

TUNNEL
BOTTOM

TOP VIEW

1½"

½"

4⁷⁄₁₆"

60°

2⅞"

85°

A

3¾"

CORNER FILLET
AT GROOVED BALL
RETURN

4⅝" R.

1³⁄₁₆"

4¼"

A

3"

1¼"

19

FACED WITH COUNTER-
TOP MATERIAL

retarding flaps in the side and end pockets next, Fig. 22. The flaps, which serve to cushion the straight drop of a ball, are supported with the free end in the pocket openings by means of holders which are three-piece assemblies made up of one piece of ¼-in. plywood 4¼ in. wide and 4¾ in. long, a spacer of the same width but only 3¼ in. long and a wood block ¾ x 2⅞ x 4¾ in. The spacer is cut from the same material as the flap. These parts are assembled as indicated and glued in place in the tunnels with the slotted (the slot being formed by the placement of the parts) end flush with the edge of the ball pocket, one holder to each of the six openings. The flaps are cut to size, fingerholes cut through as indicated, and then they are inserted into place in the open slot in each holder, Fig. 22. This manner of assembly permits easy replacement of the flaps after they weaken and possibly break from long usage. Note that the shape of part A, Fig. 19, also serves to tilt the flap as the ball drops.

Now refer to Fig. 15 and Fig. 3. The sectional view, Fig. 3, shows a ¾ x 1-in. clamping strip between the end rail (also the side rails) and the rabbeted riser, part B, which supports the inner rabbeted edge of the top rail. Note that this strip serves a threefold purpose—it clamps the bed firmly to the supporting shelf members; it provides a screw base for the countersunk screws anchoring the top rail and it serves as a nailing strip for the nails holding the riser, B. The whole assembly is easily removed, permitting the bed to be refelted when necessary. Still referring to Fig. 3, note the 1/16 x ¼-in. rabbet on the lower edge of part A. It is not shown elsewhere on details of part A. Its purpose is to permit shifting the cushion-mounting rail (part A) in order to hold the outer edge, or apex, of the cushion at a point exactly 1³⁄₁₆ in. (for a 2¼-in. ball) above the surface of the felted bed. This is important.

Referring now to Fig. 15, cut the clamping strips, the risers and the mounting rails and try them for fit with the bed in position. Once sure of the fit of the parts, glue the rubber cushions to the mounting rails with a special adhesive and wrap with cord at spaced intervals as in detail A, Fig 20. Be sure to allow sufficient cushion material at the ends of each member of the mounting rail for trimming as in detail B, Fig. 20. Use a sharp knife for trimming flush with

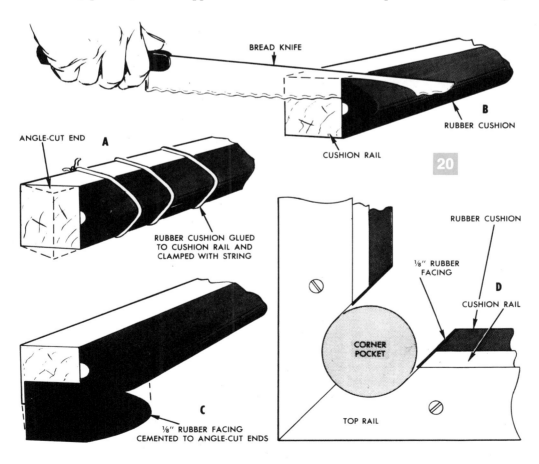

BREAD KNIFE

B

RUBBER CUSHION

CUSHION RAIL

20

ANGLE-CUT END   A

RUBBER CUSHION GLUED TO CUSHION RAIL AND CLAMPED WITH STRING

RUBBER CUSHION

⅛" RUBBER FACING

D

CUSHION RAIL

CORNER POCKET

C

⅛" RUBBER FACING CEMENTED TO ANGLE-CUT ENDS

TOP RAIL

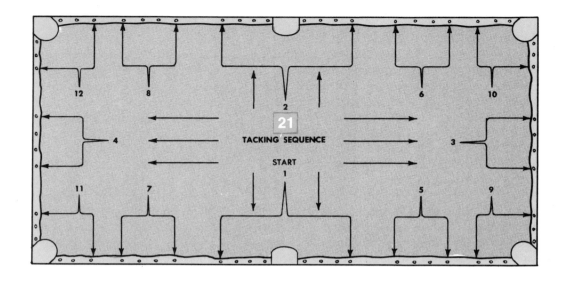

Fig. 21 — TACKING SEQUENCE / START

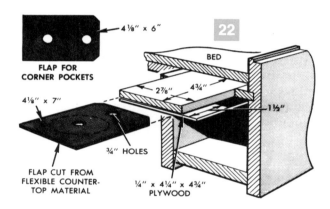

FLAP FOR CORNER POCKETS — 4⅛″ x 6″

4⅛″ x 7″

FLAP CUT FROM FLEXIBLE COUNTER-TOP MATERIAL

¾″ HOLES

¼″ x 4¼″ x 4¾″ PLYWOOD

BED — 2⅞″ — 4¾″ — 1½″

Retarding flaps are placed in the side and corner pockets as detailed above. These flaps fit loosely into holders made as detailed, and can be replaced when worn after long use. Below, the bed felt is cut and fitted around edges of the ball-pocket openings in the particle-board bed. Patterns show cuts to make

flip-top table for fun, continued

the miter at the ends. Then apply the rubber facing as in detail C and trim to the contour at the mitered ends of the mounting rails. Note in detail D, Fig. 20, that the rubber facing extends its full thickness into the pocket.

Now comes the application of the felt covering to the cushions. Note in Fig. 26 that the felting goes all the way around both cushion and rail and is butted and tacked on the back face of the rail. Cut the strips of felt 5 in. wide. Fig. 25 gives the pattern for cutting the felt for a neat fit around the rubber facing at the ends of the cushion assembly. Work carefully to get the felt in place without any wrinkles. Temporary rows of tacks are used to hold the felt while the glue dries.

Refer again to Fig. 3, parts A and B. Note that in the assembly detailed the riser B is screwed to the cushion mounting rail A and the riser B is then nailed and glued to the clamping strip. Space the nails about 6 in. apart. It's a

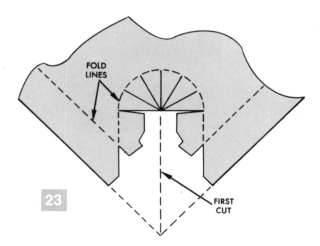

Fig. 23 — FOLD LINES / FIRST CUT

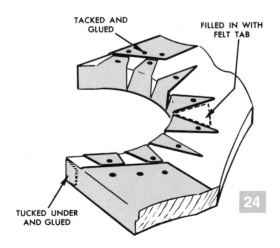

Fig. 24 — TACKED AND GLUED / FILLED IN WITH FELT TAB / TUCKED UNDER AND GLUED

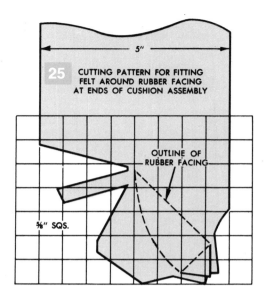

25 CUTTING PATTERN FOR FITTING FELT AROUND RUBBER FACING AT ENDS OF CUSHION ASSEMBLY

OUTLINE OF RUBBER FACING

⅜" SQS.

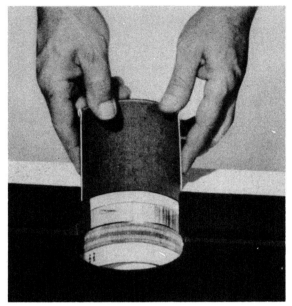

Ball-pocket liners for the side pockets differ slightly from those fitted into corner pockets, as you will see from Fig. 27 and also from the photograph in the lower left corner

good idea to drill undersized pilot holes for the nails to prevent splitting of the clamping strip. Four screws are used to fasten each clamping strip to the bed. These are located 3½ in. from the ends, the two other screws being equally spaced between the end ones.

At this stage the assembly is ready for attachment of the top rail, Fig. 18. Spacing of the countersunk holes for the screws which hold it is given in Fig. 15, the spacings being located on the center line of the rail. Drill the body holes for the No. 10 screws all the way through, then use ½-in. countersink, running the latter just deep enough to allow only 1⁄16-in. above the

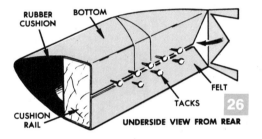

RUBBER CUSHION | BOTTOM

FELT

TACKS

CUSHION RAIL

26 UNDERSIDE VIEW FROM REAR

The rubber cushion and rail are covered with felt as shown in the detail above. Note that the rows of tacks on the back of the rail are staggered

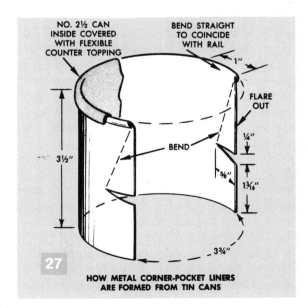

NO. 2½ CAN INSIDE COVERED WITH FLEXIBLE COUNTER TOPPING

BEND STRAIGHT TO COINCIDE WITH RAIL

1"

FLARE OUT

BEND

3½"

¼"

⅝"

1⅜16"

3¾"

27 HOW METAL CORNER-POCKET LINERS ARE FORMED FROM TIN CANS

28

screwhead when the screw is drawn tight. The screwheads are capped with pearl sighting disks, which you buy ready-made. They are slightly under ½ in. in diameter. The disks are loose-fitted to permit them to be lifted out readily when it is necessary to replace worn or damaged felt on the bed and cushions. In the final assembly of the rail, after painting, a tiny spot of putty placed on each of the screwheads will hold the sighting disks in place yet permit removal when necessary.

Now make and fit the end and side-pocket boots, Fig. 27. Each boot is made from a No. 2½ tin can and lined. The lining material is the same as that used in the ball returns and is applied with contact cement. Note that the top edge of the lining material is bent over the lip of the can section. Only the end-pocket boots are notched and bent as detailed in Fig. 27. Edges of the side-pocket liners are cut straight as indicated in the photo on page 1975. Here the can is first

formed oval shape and then cut. Approximately one half of the can is required, actual measurement being taken between the ends of the cushion facings against which the cans hook. Once fitted, the pocket boots are removed, each one being marked so that all six can be replaced in sequence. Now, remove the rail assembly consisting of the top rail, the assembled parts A and B and the clamping strip. Remove the cushion rail from the riser, again marking the parts so that they can be reassembled in sequence. Cover the felted bed with heavy paper to keep it clean, also to protect it from overspray when painting. Trim the paper to the full size of the bed so that the edges will extend under the clamping strips. Reassemble by placing the bed back in position, replacing the clamping strips, the risers and the top rail, but omitting the cushion rails. In this temporary reassembly of the parts, turn the screws in only moderately tight as the parts must again be disassembled after sanding and painting.

Now you are ready to start building the supporting base which features roomy storage compartments.

The storage unit assembly measures 20¾ x 36½ x 80½ in. and can be separated into three units for transportation, Fig. 28. The two end,

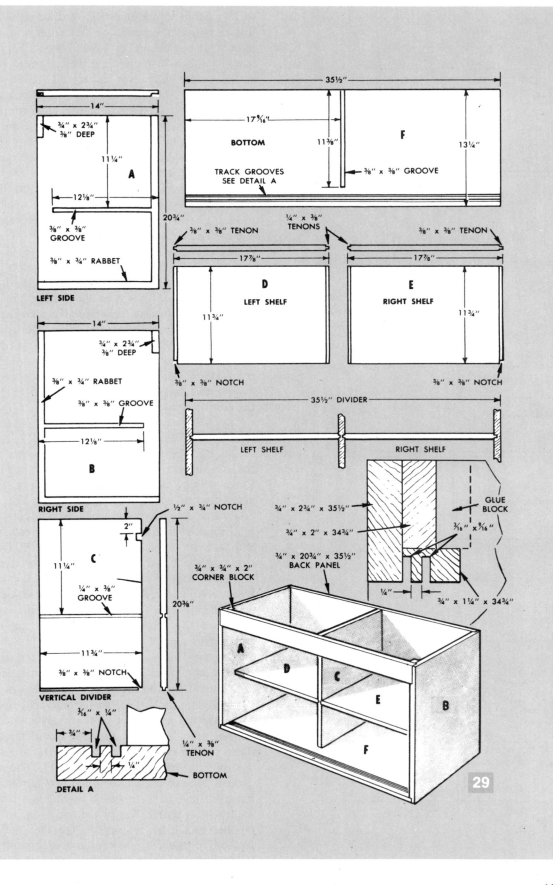

14"

¾" x 2¾"
⅜" DEEP

11¼"

A

12⅛"

⅜" x ⅜"
GROOVE

⅜" x ¾" RABBET

20¾"

LEFT SIDE

14"

¾" x 2¾"
⅜" DEEP

⅜" x ¾" RABBET

⅜" x ⅜" GROOVE

12⅛"

B

RIGHT SIDE

½" x ¾" NOTCH

2"

11¼"

C

¼" x ⅜"
GROOVE

11¾"

⅜" x ⅜" NOTCH

VERTICAL DIVIDER

20⅜"

35½"

17⁹⁄₁₆"

BOTTOM

11⅜"

TRACK GROOVES
SEE DETAIL A

F

⅜" x ⅜" GROOVE

13¼"

⅜" x ⅜" TENON

¼" x ⅜"
TENONS

⅜" x ⅜" TENON

17⅞"

D

LEFT SHELF

11¾"

17⅞"

E

RIGHT SHELF

11¾"

⅜" x ⅜" NOTCH

⅜" x ⅜" NOTCH

35½" DIVIDER

LEFT SHELF

RIGHT SHELF

GLUE
BLOCK

¾" x 2¾" x 35½"

¾" x 2" x 34¾"

³⁄₁₆" x ⁹⁄₁₆"

¾" x 20¾" x 35½"
BACK PANEL

¼"

¾" x 1¼" x 34¾"

¾" x ¾" x 2"
CORNER BLOCK

³⁄₁₆" x ¼"

¾"

¼"

¼" x ⅜"
TENON

BOTTOM

DETAIL A

A

D

C

E

B

F

29

1977

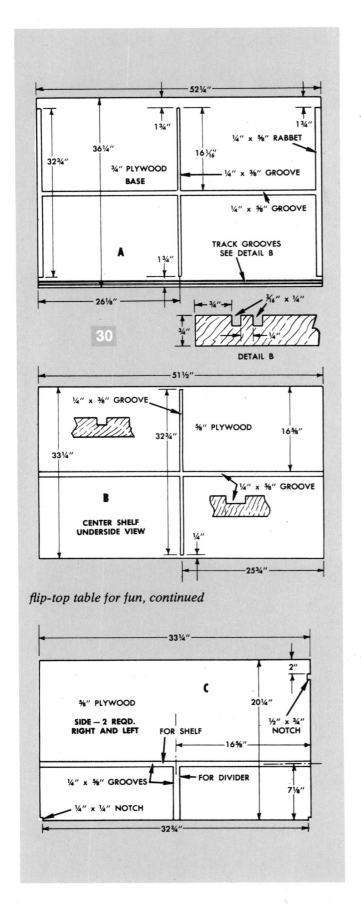

flip-top table for fun, continued

or leg, cabinets are identical and serve as the legs as well as a support for the center unit. The base of the leg cabinet is ¾-in. plywood, Fig. 29, part F, with a ⅜-in. stopped dado 11⅜ in. long at the center. Run this cut on the table saw, stopping just short of the required dimension. Finish the cut with a wood chisel. Then run 3/16 x ¼-in. door grooves, or tracks, 1 in. in from the front edge of the material.

The two sides, made right and left, come next. Notice that the parts A and B in Fig. 29 have ⅜ x ⅜ x 11⅜-in. stopped dadoes and that there are ⅜ x ¾-in. rabbets on two edges of both pieces. The ⅜ x ¾ x 2¾-in. corner rabbets are laid out and cut with a wood chisel.

The center divider, part C, Fig. 29, requires a dado located 11¼ in. from the top edge on both faces. Cut a ⅜-in. tongue (tenon) on the lower edge, and a ⅜-in. notch at the front edge. The ½ x ¾-in. notch near the upper front corner receives the upper track for the sliding doors. Detail A, Fig. 29, shows the lower tracks. Note that upper tracks are cut deeper. Two shelves, parts D and E, Fig. 29, have ends tenoned to fit into the dadoes in parts A, B, and C. Note the difference in tenon sizes.

the back panel

The back panel requires no cutting other than the overall size given. A front piece, or rail, forms a part of the upper sliding-door track assembly, as in the sectional view, Fig. 29. Study the drawing before making any cuts. Behind this rail is a backing strip, a grooved track and two corner blocks. Take extra care in constructing the upper grooved track since it must line up precisely with the grooves in the base. Duplicate all pieces as there are two end, or leg, units. Prime (with glue) all edge grain, apply glue over the priming, and nail. Set the nails and fill with a patching compound.

The base, shelf and end pieces of the center storage unit, parts A, B, and C, are detailed in Fig. 30 and the unit is shown assembled in Fig. 32, including the additional parts E, and F, Fig. 31. Only the bottom is of ¾-in. plywood. The bottom tracks detail B, Fig. 30, are identical to those on the end cabinets. Note that two sides are required, one left and one right. The shelf dado is easy to cut on the table saw all the way but you may have to finish cutting the divider dado with a chisel. Notice the two ¼-in. x ¼-in. notches in the lower corners. On the shelf the dadoes, or grooves, are centered each way; one is stopped, the other goes through to the edges.

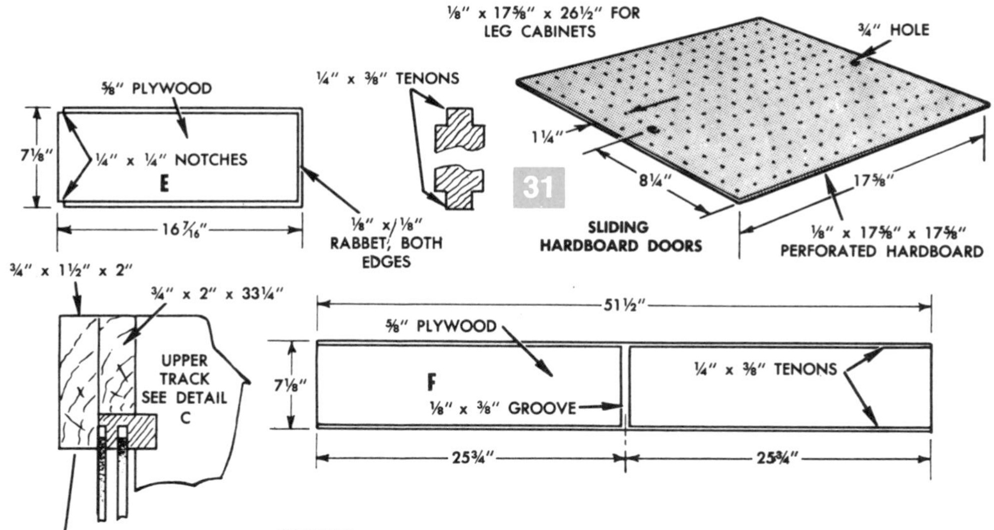
⅛" x 17⅝" x 26½" FOR LEG CABINETS
¾" HOLE
⅝" PLYWOOD
¼" x ⅜" TENONS
7⅛"
¼" x ¼" NOTCHES
E
16 7/16"
⅛" x ⅛" RABBET, BOTH EDGES
1¼"
8¼"
17⅝"
31
SLIDING HARDBOARD DOORS
⅛" x 17⅝" x 17⅝" PERFORATED HARDBOARD
¾" x 1½" x 2"
¾" x 2" x 33¼"
UPPER TRACK SEE DETAIL C
51½"
⅝" PLYWOOD
7⅛"
F
⅛" x ⅜" GROOVE
¼" x ⅜" TENONS
25¾"
25¾"

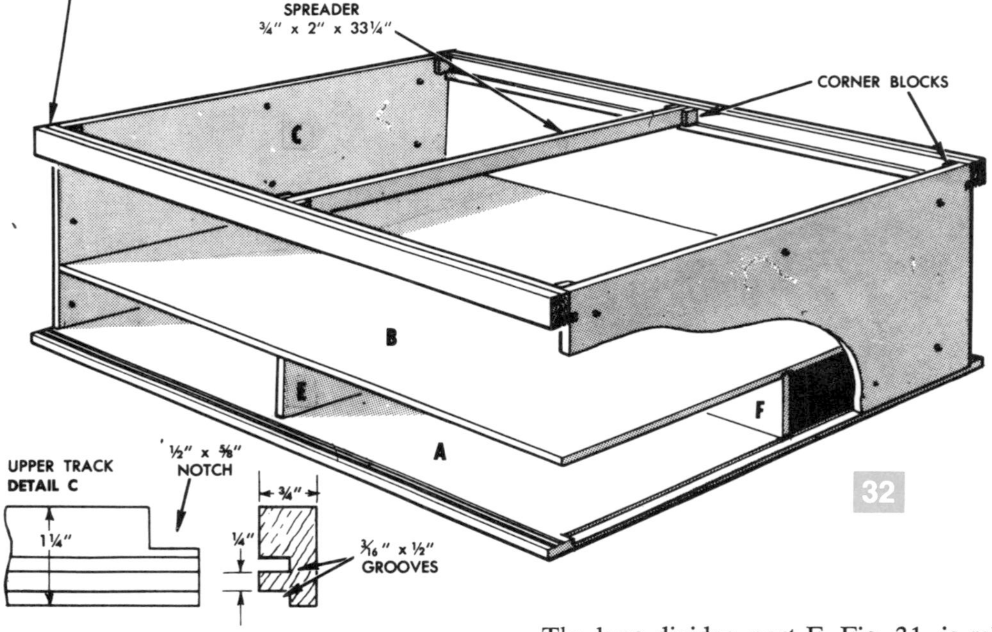
SPREADER ¾" x 2" x 33¼"
CORNER BLOCKS
C
B
E
F
A
32
UPPER TRACK DETAIL C
½" x ⅝" NOTCH
1¼"
¾"
¼"
3/16" x ½" GROOVES

The long divider, part F, Fig. 31, is rabbeted on both edges and grooved on both sides at the center to take the inner end of the dividers, parts E, Fig. 31. On the front corners of the dividers E the tenons are cut back ¼ in.

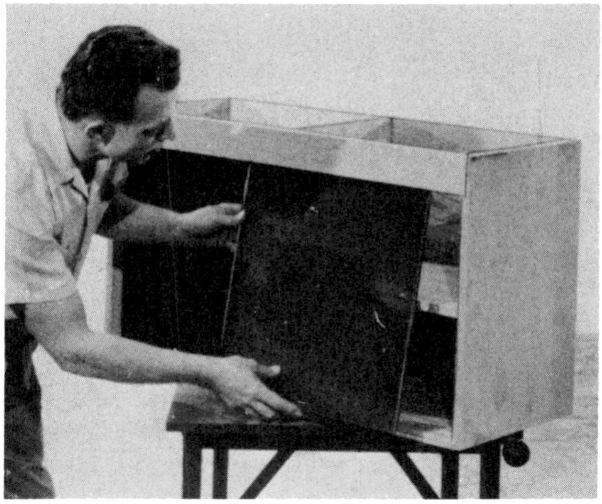

Sectional dimension and assembly of the upper track, Fig. 31, will be seen in detail C, Fig. 32. This member is 52¼ in. long. Cut duplicate ¾ x 2¾-in. facing strips, and ¾ x 2-in. backing strips. These will be assembled as in the sectional view, Fig. 31. The parts are cut from solid stock. Finally you'll need one spreader, and eight glue blocks, each ¾ x ½ x 2 in.

Now, trial-fit all the parts of the three-unit base. Make any adjustments necessary, then begin assembling, starting with the leg cabinets. Use glue in all the joints and be sure to strike nailing guide lines so that you know where to center nails into edges that are concealed in the assemblies. Use bar clamps to draw parts tightly together before nailing. Wipe off excess glue with a damp cloth.

Place the end units in position against the center cabinet, line up accurately, and clamp in position. Mark off on the inside ends of the center cabinet, and drill 8 holes in each side as indicated. Countersink and drive 1¼-in. No. 10 flathead wood screws—8 on each side. This results in a simple, rigid assembly of the three-part base. Now, to add the casters, take the three units apart, place the two end cabinets back to back, clamp together temporarily and turn the combined units over, bottom up.

The assembled table rolls on four 2-in. rubber or plastic-wheel casters (two with brakes), which are of the type fitted with a ¾-in. threaded stud and generally used on power-tool stands. Locate longitudinal center lines on the bottom of each end cabinet. Plates for the casters are made from heavy clothesline hooks of the type having mounting plates, or bases, like those in Fig. 34. Remove the hooks. Enlarge the hole in the center of each plate to take the caster stud. Then attach the plates to the casters, drawing the nuts up tightly. Now drill ¾-in. holes on the center line penciled on the bottom of each end cabinet. These holes take the studs as in Fig. 34 and must be located so that when the caster is in place, the outer edge of the plate will be ¼ in. in from the edge of the cabinet. Locate the casters with brakes on opposite corners.

Four table levelers are necessary to assure a perfectly level pool-table bed. These are made from L-shaped steel mending plates (inside-corner type). Cut a 1-in. length from one leg of each plate and bend a ¼-in. lip on one end of each of the cut pieces. Run a nut on each of four ¼ x 2-in. stovebolts. Enlarge the hole in the short leg of each of the mending plates. Pass the stovebolt through the enlarged hole. Run a second nut down on the bolt and solder (or attach with epoxy cement) the second nut to the plate. This latter assembly is attached to each side of each leg cabinet on the center line and about 1 in. below the lower edge of the table side rail as in Fig. 35. Then attach the strike plates to the edges of the side rail directly above the end of the stovebolt and you end up with four assemblies like that in Fig. 35 which enable you to level the table easily.

Cues are stored under the ball tunnel as in Fig. 33. Spring tool clips are attached to the bottom of each ball tunnel at the positions indicated, the larger clip at the high end and the smaller one, which holds the cue tip, 40 in. distant.

Use ⅛-in. perforated hardboard for the sliding doors. In laying out, remember to evenly space the holes from the outside edges, Fig. 31. Note the variations in sizes of the doors. Locate and drill two ¾-in. finger holes on each door. Smooth and slightly round all edges.

Now you're ready to make the piggyback top for the table. Refer to Figs. 38, 39 and 40 for construction details. You can purchase a two-piece folding table-tennis top, with each side

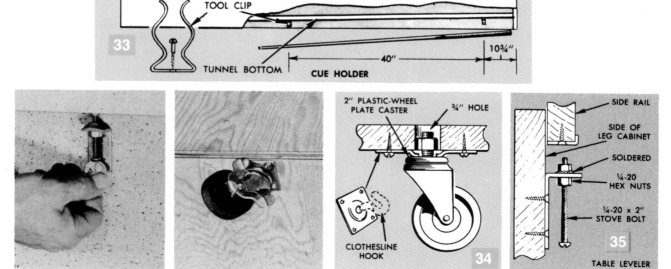

Swivel casters, two with brakes, are attached to leg cabinets as in the photo at the left, and in Fig. 34.
Fig. 35 shows how the levelers are attached to leg cabinets. Four identical levelers are needed

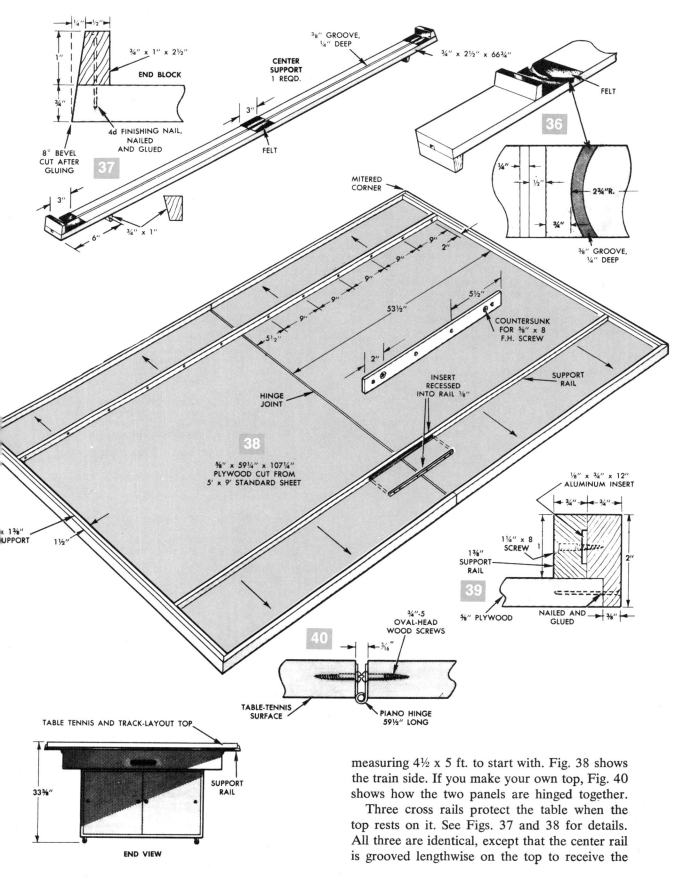

¼″ ½″

1″

¾″

¾″ x 1″ x 2½″

END BLOCK

8° BEVEL
CUT AFTER
GLUING

37

4d FINISHING NAIL,
NAILED
AND GLUED

3″

6″   ¾″ x 1″

**CENTER
SUPPORT**
1 REQD.

⅜″ GROOVE,
¼″ DEEP

3″

FELT

¾″ x 2½″ x 66¾″

FELT

36

¼″   ½″

2¾″R.

¾″

⅜″ GROOVE,
¼″ DEEP

MITERED
CORNER

9″   2″

9″

9″

9″

9″

53½″

5½″

5½″

2″

COUNTERSUNK
FOR ⅝″ x 8
F.H. SCREW

HINGE
JOINT

INSERT
RECESSED
INTO RAIL ⅛″

SUPPORT
RAIL

38

⅝″ x 59¼″ x 107¼″
PLYWOOD CUT FROM
5′ x 9′ STANDARD SHEET

x 1⅜″
SUPPORT

1½″

⅛″ x ¾″ x 12″
ALUMINUM INSERT

¾″   ¾″

1¼″ x 8
SCREW

1⅜″
SUPPORT
RAIL

39

⅝″ PLYWOOD

2″

NAILED AND
GLUED   ⅜″

¾″-5
OVAL-HEAD
WOOD SCREWS

40

³⁄₁₆″

TABLE-TENNIS
SURFACE

PIANO HINGE
59½″ LONG

TABLE TENNIS AND TRACK-LAYOUT TOP

33⅜″

SUPPORT
RAIL

END VIEW

measuring 4½ x 5 ft. to start with. Fig. 38 shows
the train side. If you make your own top, Fig. 40
shows how the two panels are hinged together.

Three cross rails protect the table when the
top rests on it. See Figs. 37 and 38 for details.
All three are identical, except that the center rail
is grooved lengthwise on the top to receive the

MATERIALS LIST
(All dimensions actual sizes in inches)

BILLIARD TOP

2 pcs.—¾ x 7½ x 92 Side rails
2 pcs.—¾ x 7½ x 48 End rails
2 pcs.—¾ x 5¼ x 86¼ Side wall of tunnel—sides
2 pcs.—¾ x 5¼ x 36½ Side wall of tunnel—ends
1 pc. —¾ x 4¼ x 36½ Unused tunnel bottom—end
2 pcs.—¾ x 4¼ x 86¼ Side tunnel bottoms
1 pc.—¾ x 4¼ x 46½ Ball-return bottom
2 pcs.—¾ x 1¾ x 91¼ Bed—shelf—sides
2 pcs.—¾ x 1¾ x 43¾ Bed—shelf—ends
2 pcs.—¾ x 1 x 80½ Cleats for table support—sides
2 pcs.—¾ x 1 x 35 Cleats for table support—ends
1 pc. —48 x 96 (Particle boards)—Playing bed
1 pc. —¾ x 3½ x 80½ Center brace under bed
4 pcs.—¾ x 1½ x 3½ Center-brace glue blocks
4 pcs.—¾ x 2⅝ x 43¾ Support slats under bed
2 pcs.—¾ x 2¼ x 48 Top rail—ends
2 pcs.—¾ x 2¼ x 92 Top rail—sides
4 pcs.—¼ x ⅝ x 8 Splines for side rails
2 ½ x ¾ x 5 Support blocks for ball return
4 ¼ x 1 x 3¾ Splines for top rail
2 pcs.—¾ x 1 x 42¼—Cushion clamping strip—ends
2 pcs.—¾ x 1⁹⁄₁₆ x 42¼—Cushion rail riser—ends
2 pcs.—¾ x 1¼ x 37¾—Cushion rails—ends
4 pcs.—¾ x 1 x 43⅛—Cushion clamping strip—sides
4 pcs.—¾ x 1⁹⁄₁₆ x 43⅛—Cushion rail riser—sides
4 pcs.—¾ x 1¼ x 38¾—Cushion rails—sides
6 pcs.—¾ x 4¼ x 4¼—Head corner pocket fillets
4 pcs.—¾ x 3 x 4¼—Foot corner pocket fillets
2 pcs.—¾ x 1¾ x 4½—Side pocket fillers
12 pcs.—¾ x 2¹⁄₁₆ x 2¹⁄₁₆—Corner pocket fillers
4 pcs.—¾ x 2⅞ x 4¾—Flap holders
4 pcs.—¼ x 4¼ x 4½—Flap holders
1 pt.—Liquid hide glue (Franklin)
1 lb.—Plastic-resin glue—powdered (Weldwood)
½ pt.—Super strong glue (Allens)
1 set—Rubber cushions—For 4 x 8 table
1 pc.—48 x 96—Billiard cloth
6 pcs.—5 x 48—Cushion cloth
⁷⁄₁₆ #4—Carpet tacks
12 Rubber cushion facing
Flexible plastic countertop material
1 pt.—Contact cement
1¼ x 10—F.H. wood screws
1½ x 10—F.H. wood screws
2¼ x 10—F.H. wood screws
6 #2½ Tin cans
1½ doz.—½—Pearl spots

CABINET BASE

2 pcs.—¾ x 13¼ x 35½—Base of end unit
4 pcs.—¾ x 14 x 20¾—Sides of end unit (2 R. and 2 L.)
2 pcs.—¾ x 11¾ x 20⅜—Center divider
4 pcs.—¾ x 11¾ x 17⅞—Shelves—end unit (2 R. and 2 L.)
2 pcs.—¾ x 2¾ x 35½—Face spreader for end unit
4 pcs.—¾ x ¾ x 2—Corner blocks—end unit
2 pcs.—¾ x 2 x 34¾—Back strip, upper-track assembly (end unit)
2 pcs.—¾ x 1¼ x 34¾—Upper grooved track—end unit
1 pc. —¾ x 36¼ x 52¼—Center-unit base
2 pcs.—⅝ x 20¼ x 33¼—Center-unit sides (1 R. and 1 L.)
1 pc. —⅝ x 33¼ x 51½—Center-unit shelf
1 pc. —⅝ x 7⅛ x 51½—Center unit—long divider
2 pcs.—⅝ x 7⅛ x 16⁷⁄₁₆—Center unit—short dividers
2 pcs.—¾ x 2¾ x 52¼—Face spreader, upper track, center
2 pcs.—¾ x 2 x 52¼—Back strip, upper track, center unit
2 pcs.—¾ x 1¼ x 52¼—Upper-track strip, center unit
1 pc. —¾ x 2 x 33¼—Spreader, center unit
8 pcs.—¾ x 1½ x 2—Corner blocks, center unit
4 pcs.—⅛ x 17⅜ x 26½—Doors for leg cabinet
4 pcs.—⅛ x 17⅜ x 17⅜—Doors for center cabinet
16 —1¼ x 10 F.H. wood screws (fasten units together)
8 —¾ x 10 F.H. wood screws (table levelers)
4 —2 x ¼ x 20—R.H. stove bolts (levelers)
8 —Hex nuts for ¼—20 bolts (levelers)
4 —⅝ x 2½ x 2½—Steel corner plates (levelers)
4 —¾ x 8 F.H. wood screws (strike plate, levelers)
4 —Spring tool holders—2 for 1¼ D. and 2 for ½ D. (cue holders)
4 —R.H. wood screws—2 1 x 10 R.H. 2⅝ x 8 R.H. (cue holders)
4 —Rubber or plastic-wheel casters (two with brake)
4 —Clothesline hooks (casters)
4 —Lock washers (caster stud)

TABLE TENNIS TOP

2 pcs.—¾ x 2 x 60—End edging
4 pcs.—¾ x 2 x 54—Side edging
1 pc. —6' length ½ x ½ continuous (piano) hinge
60 —¾ x 5 oval-head wood screws
2 pcs.—¾ x 1⅜ x 58½—Inner end edging
2 pcs.—¾ x 1⅜ x 105—Locking cleats
2 pcs.—⅝ x 4½ x 60—Table-tennis playing field
2 pcs.—⅛ x ¾ x 12—Flat alum. or steel
28 —1¼ x 8 F.H. wood screws (for side edging)
4 —⅝ x 8 F.H. wood screws (for metal strips)
4d & 6d Finishing nails
¼-lb. can patching compound
3 pcs.—¾ x 2¼ x 61¹¹⁄₁₆—Table crossrails
12 pcs.—Wood blocks ¾ x 1 x 2½ (for table crossrails)
Strips of felt—2½ wide

---

piano hinge, and grooved on the bottom to sit over the curved rims of the side-pocket backs.

To finish your table, first soften all edges by rounding slightly with medium garnet paper. Patch all nail holes and sand. Then clean the table with a vacuum cleaner. Mask the table carefully, then spray a primer coat and two finish coats of paint in a color of your choice. Or use a urethane varnish to give it a rich appearance.

See also: basements; billiards; hobby workspace; railroad model; road racing, model.

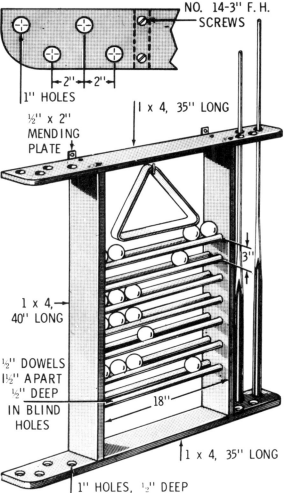

NO. 14-3" F. H. SCREWS

2"

1" HOLES

½" x 2" MENDING PLATE

1 x 4, 35" LONG

1 x 4, 40" LONG

½" DOWELS 1½" APART ½" DEEP IN BLIND HOLES

18"

1 x 4, 35" LONG

3"

1" HOLES, ½" DEEP

Pool-cue rack

BY L. DOCK

This easy-to-build rack keeps all of your pool accessories handy

■ A COMMON PROBLEM after buying a pool table is finding a place to keep the cues, triangle and other accessories. The hanging rack shown at the left is a convenient solution. The balls are cradled on pairs of ½-in. dowels. The triangle is hung on a hook made of heavy wire, such as coat-hanger wire. Holes are bored through the top piece and part way into the bottom cross-piece to take the cues. Finish the rack to match the decor of the room in which it is mounted. Mending plates are used to fasten the rack to the wall by letting them extend above the top member. The cues are inserted by passing the tips up through the upper holes first. They are then brought back down and seated in the bottom crosspiece.

Building contractors and do-it-yourselfers will do well to remember this novel treatment the next time they install board-and-batten siding. Tilt the table saw to about 30 deg. and bevel-rip a 1 x 12 into 2¼-in.-wide strips. This gives battens with beveled edges. Placed with the wide side against the wall they give a soft shadow; reverse the batten and they give a sharp, deep shadow. You can get some truly novel effects by varying the angle of the bevel-rip with your table saw.

You can carry a shovel or spade and a rake comfortably, using both hands, but add another tool and the three can become unmanageable. Just add this tool-toter bar to your garden wheelbarrow and take everything you are likely to need in one trip. It's simply a band about 3 in. wide cut from a big inner tube and snapped around the barrow handles. It doesn't interfere in any way with normal use of the barrow. Builders can make use of the same idea to carry lumber and pipe safely.

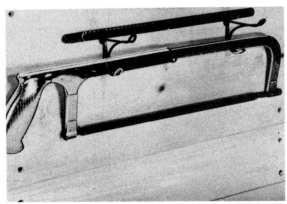

Usually it's easy to locate the hacksaw frame, but suppose you want to change the blade? Finding that spare could take time you can ill afford on a busy weekend. If you follow through with the rack shown above, the tool and a selection of blades are always handy. Screw two spaced coat hooks into the wall. Then you can hang the saw from the bottom hooks and lay the blades across the top. You'll also find this an easy way to keep track of your coping saw.

When you don't have a rosehead countersink at hand you can countersink a hole for a flatheaded screw with a twist drill. Select a drill about twice the diameter of the screw hole, chuck it in a hand drill, place the tip in the hole and turn the hand drill backwards. This will give a good countersink, especially in soft woods that splinter easily.

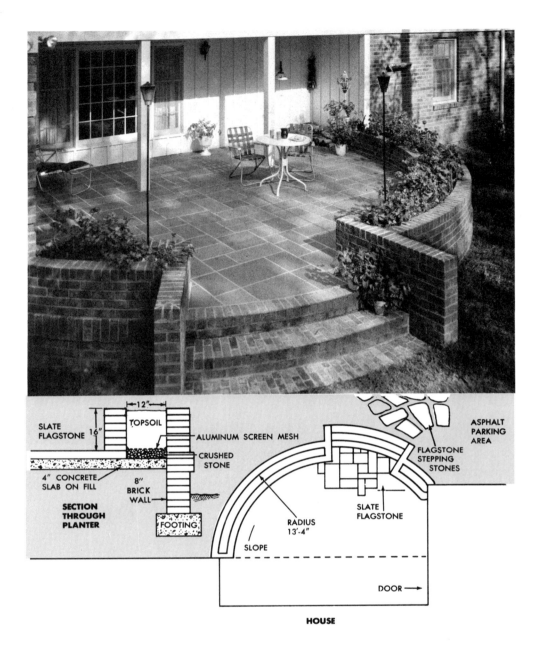

SLATE FLAGSTONE • 16" • TOPSOIL • 12" •
ALUMINUM SCREEN MESH
CRUSHED STONE
4" CONCRETE SLAB ON FILL • 8" BRICK WALL
SECTION THROUGH PLANTER
FOOTING
SLOPE
RADIUS 13'-4"
SLATE FLAGSTONE
FLAGSTONE STEPPING STONES
ASPHALT PARKING AREA
DOOR →
HOUSE

Patio porch on a curve

■ ON MOST HOMES a porch is a square, un-interesting appendage to the front door. But on the house above, a landscape architect has extended the original, small, recessed porch into an interesting semicircular patio porch.

The new porch affords a vantage point for enjoying the view of the lawn and plantings, as well as providing a fine spot for lounging and sunbathing.

The original porch was enlarged nearly three times to make it ideal for parties or family use. And the brick planters, along with the graceful curved shape, add architectural interest to the exterior of the house.

At night the patio lights give a glow to the shrubs and flowers in the planter walls.

See also: crawl space; home additions; house paints; remodeling.

port, boat: see cover, boat
portable darkroom: see darkroom, portable
portable high fidelity: see high fidelity, portable
portable radios: see transistor radios
portable vacuum cleaner: see vacuum cleaners, shop
portaging: see packs, camping

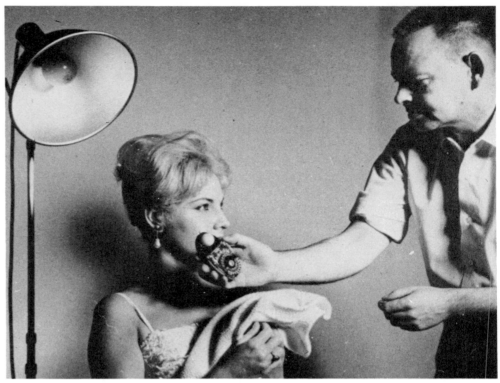

Use your light meter to guide you in placing your lamps for portrait work

Light your portraits like the pros

BY JOHN BURROUGHS

Team up your camera
with a bit of lighting know-how.
The result—striking portraits
that will rival those made
by a professional studio

Standard three-light setup as shown forms your
basic lighting arrangement. Variations start from here

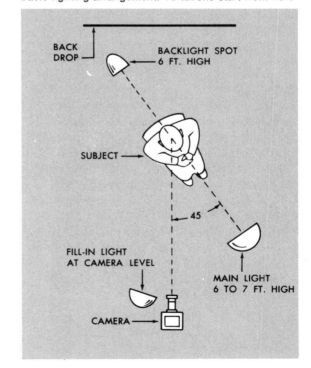

Main light is placed in front, above and in line with the subject's nose or slightly to one side

Fill light, on other side, is then positioned at the lens level to soften the shadows

Effect light, from behind and above, highlights the hair and softens a harsh shoulder line

HOME STUDIO portraiture might seem a lot more complicated than it really is. It's true that a knowledge of lighting technique is absolutely essential, but, if this scares you, you're due for a pleasant surprise—just one basic lighting arrangement is all you need to master. Best of all, despite its simplicity, this setup does not sacrifice quality; in fact, the identical positioning is used in professional portrait studios.

The three floodlights you will need of either the clamp-on or stand type, equipped with 12-in. spun aluminum reflectors, will cost from $15–$25. It's a good idea to buy 3200-deg. Kelvin, 500-watt photofloods. These radiate less heat,

have a longer life than the regular 3400-deg. No. 2 floods, and are the better choice for portraiture. You can safely use as many as four on a 20-amp household circuit since each bulb draws only 4.4 amps.

But how about camera equipment? Don't you need an elaborate bellows rig with a ground-glass back for focusing under a tent of black cloth? Nope. Any camera, even a modest one, can fill the bill for home portraits. Cameras using large-size film make it easier, of course, to produce sharp, grainless prints, and a long focal length lens is helpful in minimizing distortion. But a camera with a non-interchangeable normal-focal-

Main light for male portraits is positioned high and to the side of the subject, usually on his left

Fill light in front on other side and effect light as an "edge" light complete this lighting setup

Switching angle of the subject's shoulders will very often improve the portrait's composition

Striking bridal portrait results when the subject is seated before a dark background with rear effect light directed at the veil. Shoot from a low angle, checking to make sure veil hangs naturally

main light were used, however, portions of the face left in shadow would photograph as if they were jet black. This is usually undesirable, except in special work such as theatrical portraits. For that reason, the second flood, the fill light, is positioned to illuminate the subject from another angle at somewhat lower intensity and "fill" or lighten the shadows. The function of the effect light (or backlight spot), placed high and behind the subject, is to liven the hair with natural-looking highlights and separate the subject from the background.

The three floods are always used in the same basic pattern, but here's a refinement: the main light, depending on its placement, can provide either front-lighting or side-lighting.

Take a look at a magazine cover shot of a pretty girl or child. You'll notice that the subject's face has no deep shadow areas and that the eyes and mouth are emphasized. A pro would call this a "high-key" picture; it is achieved by the use of front lighting. The main light is positioned in line with and above the subject's nose. When properly placed, it casts a small butterfly-wing-shaped shadow, just under the nostrils. The fill light is then set up beside the camera lens on the side opposite the main light. The effect light occupies its usual spot, high and to the rear of the subject.

Side-lighting, because of its emphasis on facial

portraits, continued

A semi-candid photograph of a youngster engaged in some familiar activity will probably have more appeal than a formal pose and will banish self-conscious stiffness. Favorite pet or toys make good "props"

length lens will give you perfectly satisfactory portrait negatives when fitted with a plus-1 supplementary lens to permit close focusing.

For a head-and-shoulders portrait, the camera should be placed on a rock-steady tripod at a distance from the subject that will fill the negative as nearly as possible without distorting the person's features. Ordinarily, if a standard-focal-length lens is used and the camera is close enough so that the subject fills more than one-half of the negative, objectionable distortion will result.

Studio photographers have learned that a triangular placement of three floodlights is best for portrait work. The floods that are used in this setup are known as the main, fill and effect lights.

The main light, placed closest to the subject, should give the strongest illumination; it highlights contours and provides modeling. If only the

planes and skin texture, is especially suitable for portraits of men. Here the main light is placed high and to one side of the face to cross-light the features. It floods one cheek with light and forms a small triangular highlight on the far cheek. When positioning the main light to side-light his subject, a studio photographer watches the reflections of the light that appear in the eyes. When the catchlights are in either the 2 o'clock or 10 o'clock position, depending on which side the light is placed, the flood is in the right spot. The fill and effect lights stay at their customary locations.

With the floods approximately positioned in either arrangement, they are then balanced, that is, their relative intensity is adjusted by moving them closer to or farther from the subject. Most commercial portrait photographers favor a 2-to-1 ratio between main light and fill; the main light illuminates the subject with twice the intensity of the fill. If you switch the lights on one at a time, you can check the relative intensity of the illumination with an exposure meter.

This 2-to-1 main-to-fill ratio gives soft, transparent, natural looking shading on the face. But the 2-to-1 ratio is not sacred and there's no reason to avoid varying it if you think that changing the ratio will improve the picture. For example in shooting a side-lighted portrait of a man, you may back off the fill light enough to give a 3-to-1 or even 4-to-1 ratio. The result will be a dramatic photograph with rich shadow areas. One word of caution—remember to steer clear of these high ratios when working with an inherently

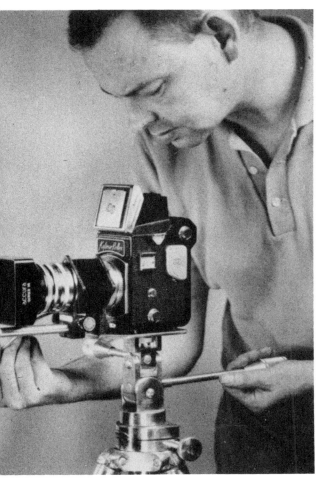

Any camera will serve, but one of the best outfits is a reflex camera with a long-focal-length lens to give you a large head image on the negative. This one has a 150-mm lens, good for 2¼ x 2¼ film size

Rigid tripod and fast shutter speeds are a must to avoid blur. Focus on eyes for best results

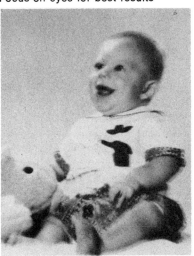

Weak fill lights leave dense shadows while strong effect lights will kill facial outlines

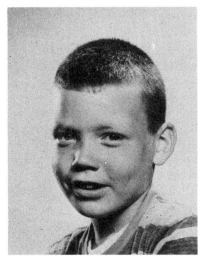

Poor tonal separation causes clothing to merge with the background, which should have been dark

portraits, continued

Selector, or "proof" sheet showing entire roll can be contact-printed with a single exposure by placing negatives on paper under glass

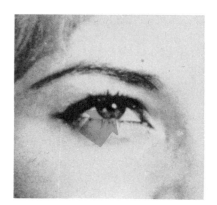

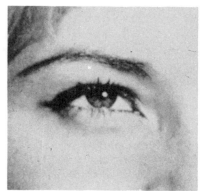

Left, only one catch light should appear in each eye. Use spotting color to remove others and sharpen outline

high contrast film, such as slow speed black and white or a color emulsion.

The most suitable relative intensity for the effect light will depend upon the color and texture of the subject's hair. Dull, dark hair requires considerably stronger backlighting than does shiny, blonde hair. As a starting point, try positioning the effect light the same distance from the subject as is the main light. If your lens is uncoated it is especially important to guard against flare by shielding the effect light.

Processing your portraits doesn't require a bank loan for darkroom equipment. You can fol-

low the practice of many a pro and simply develop and contact-proof your film, then send it to a commercial processor for enlargements. That way you won't need an elaborate darkroom setup and an enlarger. In fact, all you'll need for developing and contact printing is chemicals, a few trays, thermometer, developing tank and a sheet of glass to use as a makeshift printing frame. If you load the tank in a closet at night, with room lights off, the rest can be done in the kitchen.

See also: bird photography; darkrooms; floodlamp; light stand; photoflood control box; photography; spotlight, photo.

AN IDEAL COMBINATION for your ceramics craftwork in both the pottery and sculpture fields, this modeling wheel and hand-rest frame will help you turn out projects of professional quality and artistic appearance. The turntable can be used alone for such modeling as does not require use of a hand rest.

The base consists of an 18-in. square of ¾-in. plywood. The two uprights are sawed to their triangular shape and size, 1½ x 5 x 15 in., from two pieces of ¾-in. plywood glued together. Attach them to the base with glue and screws, not forgetting to first cut the 45-deg. compound notches, as indicated, to permit the turntable to rotate unhindered. To allow raising or lowering of the ¾ x 1 x 24-in. hardwood hand rest, 90-deg. screw hooks are spaced every 2 in. on the uprights.

The two 12-in.-dia. disks for the turntable are cut from ¾-in. plywood with either a bandsaw or jigsaw, or by hand with a coping saw. The lazy susan bearing, available at hardware stores, is first centered and attached to the underside of the top disk with screws, after which the bottom disk is attached to the bearing with ³⁄₁₆-in. flathead stovebolts. Finish the assembly with lacquer or varnish.

See also: hobby workspace.

Build a simple potter's wheel

BY MANLY BANISTER

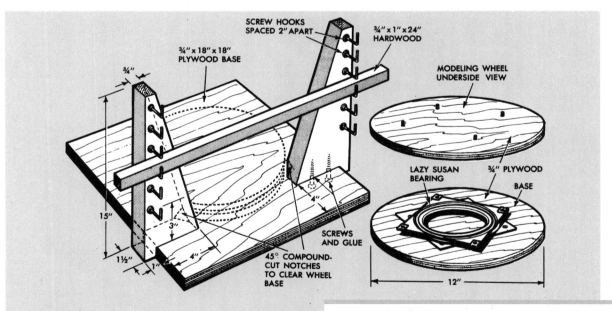

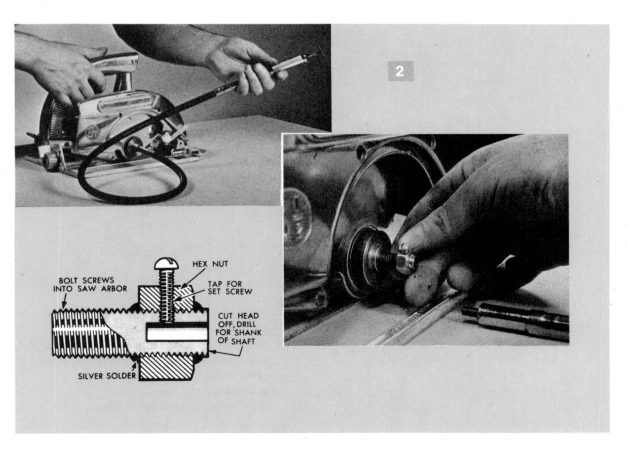

Power takeoffs
for a flexible shaft

BY JOHN BURROUGHS

RIG A DRIVE for a light flexible shaft and you have one of the most versatile, low-cost tools you can own.

Whatever your shop specialty — modelmaking, woodcarving, engraving, gunsmithing, toolmaking, lapidary work — you'll find this miniature machine tool will handle hundreds of otherwise difficult jobs.

It'll polish engine ports . . . smooth filleted welds . . . scribe your name on tools, sharpen gouges, carve plastic—even trim your fingernails! Chuck the right rotary head in the fountain-pen-sized handpiece and you can grind, rout, buff, drill, deburr, carve, file, wire-brush or sand.

The simplest power setup is to grip the shank projecting from the shaft's tail in a chuck on the spindle of any high-speed power tool. Besides the bench grinder (left), you can make use of a drill press or lathe. Just shift the tool's belt for top rpm and you're ready for business.

Or, with an easy-to-make coupling you can tap the power of your portable circular saw. Just turn a hex nut on any bolt that will screw into the saw's arbor, solder the nut in place, saw off the

BOLT SCREWS
INTO SAW ARBOR

HEX NUT

TAP FOR
SET SCREW

CUT HEAD
OFF, DRILL
FOR SHANK
OF SHAFT

SILVER SOLDER

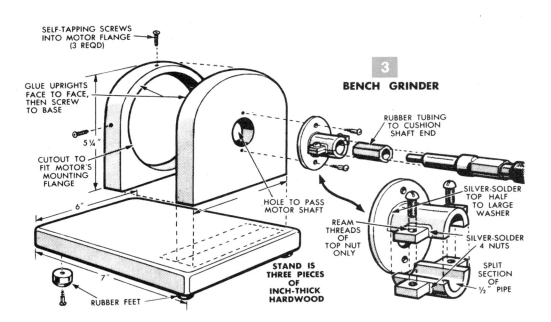

SELF-TAPPING SCREWS
INTO MOTOR FLANGE →
(3 REQD)

3
BENCH GRINDER

GLUE UPRIGHTS
FACE TO FACE,
THEN SCREW
TO BASE

RUBBER TUBING
TO CUSHION
SHAFT END

5¼"

CUTOUT TO
FIT MOTOR'S
MOUNTING
FLANGE

SILVER-SOLDER
TOP HALF
TO LARGE
WASHER

6"

HOLE TO PASS
MOTOR SHAFT

REAM
THREADS
OF
TOP NUT
ONLY

SILVER-SOLDER
4 NUTS

STAND IS
THREE PIECES
OF
INCH-THICK
HARDWOOD

7"

SPLIT
SECTION
OF
½" PIPE

RUBBER FEET →

A clamp fixture, soldered from standard parts, screws to the front of the motor mount to grip the flexible shaft's casing, eliminating the slight torque you'd feel at the handpiece if no clamp were provided. The rubber-tube insert slips onto the shaft for cushioning while the shank is coupled to motor

A wooden stand turns a universal motor (which can be salvaged from an upright vacuum cleaner) into a permanent high-speed drive for a light flexible shaft (see photo at right). A collet-chuck handpiece accepts a variety of rotary tools with ⅛ or 3/22-in. shanks for modelmaking and carving work. The shanks are shown in the foreground

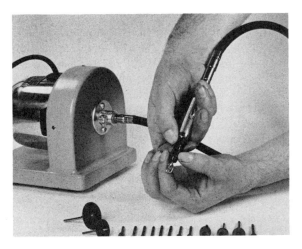

bolt head and centerdrill to accept the shank of your shaft. A setscrew makes the shank spin with the bolt coupling.

If you'd prefer a permanent assembly, hunt up a universal motor from a junked vacuum cleaner or almost any AC-DC appliance. They're usually flange-mounting, so are easy to fit into a simple stand like the one detailed above. Standard couplings are available for ¼, ⁵⁄₁₆ and ⅜-in. motor shafts.

Which of these three takeoffs is best for you? That depends, of course, on which power source is handy, what type of shaft you have, and what work you want it to do.

The cheapest shafts are imports and they work well enough for occasional use. A quality-built,

neoprene-sheathed shaft with a sleeve-bearing handpiece will run about twice as much. Shafts with ballbearing handpieces and tail couplings retail at a higher price.

Since the carving burrs and grinding points you'll be using are small in diameter, the shaft must turn at high speed—3500 rpm at least—for the tool to perform well. Very cheap shafts may heat up when run at speeds above 6000 rpm, but a sleeve-bearing shaft can be revved to 10,000 without overheating, once the bearings are run in. The no-load speed of a portable saw motor is from 4000 to 5000; vacuum-cleaner motors turn at 5000 to 8000.

See also: bench saws; carving; filing; gemstones; grinding; soldering.

Power tower rolls tools to the job

BY HAYDEN RICKER

■ ANYONE WHO USES more than one portable power tool in a home shop or on the building site will be quick to see the time-saving features of this tool tower. It has individual storage shelves and outlets for five of the most commonly used portable tools. A boxed base stores the cords when the units are not in use. There are no tools piled up on the bench or floor, no trailing cords underfoot while you're working in an unfinished room or on a project in the basement shop. A single power cord plugged into a wall or ceiling receptacle feeds the six outlets you see in the detail.

Construction is simple butt joinery, all the parts being fastened with glue and nails or screws. The top shelf is square, the second shelf is U-shaped; that is, it is fitted around the column. On the original pictured, the two lower shelves are hinged at an angle of 20-30 degrees for convenience in placing the larger tools such as portable saws; also to permit folding should it be necessary to store the tower in restricted space. These shelves are made with openings to take blades of portable saws so that the tools are supported level and in an upright position.

If you wish to add the light boom, pictured and detailed on the opposite page, cut an opening in the top shelf and support the lower end of the upright at the second shelf with cleats. Use a photoflood lamp of the clamp-on, adjustable type. Fit and hinge a door at the back or the straight side of the tower. Wire the outlets to a single junction box having a receptacle in the cover plate.

See also: belt-disk sander; drilling; electric power control; grinding; hacksaws; routing.

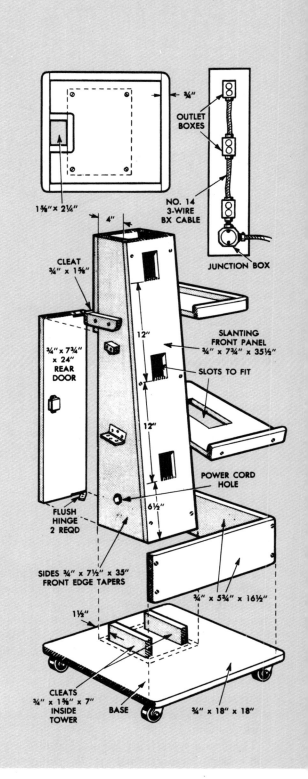

OUTLET BOXES

¾"

1⅝" x 2¼"

NO. 14 3-WIRE BX CABLE

JUNCTION BOX

CLEAT ¾" x 1⅝"

4"

12"

SLANTING FRONT PANEL ¾" x 7¾" x 35½"

SLOTS TO FIT

¾" x 7¾" x 24" REAR DOOR

12"

POWER CORD HOLE

FLUSH HINGE 2 REQD

6½"

SIDES ¾" x 7½" x 35" FRONT EDGE TAPERS

¾" x 5¾" x 16½"

1½"

CLEATS ¾" x 1⅝" x 7" INSIDE TOWER

BASE

¾" x 18" x 18"

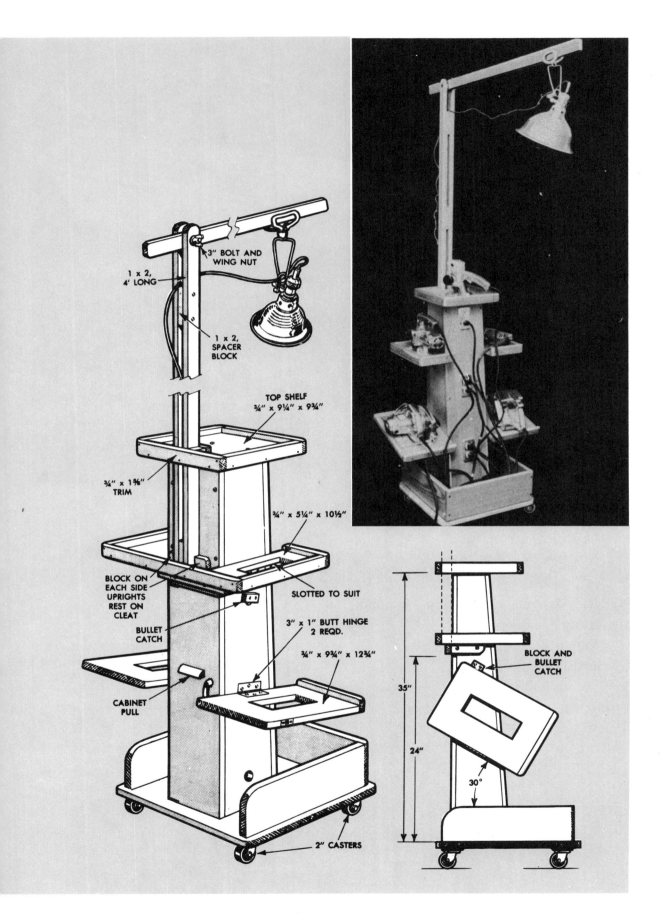

3" BOLT AND WING NUT

1 x 2, 4' LONG

1 x 2, SPACER BLOCK

TOP SHELF
¾" x 9¼" x 9¾"

¾" x 1⅝" TRIM

¾" x 5¼" x 10½"

BLOCK ON EACH SIDE UPRIGHTS REST ON CLEAT

BULLET CATCH

SLOTTED TO SUIT

3" x 1" BUTT HINGE 2 REQD.

¾" x 9¾" x 12¾"

CABINET PULL

2" CASTERS

BLOCK AND BULLET CATCH

35"

24"

30°

Break-apart boat stows camp gear

BY ARTHUR MIKESELL
DESIGNED BY WILLIAM JACKSON

Designed with camping in mind,
this sturdy two-in-one
John boat is actually a small
fishing pram with a roomy
detachable camp chest
big enough for all of your supplies
bolted to the bow

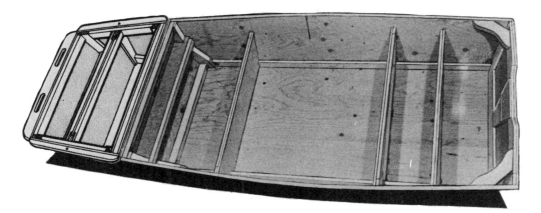

WHY THE SPLIT PERSONALITY? Well, that bolt-on bow locker is actually a sturdy camp chest which can be packed at home, attached to the pram at the launch site, then removed again when you reach camp.

Double-galvanized, annular-ring boat nails are used throughout. These cost much less than comparable screws and also make the fabricating job easier without sacrificing strength. Assuming that you plan to fiberglass the boat, all joints are both glued and nailed. If not, use caulking compound at all through-hull fastenings and planking joints. In any case, be sure to use caulking when mounting the bottom battens since these would be attached after fiberglassing the hull.

Begin by assembling the transom. Cut and

mount the inside framing on the plywood, glue-coating all contacting surfaces and spacing the 1¼-in. nails 3 in. apart. (The 1 x 4 framing on the aft surface of the transom should be mounted after you have planked the bottom.) Once the glue has cured, bevel the bottom edge 15 deg.

Next, make up the temporary building frame and the bulkhead frame which forms the bow of the pram. Since the latter must mate snugly with the rear bulkhead of the bow locker, we recommend that you build the two together. When completed, clamp them together, check the fit and then drill holes through the side frames for the two connecting plates.

The fairing operation is a little unusual since this boat isn't framed in the normal way. To

The two-man pram is light and easy to car-top. You can carry the bow locker in the car's trunk

Heavy bottom battens on the outside protect the plywood planking and act as exterior framing

The building frame is a single mold temporarily mounted amidships. Support the hull at working height on saw horses topped with 2 x 4s

determine the proper bevels for the transom and forward bulkhead, you'll have to assemble the hull temporarily, then take it apart and cut these bevels so that frames fit flush against planking.

Tack the two pieces of side planking to the transom and secure the temporary building frame 50 in. forward of this with two screws through each side. (After the seats have been installed, this frame will be removed and the screw holes sealed with wood putty backed by 1-in.-sq. plywood plates glued to the inner surface.) Bend the two side panels around the building frame and tack them in place.

Once you have marked the transom bevels, remove the transom and cut them slightly over-

break-apart boat, continued

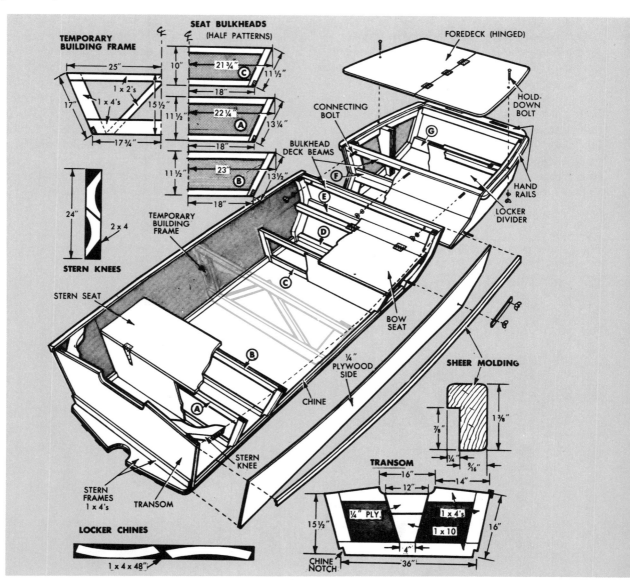

size. Then replace the transom, check the fit and sand the bevels until you have a perfect joint. Finally, coat all contacting surfaces with glue and attach the plywood with 1¼-in. nails.

The chine and sheer curves should run smoothly from the transom to the fore end of the bow locker, so before you fair the pram's bow bulkhead you'll have to frame the locker and clamp this framing to the pram. When you have marked the proper bevels, remove the clamps and fair the bow bulkhead and locker frame. After fairing, secure the side planking.

Since the locker forms a separate part of the boat, you might take time out here to finish it up before going ahead with the rest of the hull. In spite of its odd shape, the locker is simply a

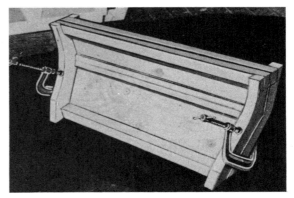

The critical joint between the bow bulkhead and the rear bulkhead of the locker must be a perfect fit. Fabricate both bulkheads in one operation

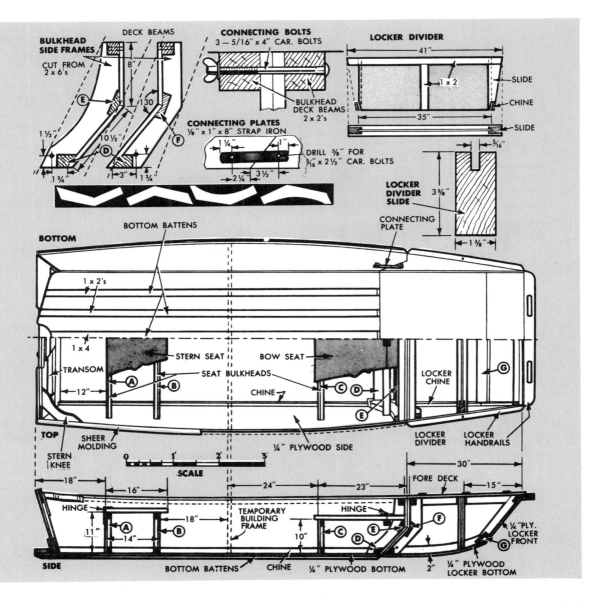

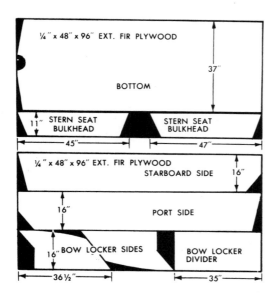

MATERIALS LIST

LUMBER (All clear fir)

1 pc.	1 x 10 x 1'	Transom framing
2 pcs.	1 x 4 x 8'	Transom framing
1 pc.	1 x 4 x 8'	Temporary building frame
1 pc.	1 x 4 x 8'	Chines (cut lengthwise)
2 pcs.	1 x 4 x 8'	Seat framing (cut lengthwise)
1 pc.	1 x 4 x 8'	Center bottom batten
2 pcs.	1 x 4 x 8'	Bottom battens (cut lengthwise)
1 pc.	1 x 4 x 8'	Sheer molding (cut lengthwise)
1 pc.	1 x 4 x 6'	Locker framing (cut lengthwise)
1 pc.	1 x 4 x 4'	Locker chines
1 pc.	1 x 4 x 4'	Bow framing (E)
1 pc.	2 x 4 x 8'	Locker framing (F & G)
1 pc.	2 x 4 x 6'	Locker handrails
1 pc.	2 x 4 x 6'	Transom knee, locker slides
1 pc.	2 x 6 x 6'	Bulkhead side frames

PLYWOOD (Fir, exterior, grade AB or better)

3 pcs.	¼" x 4' x 8'	Hull planking, seat bulkheads
1 pc.	½" x 4' x 8'	Seats, foredeck & transom

FASTENINGS*

½ lb.	1 in. boat nails	Plywood to chines, sheer and molding (#S211A)
½ lb.	1¼ in. boat nails	Plywood to chines, seat, transom and bulkhead (#S212A)
¼ lb.	1¾ in. boat nails	Bottom battens to seat, transom and bulkhead (#S214A)
2 doz.	2½ in. boat nails	Transom knees, 2 x 2 bulkhead and locker framing (#S217A)
3	5⁄16" x 4" mach. bolts	Through bulkhead deck beams to attach locker
4	5⁄16" x 2½" Car. bolts	Through bulkhead framing and connecting plates

* If boat nails aren't available in your area, you may order them by mail from the W. H. Maze Co., Peru, Ill., using the catalogue numbers listed above. Cadmium-plated 2½" No. 8 flatheaded screws may be substituted for the large 2½" boat nails listed above.

break-apart boat, continued

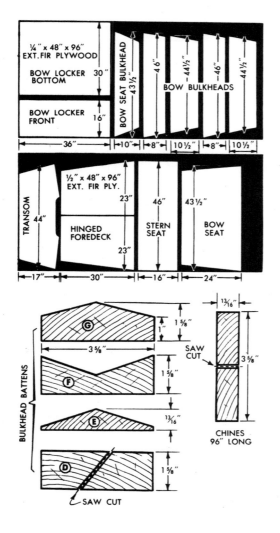

box with a center-hinged lift-off top. Make the handrails by cutting a 2 x 4 lengthwise; mount them by driving nails from inside.

Next, mount the chine battens with their edges extending slightly below the bottom edge of the side planking so that they may be faired to fit flush against the bottom planking. After fairing these battens, mount the bottom planking.

To complete the hull, make up the three seat frames and install them by driving nails from the outside through the planking. Once the stern knees have been installed, the hull will be adequately braced and you can remove the building frame. Install the ½-in. plywood seat tops with galvanized hinges—piano hinges give the best appearance—then shape the sheer moldings and mount them, using 1-in. nails.

Before painting or fiberglassing the hull, extend the connecting-plate holes in the bulkhead side frame through the side planking and seal the bolts with epoxy.

Finally, mount the bottom battens by driving nails through the planking into the framing.

See also: pontoon boat; riverboat; sailboat; sports boat.

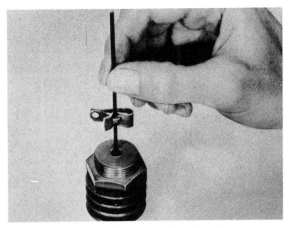

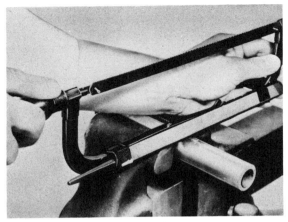

Slide a Fahnestock clip onto a length of coat-hanger wire and you have a gauge that will measure hole depth with acceptable accuracy for all but the most critical work. The clip will grip the wire with sufficient tightness to prevent it from moving out of place when transferring a depth measurement or checking depth of a hole being drilled. Once set, the distance from the edge of the clip to the end of the wire is easily and accurately measured with a rule. By using wires of different diameters you'll find it easy to make measurements in even the tightest spots. Keep this simple tool handy in your shop.

Starting a cut on round workpieces with a hacksaw can be difficult when the blade slides sidewise and refuses to take hold just where you want it. Overcome this tendency by taping a three-cornered file to the back of the saw frame. Then mark the work for length, invert the saw and file a notch on the mark or in the waste as accuracy requires. The filed notch guides the blade on the first few strokes. You'll find that this is the easy way to cut pipe or rods to length when something more than "eye accuracy" is necessary. Draw the tape tightly to hold the file securely.

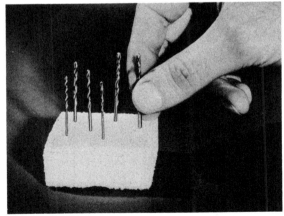

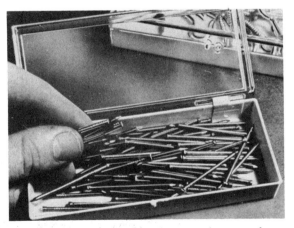

Usually when one loses a tiny twist drill he just gives up looking and goes and buys another. But that can get expensive if one uses nothing but high-speed drill bits. One way to keep tiny drills always at hand is to stick them in a square of foam plastic the instant you finish a drilling job. Unlike a regular drill stand the foam plastic grips the shanks and holds the drills even when it's turned upside down or dropped on the floor. A piece of foam plastic about 3 in. square will hold a dozen or more drills securely.

Many home craftsmen and shop men have a rule they've learned to live by: Don't throw away any small, usable container. They are the fellows who never lose anything. Mention it and they'll bring out one of those clear plastic boxes, likely the one the last bowtie came in, and there in it is the item you asked for. Small, clear-plastic boxes, also metal boxes, make it easy to keep track of small parts, nails, screws, screw eyes, washers, anything that is easy to lose and hard to find. There is always a good use for those you save.

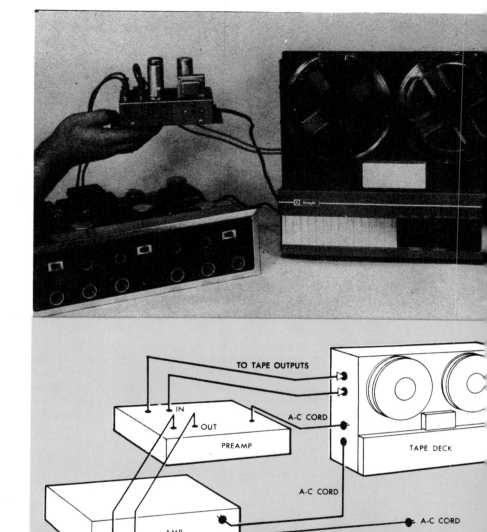

You'll cut out
scratchy surface
noise and improve
tonal quality of
your phono rig
with this simple
preamplifier

Stereo preamp
for magnetic pickups

BY OTTO FRIED

IF YOUR phonograph provides you with almost as much scratchiness as it does music, it could very well be that you have a crystal or a ceramic pickup. The pickup translates the information in the record grooves to electrical impulses, and crystal or ceramic pickups provide an output of about 3 to 5 volts. On the other hand, a magnetic pickup will provide an output measured in millivolts, so less surface noise is picked up.

While using a magnetic pickup thus results in less scratch, the voltage must be preamplified before you feed it to the amplifier. The unit described here will give that extra boost to various magnetic playback devices, such as phonos, tape or microphones.

In constructing the unit, lay out the chassis and punch all holes. Mount the major components and proceed with the wiring. Use terminal strips where required to avoid crowding at lugs. When the unit is completely wired, insert the tubes and

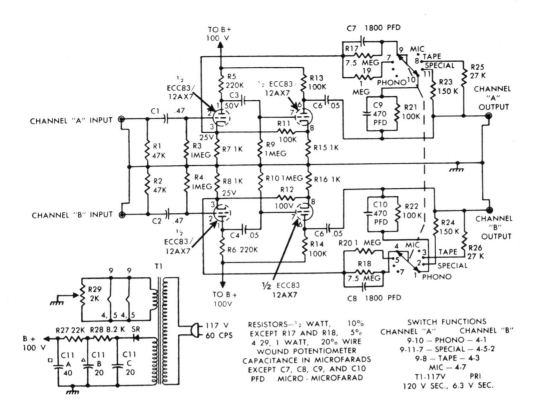

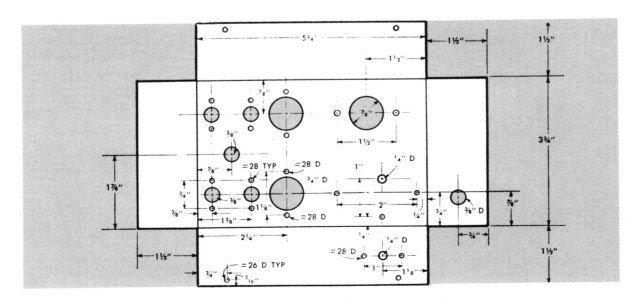

add decals to identify the various switch positions and sockets. You are now ready to test.

To test the setup, plug the magnetic sound source (we used a tape deck) into the input jacks on the preamp. Connect the output jacks to a basic amplifier. Connect the a.c. line from the preamp to a switched outlet on the tape deck. In this way, the preamp will be on only when the tape deck is on. The a.c. line from the tape deck can be plugged into a switched outlet on the basic amplifier.

Start the sound source working. If you use a tape deck, put a tape on. If you use a phono, put a record on. Turn on the amplifier and the sound source. This will automatically turn on the preamp. The result should be nearly scratch-free, high fidelity sound. The small preamp can easily be mounted behind a panel.

See also: high fidelity; high-fidelity center; high fidelity, portable; microphones; phonographs; tape recorders.

This small press does a top-quality job of reproducing type, linoleum blocks, woodcuts, etchings and, with a special cylinder, it even lithographs

Build a tabletop printing press

BY MANLY BANISTER

Center pipe core for the blanket cylinder is adjusted concentric with the end plates. Then the nuts are tightened on the threaded rod to hold the plates while the pipe is welded on

To check roller diameter, mount dial indicator on the carriage and run it along the roller with the button riding the center line. If the needle varies no more than a thousandth or two, it is within tolerance that is necessary. Be sure you check the roller carefully

HAND-WORKED BLOCKS and plates for printing are enjoying wide popularity today, and although it's possible to work a plate and then have it printed professionally, almost all artists prefer to print their own. This way they have complete control of every step of the print-making operation.

Here's a press that will not only handle print-making but many other types of printing. With it, you can print from forms made up of handset type or Linotype, from linoleum and wood blocks, from etchings and engravings, as well as from halftone plates. And it can be built in any modestly equipped shop for less than one-fourth the cost of a commercial model of the same capacity.

By replacing the steel roller on top with a cylinder covered with a rubber blanket, the press is set up for offset lithography from a lithographic stone as well as from zinc and aluminum plates which are standard in the printing trade. You even have a choice of hand or motorized operation.

In order to insure top quality of the prints it turns out, the press must be of heavy construction throughout. The model shown weighs about 150 lbs., including the top roller and bed. A further advantage of this design is that the builder can scale the dimensions up or down to produce a press of greater or lesser capacity to suit his own needs or his workshop equipment.

With the standard bed, the press will print any block up to nearly 14 in. wide and 24 in. long. However, a bed of any greater length can be substituted for printing streamers or banners of any length desired.

The size limits for lithographs are restricted by the dimensions of the rubber blanket (approximately 14 x 16 in.).

Standard gears are used in the gear train, and these, plus the four bronze bushings, can be ordered from the Boston Gear Co. A reduction ratio of 1:8 is provided, making hand operation extremely easy, and as little as $\frac{1}{20}$ hp in a gear-reduction motor can be utilized for motorized operation.

A good place to begin construction is with the rollers. A metal-turning lathe with a 6-in. swing will do all the work required on the rollers except turning down the blanket cylinder. After I had welded up the rough cylinder, I had it turned at a machine shop, then mounted it between centers in my 6-in. lathe and finished up the surface with a file and emery cloth.

The drive roller and steel printing roller are made of standard 3-in. pipe—double-thickness wall ($\frac{5}{8}$ in.) if it is available, though single thickness would do. The nominal o.d. of 3-in. pipe is $3\frac{1}{2}$ in., and most of this is retained in

Blanket cylinder should not be allowed to rest on the rubber blanket, so you will have to make up a storage cradle from scrap plywood to hold the cylinder when it is not being used. This cradle was fabricated from ¾-in. plywood scrap stock

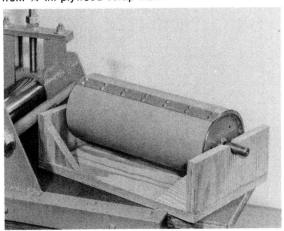

Ready to print, the block is locked up in the chase with "furniture"—wooden blocks—around it. Construction of the chase, bed and other parts is shown in the drawings and photos. The bed moves back and forth to make the paper impressions

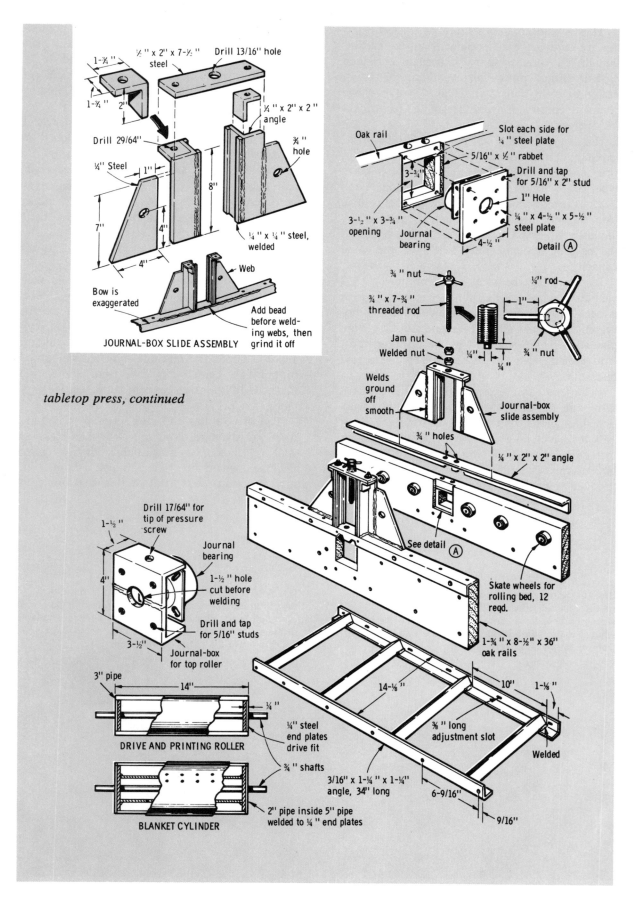

½ " x 2" x 7-½ " steel

Drill 13/16" hole

1-¾ "

1-¾ " 2"

Drill 29/64"

¼ " x 2" x 2" angle

¾ " hole

¼" Steel 1"

8"

7"

4"

4"

Web

Bow is exaggerated

¼ " x ¼ " steel, welded

Add bead before welding webs, then grind it off

JOURNAL-BOX SLIDE ASSEMBLY

Oak rail

Slot each side for ¼ " steel plate

5/16" x ½ " rabbet

Drill and tap for 5/16" x 2" stud

3-¾ "

3-½ " x 3-¾ " opening

Journal bearing

1" Hole

¼ " x 4-½ " x 5-½ " steel plate

4-½ "

Detail Ⓐ

¾ " nut

¾ " x 7-¾ " threaded rod

Jam nut

Welded nut

¼ "

¼" rod

1"

¾ " nut

¼ "

tabletop press, continued

Welds ground off smooth

Journal-box slide assembly

¾ " holes

¼ " x 2" x 2" angle

See detail Ⓐ

Skate wheels for rolling bed, 12 reqd.

Drill 17/64" for tip of pressure screw

1-½ "

Journal bearing

4"

1-½ " hole cut before welding

Drill and tap for 5/16" studs

Journal-box for top roller

3-½"

1-¾ " x 8-½ " x 36" oak rails

3" pipe

14"

¼ "

DRIVE AND PRINTING ROLLER

¼" steel end plates drive fit

¾ " shafts

3/16" x 1-¼ " x 1-¼ " angle, 34" long

14-⅛ "

⅜ " long adjustment slot

10"

1-⅛ "

Welded

BLANKET CYLINDER

2" pipe inside 5" pipe welded to ¼ " end plates

6-9/16"

9/16"

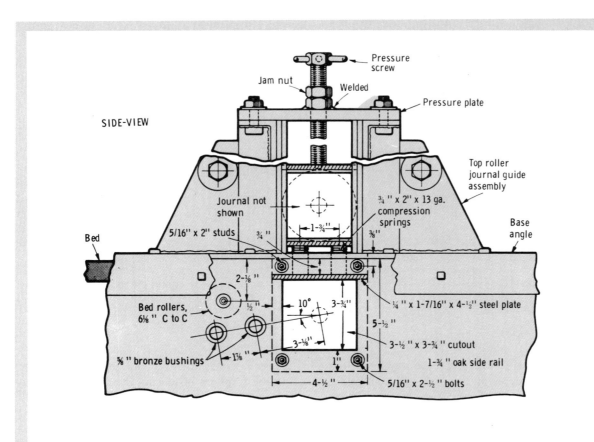

SIDE-VIEW

Pressure screw

Jam nut

Welded

Pressure plate

Top roller journal guide assembly

Base angle

Journal not shown

3/4" x 2" x 13 ga. compression springs

5/16" x 2" studs

3/4"

3/8"

Bed

1-3/4"

2-1/8"

1/2"

10°

3-3/4"

1/4" x 1-7/16" x 4-1/2" steel plate

Bed rollers, 6-1/8" C to C

5/8" bronze bushings

1-7/8"

3-1/8"

1"

5-1/2"

3-1/2" x 3-3/4" cutout

1-3/4" oak side rail

4-1/2"

5/16" x 2-1/2" bolts

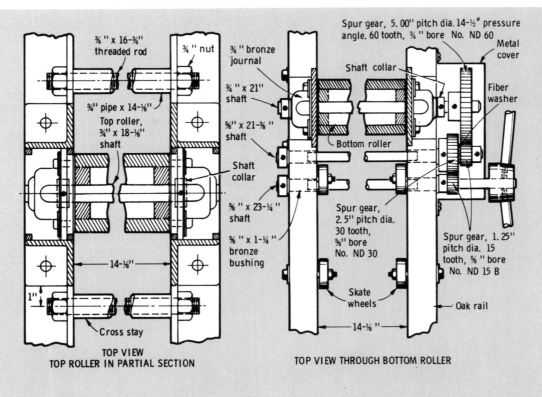

3/4" x 16-3/4" threaded rod

3/4" nut

3/4" bronze journal

Spur gear, 5.00" pitch dia. 14-1/2° pressure angle. 60 tooth, 3/4" bore No. ND 60

Metal cover

Shaft collar

3/4" x 21" shaft

Fiber washer

3/4" pipe x 14-1/8"

Top roller, 3/4" x 18-1/8" shaft

5/8" x 21-3/8" shaft

Bottom roller

Shaft collar

5/8" x 23-1/4" shaft

5/8" x 1-1/4" bronze bushing

Spur gear, 2.5" pitch dia. 30 tooth, 5/8" bore No. ND 30

Spur gear, 1.25" pitch dia. 15 tooth, 5/8" bore No. ND 15 B

14-1/8"

1"

Cross stay

Skate wheels

Oak rail

14-1/8"

TOP VIEW
TOP ROLLER IN PARTIAL SECTION

TOP VIEW THROUGH BOTTOM ROLLER

The simplest method of cutting the rabbets for the journal plates is to use an electric router with guides clamped to the plank, as shown. If you don't have access to a router, you can do the job with a sharp wood chisel and mallet

Before drilling the holes for the bed-roller bolts, be sure to check the location of them by lifting the drive roller as high as it will go in the journals and measuring it with a square. Add the bed-roller radius to this figure before you drill

the turning. Final diameter can be anything between 3¼ in. and 3⅜ in. You can use standard-thickness 5-in. pipe to keep the weight within reason. The nominal o.d. is 5½ in. and you should have at least 5¼ in. left after turning.

The best way to make the end plates for the 3-in.-plus rollers is to saw them oversize from ¼-in. steel plate on a metalcutting bandsaw. Drill a ⅜-in. hole through the center of each, then stack them on a ⅜-in. bolt that has its head

tabletop press, continued

When drilling center holes of the journal plates on the drill press, shown left, clamp the work to the table, backing it with scrap plywood to take the point of the drill bit. The journal plates can be clamped and drilled at one time. Use a metal-cutting bandsaw to cut the journal bases down to the required 3¼-in. square. A piece of steel or wood clamped to the table makes a good fence to assure accuracy. First cut ¼ in. off each of the two adjacent sides, then reset the fence to trim ¼ in. off the other sides. If a metal-cutting bandsaw isn't available, the job also can be done by hand. If you do this, make sure you make all of the cuts accurately. In sawing the journal bases down to the right size, be careful that the measurements are correct

drilled to receive the lathe tail center. Run down the nut on a lock washer, then grip the nut in the lathe chuck and bring up the tail center. Machine the o.d. of the group to a press fit in the i.d. of the pipe. Dismount the plates and bore out the center holes to fit the ¾-in. cold-rolled steel shafting, holding them in the universal chuck and using a boring tool for close tolerance.

Insert the plates about ¼ in. into the ends of the pipe and weld them, then insert the shaft and weld it to the plates at both ends.

The end-plate unit is prepared for the blanket cylinder by inserting it into the 5-in. pipe and welding it in, the threaded rod being replaced with ¾-in. cold-rolled steel shafting. The center pipe is a piece of 2-in. with the ends faced off square in the lathe.

After the blanket cylinder has been machined and polished, a double line of holes ½ in. apart is drilled along one side as shown in the drawing on page 2006. The rubber blanket is then wrapped around and clamped down under a strip of ⅛ x 1-in. aluminum.

blanket is standard equipment

The rubber blanket is standard lithographic equipment and can be purchased from a dealer in lithographic supplies (the California Ink Co., for instance, which has offices in most large cities). The blanket comes marked with parallel black lines on the back and goes on the cylinder with the lines wrapped around it. The blanket is cut to fit the cylinder and punched (with a paper punch) at each end for the clamping screws. One end is fitted loosely under the clamp and the screws inserted. The other end is then brought around, inserted under the clamp, and the screws tightened.

There must be no bulges or looseness in the fit of the blanket.

All roller shafts must be center-drilled for mounting between centers on the lathe. Owners of small lathes can have the shafts center-drilled at a machine shop. Also, since the top and bottom rollers revolve independently of each other, they do not have to be miked to equal diameters.

With the rollers finished, work can go forward on the press frame. I made the side planks of solid 2 x 8 oak, but I would rather recommend that these be built up to the required 1¾-in. thickness by laminating plywood (¼-in. ply glued between two ¾-in. pieces) or hardboard (seven layers of ¼-in.). Either would be less expensive than the oak and would obviate some

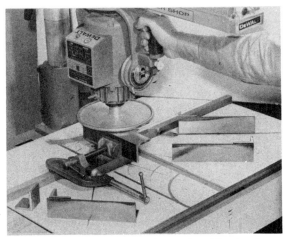

The faces of the angles used to make sides for the top-roller journal boxes must be at exact right angles to each other and perfectly smooth. To get the metal to perfection, use a sanding disk on a radial-arm saw with No. 50 aluminum oxide paper

A filler block cut to fit and clamped between the guide units makes it possible to drill the pressure plate and lugs accurately. After you have completed the drilling job, clamp the assembly to a welding table and weld the unit to the base angle

Clamp the steel slides to the planks with lag screws so the sides will not move. Then install the journal plates and weld the top edge of the plate to the edge of the base angle to make the journal plate and steel frame a single unit. Make sure clamps are tight

When welding the crossframe, clamp
long members to the table and hold the
cross-members with clamps. Refinement
is shown above: a speed-reducer motor
with a gear head for even feed-through

difficulties in working presented by the oak, such as warping and splitting.

Work the planks together, squaring both to exactly the same dimensions. Rout out the journal plate seats on the inside faces of the planks. The base angles holding the steel upper frames to the planks must, of course, be square with the planks.

The photo on page 2008 illustrates an important step in ascertaining where to place the bed rollers. The planks should be drilled for the bed-roller bolts as well as for those holding the cross frame.

Construction of the welded steel slides for the top-roller journal boxes is detailed at the top

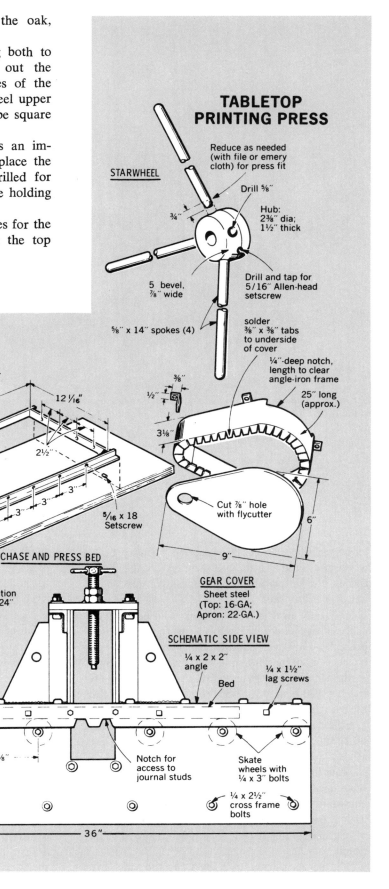

TABLETOP PRINTING PRESS

STARWHEEL

Reduce as needed (with file or emery cloth) for press fit

Drill 5/8"

Hub: 2 3/8" dia; 1 1/2" thick

3/4"

5 bevel, 7/8" wide

Drill and tap for 5/16" Allen-head setscrew

5/8" x 14" spokes (4)

solder 3/8" x 3/8" tabs to underside of cover

1/4"-deep notch, length to clear angle-iron frame

25" long (approx.)

3/8"

1/2"

3 1/8"

Cut 7/8" hole with flycutter

6"

9"

GEAR COVER
Sheet steel
(Top: 16-GA;
Apron: 22-GA.)

1/8 x 3/4 x 3/4" angle iron

12 1/16"

16 1/16"

2 1/2"

3"

3"

3"

3"

5/16 x 18 Setscrew

Weld all corners

4-ply lamination of 1/4 x 14 x 24" tempered hardboard

CHASE AND PRESS BED

SCHEMATIC SIDE VIEW

Find this dimension after installing drive roller

5/16 x 1 1/2" lag screws

1/4 x 2 x 2" angle

Bed

1/4 x 1 1/2" lag screws

8 to 8 1/2"

1 1/4"

6 1/8"

6 1/8"

Notch for access to journal studs

Skate wheels with 1/4 x 3" bolts

1 1/2"   1 11/16"

1/4 x 2 1/2" cross frame bolts

36"

Use a straightedge when installing the bedrollers so they line up level with the top edge of the driver roller. If roller must be moved, grind out bolt hole with a bit or a rotary file

tabletop press, continued

of page 2006. There is a good possibility that, when the guide units are welded to the base angles, the latter may bow (unless clamped to a heavy welding table).

The bow of the base angles will be toward each other, making assembly of the press impossible. However, if this does happen, it can be corrected by following the procedure shown in the drawing on page 2006. After grinding off the bead indicated, check the straightness of the base angle with a straightedge. If it is still bowed a trifle, another bead welded over the ground-off remains of the first will be in order. The base angles must be perfectly straight.

Now the press can be assembled. If the bronze bushings for the gear shafting turn with the shaft, eliminate this by cutting a notch in the bushing flange and mounting a small brass plate on the plank, the plate having a tongue to engage the notch.

The same journals are used for the steel top roller and the blanket cylinder, so you'll have to make only one pair. Because of the separation of the rollers, the bed must be 1 in. thick. For most uses, this can be laminated from four thicknesses of ¼-in. hardboard. However, if considerable printing involving metal type is contemplated, the top layer of hardboard may be omitted and a ¼-in. steel plate or aluminum sheet substituted.

Aluminum sheet is smooth-surfaced and may be used as is, but steel plate should be surface ground both sides to a uniform thickness by a firm specializing in this work.

If metal is used on the bed, make some arrangement that will prevent the bed from falling out at either end of the press.

In the construction of the chase, the hollow-head setscrews installed along one side and one end provide the pressure needed to keep the printing form and furniture in place. Note that a strip of ⅛ x ¾-in. aluminum is placed between the screws and the blocks to take the thrust.

The drive-gear setup has 1:8 reduction ratio for easy hand operation. Or use it with a low-horsepower motor

Motor rated at $\frac{1}{20}$ runs press at 5 ft. per minute with 9-tooth sprocket on motor and 12 on the shaft

When using the press for lithography, the blanket cylinder will be installed in place of the steel printing roller. The height of the journal boxes in the slides will vary, depending on whether you're printing from plates or lithographic stone. This height must be determined from the situation at hand, and the space between the journal boxes and the springs filled with a block of hardwood, cut to size.

In other forms of printing, where the steel roller is used, linoleum or plates should be mounted on blocks ¾ in. high.

Before printing, the top roller must be adjusted to the height of the printing block or form, and to the pressure required. The block is then padded with more or less packing, as required. First, the printing paper is laid on the inked block, then a sheet of manila or tympan paper (available from printing supply houses) is laid over it, followed by five or six sheets of newspaper. This is topped off by a sheet of thin cardboard to prevent the paper padding from bunching and creasing under the roller.

This same amount of padding should be placed on the adjusting blocks and both adjusting screws tightened down until they cannot be turned further. Then back off both screws a full turn and try the printing block (padded but uninked) under the roller.

Any further adjustment of the roller is done equally at both ends by turning each pressure screw the same.

not much pressure required

Usually, not much more pressure is required than enough to make the top roller turn by friction as the form is fed through the press. Further adjustment is determined by inking the block and pulling proofs on newsprint. Examination of the proof will show whether more ink or more pressure (or less pressure and less ink) is required.

To operate the press, start turning the star-wheel, and at the same time push the form against the roller. Turn the wheel rapidly, without hesitation, until the form has completed its pass.

Inspect the print before stripping it from the block. If the image is lighter on one side than the other, the rollers are not parallel. However, the print can be saved by turning the block around and running it through the press again. The roller can then be adjusted by turning down the screw on the light side. When the press is adjusted, the locking nuts are run down on the pressure screws.

Once adjusted for a given block, the press is adjusted for all future blocks of the same height. Where small increments of adjustment are involved, the pressure can be regulated by adding or removing a sheet or two of the newsprint packing.

See also: copy machine; duplicator; linoleum-block press; rubber stamps; tracing projector.

Rear-projection theater for slides

BY MANLY BANISTER

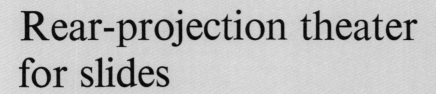

This handsome cabinet contains a whole new concept in home slide viewing. It stores your projector in an end compartment for quick setup. The doors swing open to present a big TV-type screen

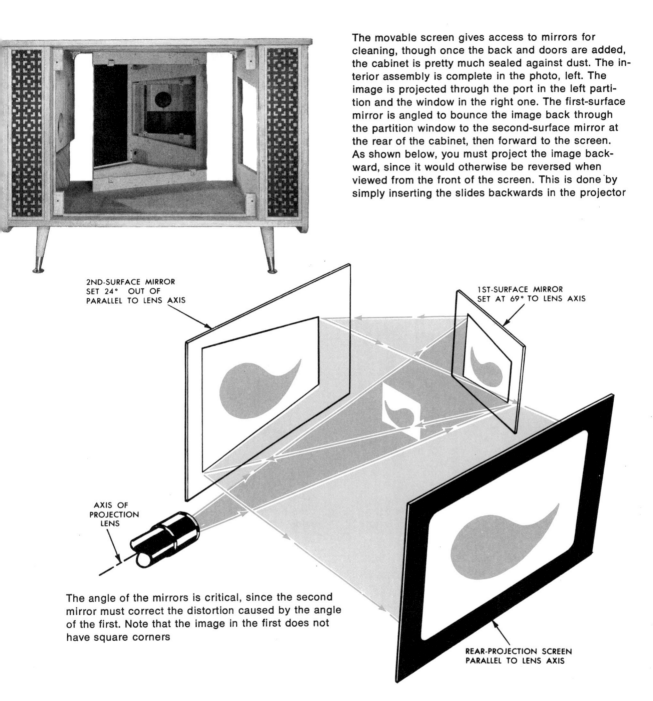

The movable screen gives access to mirrors for cleaning, though once the back and doors are added, the cabinet is pretty much sealed against dust. The interior assembly is complete in the photo, left. The image is projected through the port in the left partition and the window in the right one. The first-surface mirror is angled to bounce the image back through the partition window to the second-surface mirror at the rear of the cabinet, then forward to the screen. As shown below, you must project the image backward, since it would otherwise be reversed when viewed from the front of the screen. This is done by simply inserting the slides backwards in the projector

2ND-SURFACE MIRROR SET 24° OUT OF PARALLEL TO LENS AXIS

1ST-SURFACE MIRROR SET AT 69° TO LENS AXIS

AXIS OF PROJECTION LENS

The angle of the mirrors is critical, since the second mirror must correct the distortion caused by the angle of the first. Note that the image in the first does not have square corners

REAR-PROJECTION SCREEN PARALLEL TO LENS AXIS

YOU'VE PROBABLY often wished for a more graceful way to share your slides with friends— one that would avoid all the fuss and formality of setting up a clumsy screen. Well, here it is— and, as a bonus, this system gives you a modern lo-boy for your living room or den. Slide shows can now be as easy and relaxed as television viewing. There'll be no more heads bobbing into the frame—or those distracting shadow-faces restless children like to make by thrusting their fingers into the beam.

Like most good magic, it's done with mirrors,

as shown in the photo and diagram above. The smaller mirror is a special type, silvered on the face instead of the back. The bigger one, at the rear of the cabinet, is a standard mirror you can buy at any mirror shop—but be sure it's made of ¼-in. polished plate glass; a window-glass mirror is too wavy to produce an undistorted image. The screen is Kodak's black rear-projection type, mounted with the dull side out to eliminate reflections from the room's lamps or windows. In this big 20 x 24-in. size, the screen may have to be ordered from a mail-order opti-

The first assembly step is to nail the ends to the bottom. Then true with a carpenter's square, tack temporary rails across the top, add glue blocks and metal corner braces

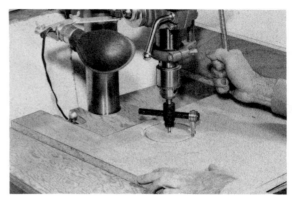

A fly-cutter in your drill press cuts a clean projection port in the left partition, though the hole can also be jig-sawed and rasped. The partition is made of particle board and won't splinter

The three-piece projection bay is assembled with glue and nails before it is attached across the gap. The window partition is added next

Now the top is attached by nailing through the ends into cleats which have been mounted on the underside, then securing with metal corner braces

cal house. Edmund Scientific Co. (Barrington, N.J. 08007) lists it as Item No. 85,002. (They can also supply the 10 x 14-in. first-surface mirror, Item No. 85,036.)

Built to the specifications on the following pages, your cabinet will be a precision optical instrument that you could even use for movies, if you don't mind the fact that printing will appear backwards. An 8-mm movie projector has no provision for "flopping" the film. With slides, you simply insert them with the "wrong" face toward the lens.

As dimensioned, the cabinet is just right for Kodak's popular Carousel (Model 550 or 570) automatic projector. Its 4-in. projection lens will blow up a standard 35-mm slide to the proportions shown in the bottom photo on page 2014. The "margin" lets you show vertical slides without masking off top and bottom. If you take the larger, square "super" slides, you'll want to use a 5-in. lens in the projector—or invest in a zoom

lens which lets you adjust for mixed slides. Since most good projectors now feature remote control of both slide-change and focus, you'll be able to sit "out front" with your audience.

With a little experimentation, you can adapt the cabinet to any other slide projector—or a movie projector. Since the latter requires a greater projection length to blow up the tiny 8-mm image, you'll have to provide an outboard bench of the proper height—and a bigger projection port.

The cabinet is constructed of ¾-in. particle board, shop grade, faced with hardwood veneer. It's cheaper than hardwood plywood and its stability and easy machining recommend it for this type of construction. You'll need one and a half 4 x 8 panels for the case and partitions. As with plywood, all exposed edges must be covered with a matching veneer tape.

You'll also need solid hardwood stock (to match the veneer) for the door and screen

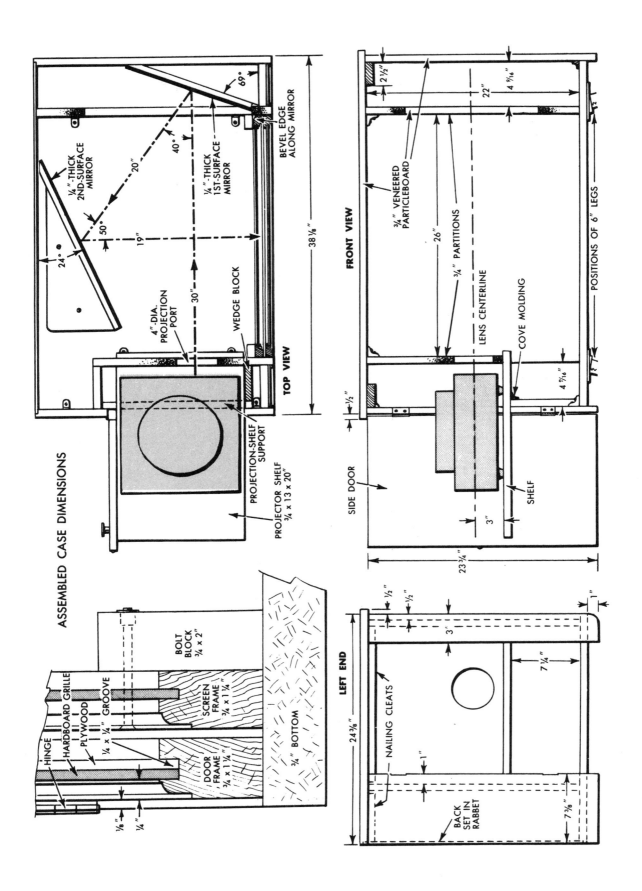

ASSEMBLED CASE DIMENSIONS

TOP VIEW

69°

BEVEL EDGE ALONG MIRROR

1/4"-THICK 1ST-SURFACE MIRROR

1/4"-THICK 2ND-SURFACE MIRROR

40°

20"

50°

24°

19"

30"

38 1/8"

4" DIA. PROJECTION PORT

WEDGE BLOCK

PROJECTION-SHELF SUPPORT

PROJECTOR SHELF 3/4 x 13 x 20"

FRONT VIEW

2 1/2"

22"

4 9/16"

POSITIONS OF 6" LEGS

3/4" VENEERED PARTICLEBOARD

26"

3/4" PARTITIONS

LENS CENTERLINE

COVE MOLDING

1/2"

4 9/16"

SIDE DOOR

SHELF

3"

23 3/4"

BOLT BLOCK 3/4 x 2"

HINGE

HARDBOARD GRILLE

PLYWOOD

GROOVE

1/4 x 1/4"

SCREEN FRAME 3/4 x 1 1/4"

DOOR FRAME 3/4 x 1 1/4"

3/4" BOTTOM

1/8"

1/4"

LEFT END

1/2"

1/2"

3"

1"

24 3/8"

NAILING CLEATS

1"

7 1/4"

BACK SET IN RABBET

7 3/8"

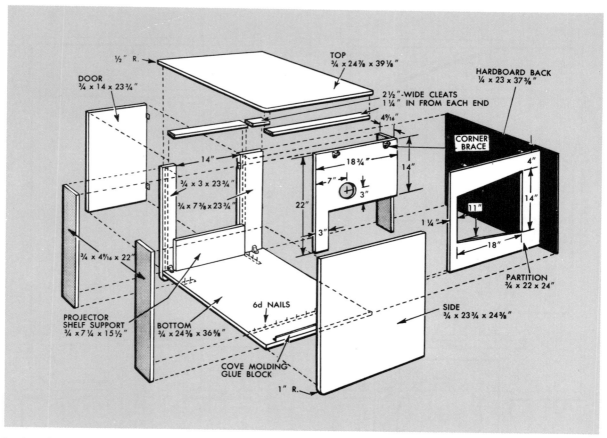

rear-projection theater, continued

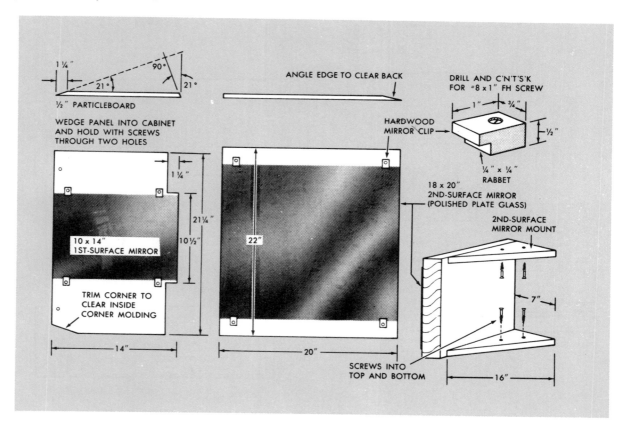

frames, and a set of four 6-in. hardwood legs, with angled mounting plates, that you can finish to match. To back up the hardboard grilles on the doors, you'll want ⅛-in. plywood in a matching veneer—or a prefinished hardboard. The mirror mounts can be plain (unveneered) ½-in. particleboard, or plywood.

You needn't be an experienced cabinetmaker to build this unit. We've purposely kept construction simple by using butt joints tied together with glue blocks and standard metal corner brackets. And though the grille feature gives the piece its distinction, the effect is easily achieved with die-cut hardboard. You can paint the grille to match a dominant color in the room decor.

When the basic construction is done, apply an overall natural finish to all veneer faces, including the door panels, if you're using plywood here. The finish on the unit shown (which is cherry) involves three coats of Deft, sanded with 6-0 cabinet paper between coats, and the final coat rubbed with 3-0 steel wool. A good paste wax was applied for the final sheen.

After finishing, lay the hardboard grille panels over the front surfaces and add the trim molding (in the case of the narrow side panels) or the hardwood frames (the two front door panels).

how to fasten mirrors

To fasten the mirrors to their mounting panels, you can either rabbet hardwood blocks as shown in the sketch or use commercial mirror clips. After a trial assembly to check optical performance with your projector (and to fasten the rear mirror-mount in position as shown) remove the screen and the first-surface mirror mount; also detach the second-surface mirror from its mount, but leave this mount in place. Paint the entire interior flat black—including both mirror boards, the inside end of the projector shelf, the edge of the projection port, the inside of the hardboard back panel, and the back of the screen frame. This eliminates reflections.

In handling the first-surface mirror, never touch the silvered surface with your fingers, and don't wipe it with a rag. To remove dust, flick it lightly with a soft-bristle brush.

The frames for the front doors and screen can be either mitered or mortised at the corners. If you intend to miter the pieces, the quickest way to cut the bead on the inner edge is on a shaper, before you cut the miters. But if you join the corners with mortise-and-tenon or slip joints, assemble the frame temporarily and shape the edges with a portable router, then disassemble

Adjust the rear mirror after the first-surface mirror is mounted. Set up the projector, aligning it square with the cabinet. Move the mirror mount until the image is centered on the screen as viewed from the back. Anchor with screws

To avoid fuzzing the edge of the projection cone, you must bevel the rear face of the screen's right stile, where it laps the first mirror. The bevels should be cut as shown in the lower sketch on page 2018. Check the angles carefully

Clearance bevels are required by compact construction. Bevels on mirror-mount panels are critical for positioning. Here a two-knife shaper head with square cutters is mounted on the arbor of a radial-arm saw and the panel is pushed past

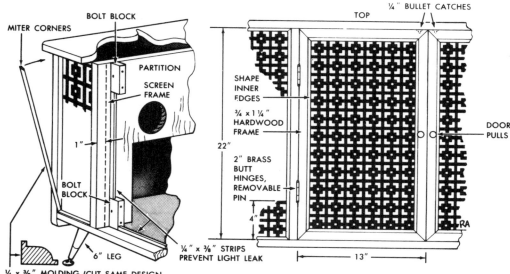

Molding trim completes the decorative side panels. Finish the veneer before fastening the hardboard grille with brads along its edges. Brads are covered by the molding, which requires no nailing, only glue for mounting

to insert the panels. The cutter for the design shown is a ⁵⁄₃₂-in.-dia. Roman ogee bit.

Since you don't glue the screen panel in its frame, these joints need to be particularly strong; the frame must be removable, because once the back is bradded into its all-around rabbet, there's

no other access to the interior of the cabinet. If you miter the screen frame, reinforce each corner with a screw.

The projector shelf is a simple loose panel, but a small cleat (a scrap of molding will do) should be glued across its undersurface to bear against the inside of the removable support panel. This prevents the shelf from being accidentally pulled free when you shift the projector for best position. The shelf, of course, is supported by the fulcrum action of the support, which holds it up against the lower edge of the partition. To keep the support board from falling inward, you wedge a block between it and the partition leg.

When the cabinet is not in use, simply lift out the shelf and the support, and slip the projector in under the partition for storage. The shelf is stored on end in the projection bay. When you close the cabinet's three doors, your self-contained "theatre" again becomes a handsome modern lo-boy—until the next show.

See also: cameras, used; hobby workspace; photography; slide projectors.

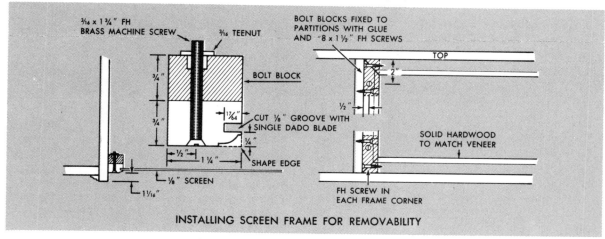

INSTALLING SCREEN FRAME FOR REMOVABILITY

Air-layering starts new shrubs

BY O. E. HOPFER

■ AIR-LAYERING of shrubs is a method of propagation the Chinese developed hundreds of years ago. And the "pot-layering" illustrated here is simply an American adaptation of this old system. It is effective with camellias, rhododendrons, azaleas and coniferous evergreens or almost any woody plant.

Essentially, pot-layering is starting a cutting while it's still attached to the parent plant. After making a cut in the branch to be removed, a slitted pot is mounted on the branch over the cut and filled with a potting mixture. Then, after waiting about a year for a good rootball to form, the branch is removed and either repotted in a larger container or set out in the garden.

Once pot-layered branches are removed, dormant buds on the parent plant develop into new branches to balance the root system and foliage.

See also: insect control; landscaping; lawns; tree felling; tree stumps; weed killers.

see next page

1 Saw a pot half way through. Plastic or asphalt-impregnated sawdust pots are suitable

2 An upward cut through one third of the branch's diameter won't weaken it seriously

3 Wedge the cut open with a nail. Otherwise, it will callus over and prevent rootball formation

4 Cut a hole in the pot's bottom to fit the diameter of the branch. Make this a close fit

5 Position pot over the branch so the cut is in the center and can be covered with potting mix

6 Twist wires around top and bottom of the pot, making sure sawed edges match for a snug fit

7 Tie a nylon cord about the branch below the pot to prevent it from sliding

8 Potting mix consists of two parts leaf mold and one part peat moss. Keep it loose

9   After a year, check root formation. If roots haven't formed, make sure cut is open and rewire

10   Use pruning saw to cut off branch below pot, leaving pot bottom in place to protect roots

11   The new plant may be planted in the garden under perfect conditions, but repotting is best

12   Repot in a large can with sufficient holes punched in the bottom for good drainage

13   Fertilize with 45 percent nitrogen mixture; rootball is too small to support the foliage

14   Keep in new pot for another year, protecting from direct sun and wind. Fertilize monthly

Dusting your favorite plants with insecticides on a windy day can be a hopeless task. It always seems that you're getting more dust in your eyes than on the plants. However, if you drop an old lamp shade over each plant before dusting, you'll find that you have a perfect windbreak for confining the spray to the plants. Keep the old shade in your garage so it will be handy whenever you need to dust.

A rigid sleeve for attaching an extension handle to a paint roller can be improvised from newspapers. Roll several layers to form a tube, slip the handles into either end of the newspapers and secure them by tying them tightly with cord.

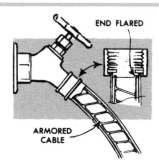

Plastic hose will sometimes collapse and bend at the hydrant coupling. This can be prevented by reinforcing it with a length of flexible armored cable (BX) from which the insulated wires have been removed. Flare the end of the cable.

This short handle for an improvised trouble light is especially handy when working in cramped conditions such as those often encountered in basement and attic crawl spaces. To make it, tie the socket to a stick or dowel. The handle also can be pointed to stick in the ground. This leaves your hands free for the job at hand.

Shop tool in a bottle

BY JERRY PARKER

Old paint is softened almost immediately by a furnace-hot flame from a propane torch. Follow up with a scraper

A torch thaws frozen hydrants or water pipes. Use a pencil flame and direct it at the point where the water is frozen in the pipe

Gutter leaks are easily stopped by flowing solder over the small openings at joints. The surface must be thoroughly cleaned

Replacement floor tiles will drop easily into place and take the floor contours when heated with the propane torch

THERE ARE FEW portable tools that can do so many jobs with so few accessories as a propane torch. It's a one-hand tool, a household appliance, a service-kit workhorse few homeowners, craftsmen, plumbers and electricians do without. It's 2300 deg. of heat concentrated at the end of a burner no larger than your finger. The fuel cylinder gives about 15 hrs. of normal service.

Figs. 1 through 17 are examples of what you can do around your home, to say nothing of home-shop applications if you're a crafter or modelmaker. Notice in the illustration at the right the convenient size of the cylinder and that bend in the tube between valve and burner. The combination of bend and size of cylinder gives you all the advantages of a pistol grip when you're aiming the flame.

The flame can be directed downward, Figs. 4, 9 and 14, or straight ahead as in Figs. 1, 2 and

5 Joints in copper tubing are soldered in a jiffy with the torch. First, make sure the joining parts are thoroughly clean and the metal is bright. Then, flux the joint, or use a rosin-core solder, and bring parts to soldering heat. Hold the torch so that the flame spreads and wraps around the tubing. Withdraw the heat from the tubing when the solder melts

6 A complete kit for soldering copper plumbing, including an igniter, tubing cutter and flaring tool. A heavy-duty torch tip is included

7 You can burn out troublesome ant colonies that infest your lawn. One or two passes of the flame gets rid of them permanently

8 Light a blaze in your fireplace without using a whole box of matches, fanning with a newspaper or frantically pumping bellows

9   It takes only a few seconds to thaw dangerous ice patches (above) on your doorsteps. A torch kit (right) consisting of an igniter, two torch tips and soldering tip is useful in any home

15, or straight up as in Fig. 5. And in none of these working positions is the hand holding the torch forced to assume a cramped hold.

Some burner tubes are made with an S-shaped bend and come with a smaller fuel cylinder, Fig. 16, for added convenience in reaching a hard-to-get-at work point. There also are torch kits, Fig. 6, in which the torch is supplied with a number of accessories suitable for soldering, plumbing (with copper tubing), brazing, paint removal, etc.

The kit comes in a neat metal case with a sturdy handle and latch. Everything fits inside the case. Some kits even include a supply of solders for various purposes. In addition to the utility tip regularly supplied with the torch,

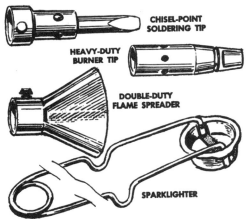

CHISEL-POINT SOLDERING TIP

HEAVY-DUTY BURNER TIP

DOUBLE-DUTY FLAME SPREADER

SPARKLIGHTER

10   Common torch tips and an igniter, or spark-lighter, are included in your propane-torch kit, shown at right

11   A chisel-point soldering tip gets hot enough to brand initials on wooden clamp jaws and projects. It is a special-purpose tip

12   Here's a fast way to remove that part of a broken handle that gets stuck in the head of a hammer or sledge

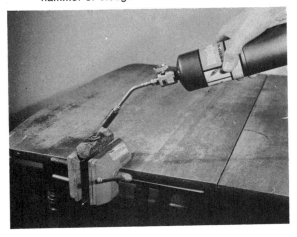

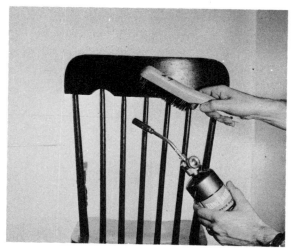

13 Heat from a torch will not only soften aged varnish, but also can be used to put attractive finish on old wood. Keep moving the flame to prevent charring of the wood

14 If you are having trouble lighting charcoal briquettes, try your propane torch. You'll find it is the fastest "match" you ever used. No paper or kindling is needed

15 Old putty can be softened in a single, slow pass of a torch flame. Move the flame just fast enough to prevent charring the wood. Remove the putty while it's still soft

several other special-purpose tips are available, including an igniter, or sparklighter.

The spreader tip is handy where a wide, spreading flame is needed, as in Figs. 1 and 17. For light soldering you can't beat that chisel-point tip. It's better than a soldering iron for some jobs.

When using a torch there are precautions to be taken. Fire is fire and 2300 deg. of it can ignite most any flammable material instantly. Don't work near anything flammable and be sure you follow instructions in all details.

See also: barbecues; gutters; house paint; plumbing; refinishing; soldering; tile, floor.

16 Remove a stubborn pipe fitting by heating it with a torch, using flame spreader, Fig. 10. The heat expands the fitting to the point where it will let go easily

17 Laboratory glass tubing can be bent into almost any desired shape if you heat it slowly with a spreader flame tip. Be sure to protect your hands because the glass is hot

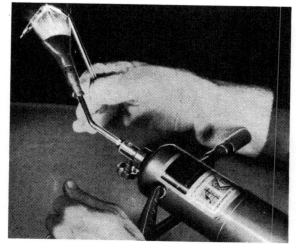

The perfect prop for your outboard

BY PACK BRYAN and MARC MICHAELSON

For every rig there's just one prop that will deliver top performance,
efficiency and economy. Here's the way you can find that ideal wheel

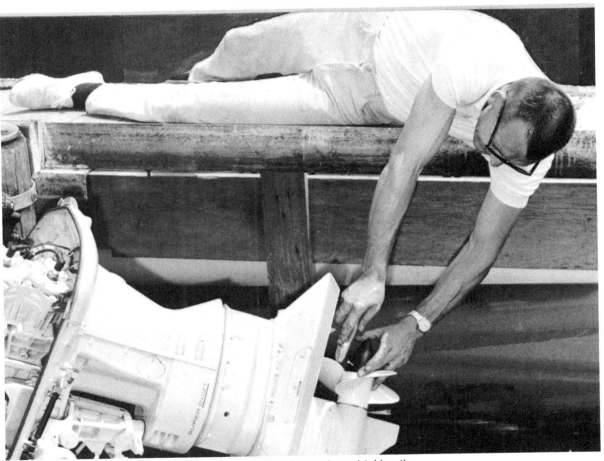

Changing props at dockside is a simple matter of removing a pin and taking the
prop off the hub. A number of propellers on the market can be tested in a short time

FOR EVERY BOAT AND MOTOR combination there is one propeller that will produce optimum performance. The finest engine-tuning job and the slickest hull in the world will not give you full value unless they are combined with the right prop.

Whether you're operating a runabout or a houseboat; looking for speed or economy, ease of handling or pulling power for water skiers, you must—for peak operating efficiency—do some personal research to find the correct propeller for the particular job.

When the U.S. Coast Guard entered two boats in the punishing 188-mile Miami-Nassau race as part of a small-boat evaluation program, they chose two 30-ft. Pearson fiberglass utility hulls

prowler alarm: see alarms, burglar

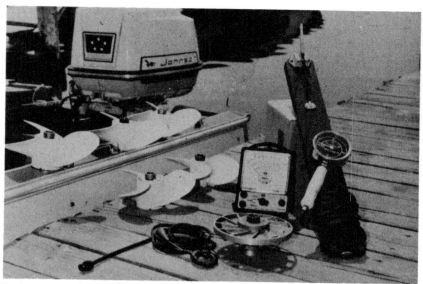

Equipment for a complete test includes a variety of props, a tachometer, a speedometer and a factory test wheel. The operating specifications for the motor and prop recommendations for boat and motor are also necessary

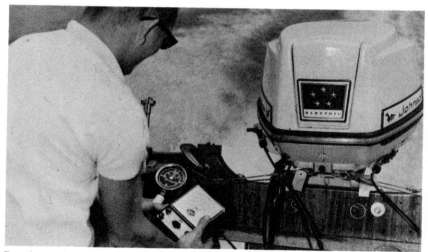

Running at full throttle on open water, a speedometer is used to compare the boat's speed with the reading of the tachometer, which will tell if a particular prop is allowing the motor to operate within its proper range

powered by paired Cummins 588-cu.-in. turbocharged diesels. Designed for rough water, the boats were to be raced in "semi-stock" condition, leaving on board most of the extra equipment that a rescue craft would ordinarily carry. The only changes from "stock" were in the engines, which were revamped to produce well over 300 hp per engine.

Each boat weighed about two tons and with the addition of a full load of fuel and the problem of rough water, you might think that a flat-pitch work propeller would be needed.

But it did not work out that way. The first props they tried were not capable of utilizing all the power the big diesels were putting out, allowing the engines to hit maximum rpm before top speed was reached.

A prop was needed to match the powerplant and the boat's design, giving constant thrust and "bite" even on high-speed turns. Finally, the Columbian Bronze Corp. of Freeport, L.I., came up with a deep-pitch prop whose blades were 50 percent wider than usual and contained a special section in each blade to give it added lift. With these special props custom-matched to the boat and motors, the Coast Guard took first place in their class.

The same lesson also applies to your own boat

A dockside test requires a tachometer and a test wheel, a hubbed wheel into which predetermined water resistance has been built. With the test wheel on the hub, the boat's motor should reach its top rpm when the throttle is opened all the way

and motor. Using simple tests to make sure that your engine is operating at peak efficiency, you can then match it with the best possible propeller.

The equipment you need is available at most dealers and the majority of them will either lend or rent it to you for the few hours it will take to get the job done. You'll need a tachometer and a speedometer, the correct operating specifications for your motor, a list of recommended propellers for your own boat and motor combination, and the factory test wheel for your motor.

A test wheel is literally what its name implies, a hubbed wheel or disk with a calibrated amount of water resistance built into it. Every manufacturer provides such a wheel to match each of the motors he produces. The wheel puts the correct load on the motor when running at peak rpm and will help you to set the standard against which you'll compare various propellers. It can be used with the motor in a test tank or on the transom at dockside.

Having checked plugs, magneto, timing and carburetion to see that they match manufacturer's recommendations, replace the existing propeller with the test wheel, put the lower unit into the water, and hook up the tachometer. Start the motor and allow it to warm up for a few minutes. Then open the throttle wide and when the tachometer steadies, take a reading. If it goes to the top of the recommended rpm range in the specs, you're all set. If not, make the necessary adjustments to timing and carburetion (you can probably do this when the engine is running) until the needle climbs to the point you're after.

Once you know that the engine will put out the power it's supposed to, you can begin your search for a perfect prop. However, there's a key step you'll want to take care of first. Check the bottom of the boat.

If the boat has been in the water for any length of time, it will probably have accumulated a slippery growth that's slicker than glare ice. You would think this might increase the boat's top speed, but it can actually cut your speed many

	Prop	R.p.m.	Speed	Notch	Load	Comments
1st	10 x 11	4000	32	2d	600	First test, recommended wheel
	10 x 11	4300	33	3d	600	First test, recommended wheel
	10 x 11	4400	33½	4th	600	Bow wild, required over steering
2nd	10¼ x 10	4500	32½	3d	600	Notable improvement
	10¼ x 10	4500	34	3d	200	Notable improvement
3rd	10 x 9¼	4800	33	3d	200	Fast getaway, best all around prop
	10 x 9¼	4600	33	3d	600	Fast getaway, best all around prop
4th	9½ x 10	4900	33½-34	3d	200	Original wheel, kept as spare
	9½ x 10	4900	33½	3d	400	Original wheel, kept as spare

PROPELLER SELECTION TEST*

* Cruisers, Inc. #100 14-Foot Lapstrake Runabout with 60 hp. Johnson

miles an hour and should be thoroughly removed. We've found that a plastic scouring pad will cut it better than anything without harming the finish. While you're at it, fill any nicks or gouges and, if there's time, wax the bottom with a good grade of auto wax.

With your present propeller on the shaft, rig the boat as it will run during normal activities. Your first test will be to run straight, without "optional load (O.L.)." Under O.L. include any-

thing not considered the standard equipment always carried in the boat. This could be extra fuel, passengers, camping equipment or anything else not used in day-to-day running.

Your standard equipment might be two full fuel tanks, water skis, anchor and rope, safety cushions and life jackets, fire extinguisher, first-aid kit and boat hook or paddle. The idea is to test the boat under conditions as close to normal as possible, rather than setting it up for absolute

This Coast Guard boat won its class in the Miami-Nassau race. The craft required special props that had a deep pitch and were 50 percent wider than usual. This was necessary to utilize the output of two powerful diesel engines

maximum speed in a superlight condition and then finding it unable to get on plane when you take the family out for a spin. For the first, or base, test, you'll be in the boat alone with all the standard equipment. Move equipment around until the boat is trimmed on an even keel.

Head for open water where you can safely run at full throttle. Once on plane, when you can hear that the engine rpm has leveled off at a peak, check both speedometer and tachometer and record the readings. (Having a speedometer on board for these tests is important, because while the tachometer will tell you that a particular propeller is allowing the engine to run within its proper range, it won't tell you how efficiently.) Throttle back slowly to idle, let the boat come to rest and then repeat the process, this time noting how quickly the boat gets on plane and reaches top speed.

why a prop lugs

The first propeller you've tried will most likely be the one recommended by the factory for your boat and motor combination. It's a compromise selection picked for average performance over a wide range of uses to which you might put your boat; it's probably not ideal for any one of them. If the engine rpm did not reach the peak it registered with a test wheel, that means it's working too hard (lugging) and you'll next want to try a flatter pitch. In view of the fact that a flatter pitch implies getting closer to a work propeller, you may feel that this will cut your speed. Just the opposite will probably happen, for as the engine gets running closer to its peak rpm, it also is capable of more work and will push the boat faster.

With the flatter-pitch prop, repeat your tests, noting once more the top speed, peak rpm reading, and how fast the boat gets up on plane. You may have hit the peak with this second try, or you may have to experiment with one or two other propellers, but we'll go on to the next step.

Take someone on board with you and repeat the test; then once more with two passengers. This is part of your "optional load," so keep these readings handy for future reference. With the extra load on board, your speed will probably decrease slightly and engine rpm will go down. You've reached the critical point in the tests, for the object has been to find the propeller that will permit your engine to turn at peak rpm with a light load while still turning within the recommended operating range when an extra load is added. Lower than recommended rpm at full throttle means possible engine damage and wasted fuel.

Once you've selected the propeller which will give you the top speed at the proper tachometer reading, experiment with your tilt-pin setting. You may find that handling will be improved or that the boat will get up on plane faster. Although acceleration is usually a function of engine and propeller performance (note on the chart that one prop gave better acceleration while not achieving top speed as compared to its neighbor on the chart) your tilt-pin settings are critical factors in achieving top performance.

For absolute top speed, you may want to experiment with "rev sticks." These are nothing but ¼-in. slats designed to raise the motor on the transom in small increments. In most cases, with a standard motor and transom, you won't have to get into this experiment, but here's the way if you want to try it.

should ride parallel

The anti-cavitation plate on your motor's lower unit (the flat, horizontal fin just above the prop) should ride approximately parallel to the boat bottom just below the surface of the water when the boat is on plane. If it's too low, you're adding needless resistance and wasting fuel. If it's too high, your propeller will cavitate, over-spinning as air bubbles displace the water it should be pushing. This can damage the engine quickly and expensively, so keep a fast hand on the throttle as you experiment. Add one rev stick at a time until the prop just begins to cavitate. Then remove one stick and install transom through-bolts with the engine in the new position. You may want to replace the rev sticks with a single piece of wood, cut and finished to match the transom.

The importance of the prop in boat performance is best illustrated by an inventory of Columbian Bronze Corp., a propeller manufacturer whose activity in the outboard and outdrive field is confined to replacement props only. They stock more than 2000 varieties of props that vary in diameter, pitch, blade shape and number of blades (plus right-and-left handed props for twin installations). And they're not the only prop manufacturer.

So for better performance this year, plan a test session early in the season. It'll pay off in efficiency, economy and better boating.

See also: boats, buying; boats, used; carburetors, outboard; outboard motors, overhauling; outboard motors, repair; outboard motors, storage; outboard motors, used; remote controls, outboard; sparkplugs, marine.

Psychrometer tells you the humidity

BY DUANE LOEWEN

■ IT's THE HIGH HUMIDITY that makes you feel uncomfortable on a summer day. But in winter low relative humidity can make you uncomfortably chilly in a warm room. Modern homes, gasketed and weatherstripped, insulated and vapor sealed, are almost airtight. That's why it's becoming necessary to condition the air in the rooms winter and summer by dehumidifying in summer and humidifying in winter to hold relative humidity at comfortable levels during seasonal extremes. But before you can control humidity in the home you must have some method of measuring it accurately. That's why it will pay homeowners to make this simple wet-bulb hygrometer, or more properly, a sling psychrometer.

how it works

Relative humidity is the percentage of saturation of the air measured from 0 to 100 percent, the latter figure representing the maximum

amount of moisture that a given amount of air will hold at a given temperature. This is inversely proportional to the rate of evaporation from any moist object, and is the principle on which the psychrometer works. Evaporation of moisture on the bulb of one thermometer (two are used) lowers its reading relative to the other thermometer which gives the ambient (actual) room temperature. The readings are compared and then are converted to relative humidity, using the table on the opposite page.

how it's made

Details on the opposite page show clearly how to construct the psychrometer. Two ordinary matched thermometers (they must read alike at any given temperature) are joined back to back and attached to a length of light wire chain. The free end of the chain is joined to a 6-in. length of hardwood dowel. To one of the thermometers you cement a plastic vial to hold a cottoncloth wick which is inserted in the vial and carried up around the bulb of the thermometer glass. The wick should entirely enclose the bulb; hold it in place with a loop of thread tied loosely just above the bulb. Before using, be sure screws and bolts holding the two thermometers and chain are tight.

use of instrument

It will be noted that distilled water is called for in the materials list. This is not essential unless your water is very hard, that is, has a high mineral content. Then it is best to use distilled water. The small quantity required can be obtained by condensing steam from a teakettle. The first step in the use of the psychrometer is to place a few drops of the distilled water in the vial, enough so that the wick is saturated. Then, immediately whirl the thermometers slowly in a clear area in the room at a uniform rate, continuing until the wick is dry and the wet-bulb thermometer will not drop further in temperature. This usually takes two to three minutes. Then quickly take the readings of both thermometers and compare with the table which converts the readings to relative humidity. As an example, suppose the dry-bulb thermometer shows a temperature of 72 deg., but the wet-bulb thermometer shows only 59 deg. As you will see from the table the humidity would be 46 percent, which is a good average for health and wintertime comfort.

See also: airconditioning; condensation; humidifiers; insulation; weatherstripping.

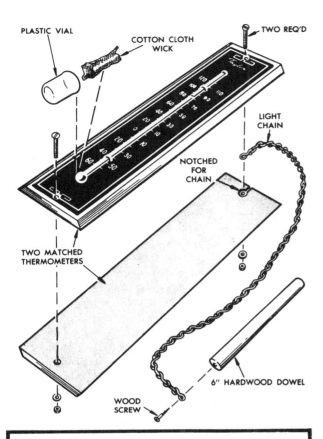

PLASTIC VIAL

COTTON CLOTH WICK

TWO REQ'D

LIGHT CHAIN

NOTCHED FOR CHAIN

TWO MATCHED THERMOMETERS

6" HARDWOOD DOWEL

WOOD SCREW

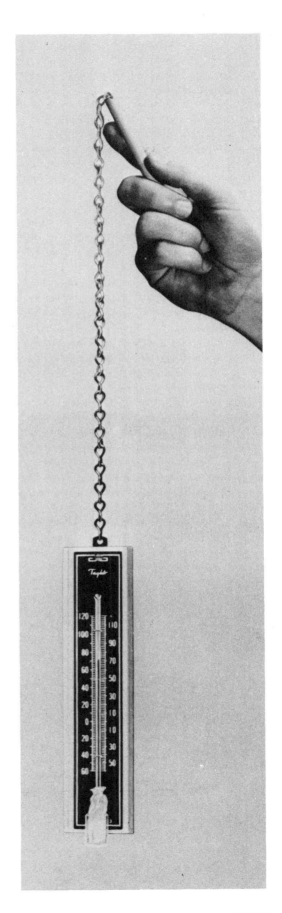

RELATIVE HUMIDITY TABLE
Wet Thermometer (F)

	70	69	68	67	66	65	64	63	62	61	60	59	58	57	56	55	54	53
80	61	57	54	51	47	44	41	38										
79	63	60	57	54	50	47	44	41	37									
78	67	64	60	57	53	50	46	43	40	37								
77	71	67	63	60	56	52	49	46	42	39	36							
76	74	70	67	63	59	55	52	48	45	42	38	35						
75	78	74	70	66	63	59	55	51	48	44	40	38	34					
74	82	78	74	70	66	62	58	54	51	47	43	40	37	34				
73	86	82	78	73	69	65	61	58	54	50	46	43	40	36	33			
72	91	86	82	78	73	69	65	61	57	53	49	46	42	39	35	32		
71	95	90	86	82	77	73	69	64	60	56	53	49	45	41	38	34	31	
70		95	90	86	81	77	72	68	64	60	56	52	48	44	40	37	33	30
69			95	90	86	81	77	72	68	64	59	55	51	47	44	40	36	32
68				95	90	85	81	76	72	67	63	59	55	51	47	43	39	35
67					95	90	85	80	76	71	67	62	58	54	50	46	42	38
66						95	90	85	80	76	71	66	62	58	53	49	45	41
65							95	90	85	80	75	70	66	62	57	53	48	44
64								95	90	85	79	75	70	66	61	56	52	48
63									95	90	84	79	74	70	65	60	56	51
62										94	89	84	79	74	69	64	60	55
61										94	89	84	79	74	68	64	59	
60											94	89	84	78	73	68	63	

Dry Thermometer (F)

MATERIALS
Two matched thermometers (see text)
Light chain (approximately 12 in. long)
Plastic vial
Wick (made of open-weave cotton)
Hardwood dowel (½ x 6 in. for handle)
Distilled water (see text)

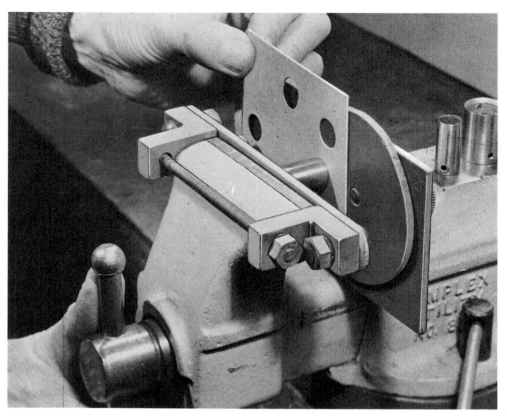

Put punch in your vise

BY WALTER E. BURTON

For an accessory that won't cost you anything,
    this hollow punch, made from scrap, can be
amazingly useful. It enables you to create
        cutters in a variety of shapes and to cut
clean holes in sheets of leather, cardboard,
    thin plastic or sheet metal, and wood veneers

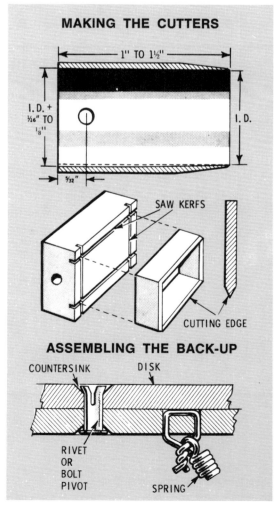

MAKING THE CUTTERS

1" TO 1½"

I. D. + ¹⁄₁₆" TO ⅛"

I. D.

⁵⁄₃₂"

SAW KERFS

CUTTING EDGE

ASSEMBLING THE BACK-UP

COUNTERSINK

DISK

RIVET OR BOLT PIVOT

SPRING

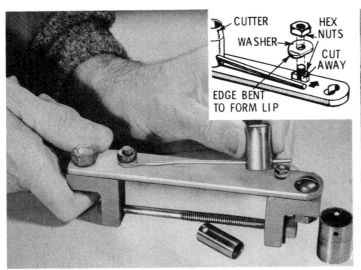

Changing cutters is simple matter of slipping one off pivoting wire, the other on. Free end of wire is tucked against half nut and held by lipped washer (inset). When top nut is tightened, tension is created on wire to keep cutter in position. Same holds true for block-mounted cutters. Photo at right shows how rivet is spread for disk pivot. Coil-spring loops pass around vise jaw to hold the back-up unit in place

IT's ALWAYS A PLEASURE to add a piece of equipment to your shop that doesn't cost you anything—especially a gizmo as useful as this one. You can custom-make it from scrap to fit your bench vise. The great pressure you're able to exert with the vise screw lets you punch your way neatly through leather, cardboard, thin plastic or sheet metal, and wood veneers. The easily made tubular punches let you retrieve the cuttings, if you're making disks or washers. And you can create cutters in many shapes—square, triangular or even cookie-cutter-type designs—from knife-edged steel strip.

The gadget consists of three parts: the punch assortment, punch holder, and back-up pad. The round punches shown in the photos are sections of tube with the outside of one end filed, ground or turned to form a sharp edge. For greatest efficiency, the tube should be machined on a lathe so that its interior diameter tapers slightly, as indicated in the sketch on the facing page. This permits the cut disks to move easily to the rear, so you can make repeated cuts without clogging.

If you don't have the equipment for machining, you can make the punches by filing or grinding a cutting edge on a length of thin-walled steel tubing, but you should harden and temper the cutting edge. If the tubing is low-carbon steel, use a case-hardening compound. Still another method is to ream out one end of the tube, putting the cutting bevel on the inside and leaving the outside diameter uniform. This is recommended when

you must cut accurate holes in fairly thick materials. But such punches will load quickly unless emptied after a few cuts.

An oval punch can be made by flattening a round punch slightly in the vise before hardening. The built-up punches can be bent from any steel strip having one edge sharpened like a knife blade. Printer's cutting rule is most convenient, but you can grind a hacksaw blade and anneal it for bending. Once you've got the shape you want, you fasten the blunt edge of the strip to a drilled block of metal or plywood, either forcing it into matching grooves or seating it in epoxy, metal paste, or solder. The drilling is to let you "string" the finished punch on the holder rod.

Construction of the punch holder depends on the shape of the vise jaws. The holder shown consists of a 3/16 x 1 x 6-in. steel bar bracketed to the jaw with two heavy angles on a long 1/4-in. bolt.

To protect cutting edges, the material to be punched is backed up by a pad. The one shown is a 3⅜-in. disk of ⅛-in. tempered hardboard, pivoted on a panel of the same material. The disk revolves to present fresh surfaces, and after the face becomes badly chewed, you just remove the rivet and replace the disk with a new one. The disk could also be zinc, or soft aluminum, and the pivot could be a flat-head bolt, as long as the head is countersunk so that the work lays flat against the disk. A means of attaching this unit to the vise is shown above.

See also: clamps; drill presses; vises.

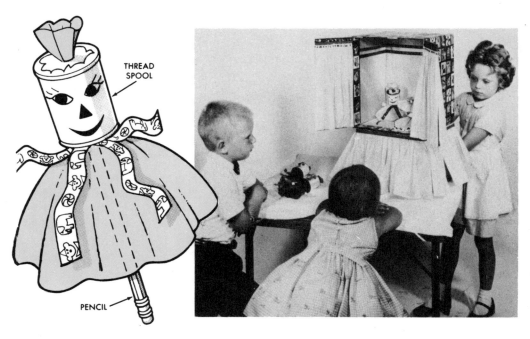

THREAD SPOOL

PENCIL

Rainy-day puppet stage from cartons

■ A SHARP KNIFE, two cardboard cartons and a few scraps of cloth are practically all you need to make this puppet theater. Start by removing the top of one box and partially cutting away one side to leave a "flange" 2 in. wide along three edges. (See drawing, below.) Then cut two holes about 5 in. in diameter in one side of the box. A few slots extending from the holes will permit freer movement of the puppets. The second box rests on top of the first and is secured with tape, staples or glue. The outside of the stage is dec-

orated by wrapping the boxes with colored foil before adding stage curtains and skirt. Sew them in place, or use staples, which may be covered with adhesive gift tape for appearance.

The puppets are just as simple. Pencils form the bodies. Thread spools, painted or wound with tape, become the heads. The costumes are merely rags and other scraps of cloth. Use your imagination to create unusual puppet characters.

See also: dollhouses; dolls; magic; playhouses; toys.

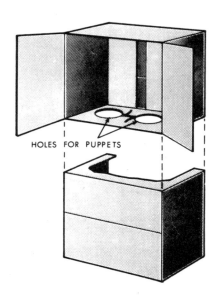

HOLES FOR PUPPETS

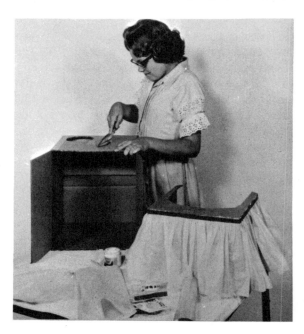

Puppet theater keeps 'em busy

BY H. J. KENNARD

■ IN THE warm and wondrous summer months, birds, buds and kids flourish. The flowers may take some tending, but it's the kids who have to be watched and kept out of mischief.

The best way to keep them out of trouble is to keep them busy doing something in which they can participate—something which will put their active imaginations to work. The little puppet "theater" illustrated above is ideal for this. You'll get a bang out of eavesdropping on their dramatized versions of bedtime stories, TV adventures, movies and anything else around which they can wrap their inventiveness. The theater is a screen made of ¼-in. plywood, the center panel measuring 24 x 48 in. and the hinged wings 12 in. wide. An opening is cut near the top of the center panel to serve as the stage and a sash curtain spring and a ½-in. dowel support the stage curtains and the backdrop. The dimensions suggested will afford ample room for the more ingenious members of the troupe to "work" behind the scenes in a kneeling position.

purple martin birdhouses: see birdhouses

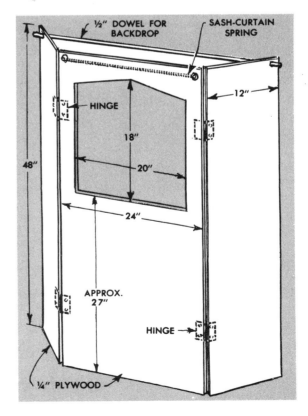

½" DOWEL FOR BACKDROP

SASH-CURTAIN SPRING

HINGE

18"

20"

12"

48"

24"

APPROX. 27"

HINGE →

¼" PLYWOOD

SECTION OF SAW BLADE

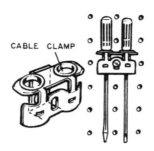

CABLE CLAMP

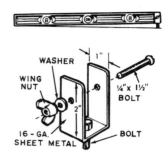

WASHER
1"
WING NUT
¼" x 1½" BOLT
2"
16 - GA. SHEET METAL
BOLT

To add a scraper to a hammer, just mount a short section of saw blade on the top of the head as shown. It's great for quickly removing concrete scale from construction form boards.

Cable lamps from switch boxes can be put to work to serve as neat toolholders for screwdrivers, chisels and other thin tools. Just mount them on the wall or fasten them to pegboard.

This homemade pitch-gauge attachment clamps to the end of your level. Bend it from sheet metal, as shown, and solder a hex nut to the upper surface of the lower section of the gauge.

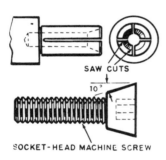

SAW CUTS
10°
SOCKET-HEAD MACHINE SCREW

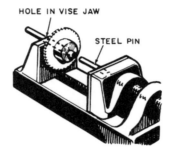

HOLE IN VISE JAW
STEEL PIN

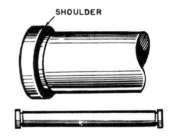

SHOULDER

An expansion arbor for working with short tubular shapes will let you finish the outside as well as the inside surface. You can make one easily. Just follow the diagram above.

Pressing shafts in or out of small gears is easy with a drill-press vise. Just drill a hole through one jaw. Then drill a corresponding blind hole in the other.

To protect test bars from being nicked or burred if dropped accidentally, add press-fit end collars. New bars can also be protected this way. Add the collars when they are machined.

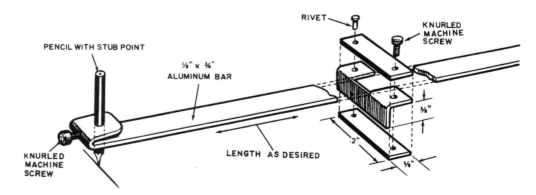

RIVET
KNURLED MACHINE SCREW
PENCIL WITH STUB POINT
⅛" x ¾" ALUMINUM BAR
KNURLED MACHINE SCREW
LENGTH AS DESIRED
⅜"
2"
⅜"

This marking gauge made from aluminum uses a stubby pencil instead of a steel pin, eliminating any danger of gouging. The marking bar can be any length desired, and can be easily calibrated with an accurate rule.

Walking box is a real puzzler

BY ROY L. CLOUGH, JR.

■ THERE IT SITS: a little black box that has no wheels, treads, or air jets to push with. Its bottom is smooth and flat. It seems a most unlikely prime mover—but just let a curious friend plug in the cable from its little red battery wagon, and away it goes, chuffing like a locomotive and towing its power supply.

If your puzzled friend puts his finger in front of it, the box nudges the finger along with a steady, pulsating thrust. Odder still, if he pushes it gently, he discovers that the box resists being urged along faster than it wants to go. If friend pushes it backward, he hears the driving mechanism labor in protest.

"Does the box run only on a flat surface?" your friend demands. In reply, you tilt the table under it to form a grade up to five percent. Undaunted, the box pumps onward and upward.

"Okay, okay!" says friend, impatiently: "What makes it go?"

Your reply can again be wordless. Just hand him this, opened to the following page.

But before you do, see if *you* can solve the mystery with these additional clues:

The box moves because it contains a source of thrust that is independent of its exterior. This

When you plug in power
the box moves, pulling its battery wagon behind.
Can you figure out what makes it go?

thrust operates in both directions, but pushes a bit harder forward than it does backward.

That's right: action with modified reaction, in that part of the reaction is taken up by the acceleration of the earth's gravity field. It's not a "bootstraps" drive, however. Equal amounts of energy are expended in both directions: the equation balances. But the energy is removed suddenly in the forward direction and more slowly in the reactive direction. As a propulsion system it is utterly impractical. The test? Suspend the box, or place it on wheels. It won't budge an inch! Got your solution? Turn the page.

See also: engine models; games, children's; magic; oscillator, audio; soldering.

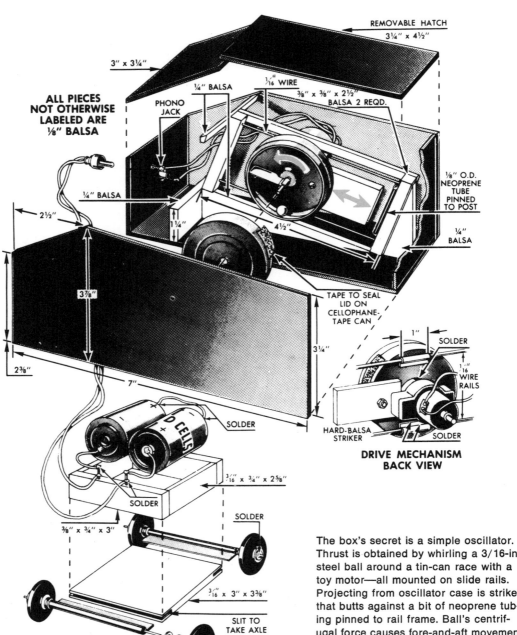

REMOVABLE HATCH
3¼" x 4½"

3" x 3¼"

ALL PIECES
NOT OTHERWISE
LABELED ARE
⅛" BALSA

¼" BALSA

PHONO
JACK

1/16" WIRE

⅜" x ⅜" x 2½"
BALSA 2 REQD.

⅛" O.D.
NEOPRENE
TUBE
PINNED
TO POST

¼"
BALSA

¼" BALSA

2½"

1¼"

4½"

3⅞"

2⅜"

3¼"

7"

TAPE TO SEAL
LID ON
CELLOPHANE-
TAPE CAN

1"

SOLDER

1/16"
WIRE
RAILS

HARD-BALSA
STRIKER

SOLDER

**DRIVE MECHANISM
BACK VIEW**

SOLDER

D CELLS

3/16" x ¾" x 2⅝"

SOLDER

⅜" x ¾" x 3"

SOLDER

3/16" x 3" x 3⅜"

SLIT TO
TAKE AXLE
BRACKET

TIN-CAN STOCK CURLED
AROUND AND SOLDERED TO
1/16" WIRE 4" LONG

1¼" MODEL
PLANE WHEEL

The box's secret is a simple oscillator. Thrust is obtained by whirling a 3/16-in. steel ball around a tin-can race with a toy motor—all mounted on slide rails. Projecting from oscillator case is striker that butts against a bit of neoprene tubing pinned to rail frame. Ball's centrifugal force causes fore-and-aft movement of case. Forward force, stopped by rubber bumper, is transmitted to box and drives it ahead. Rear force is not limited, so lift and rail friction absorb it. To make, solder front bearing of an aluminum-cased motor into hole punched at center of bottom half of cellophane-tape can, then solder tin-can-stock paddle to motor shaft. Solder tin brackets (or brass tube) at back to mount unit on rails of tilted frame.

Clamp the octagonal pieces together and finish with a rasp to assure uniformity

To provide clearance, the fixture chain which holds the rack should be at least 6 in. long

Lazy susan hardware rack

BY J. CANINE

■ THIS 80-JAR revolving rack, hung from the ceiling over your workbench, will keep track of every screw, nut and bolt—all within easy reach.

It's an octagonal frame to which lids of baby-food jars are fastened. The glass jars let you see at a glance, and a half-twist permits easy removal from the rack.

The frame is made from three octagons cut from ¾-in. pine, and eight 24-in. lengths of ½ x ¾-in. stock molding, called parting stop, all assembled with 1-in. No. 6 F.H. screws. The axle is a ⅜ x 28-in. brass curtain rod drilled at each end for a cotter pin. It rides in ⁷⁄₁₆-in. center holes and is suspended from two lengths of fixture chain which, in turn, are held by screw eyes anchored into the ceiling joists.

See also: bolts; fasteners; hardware; nails; maintenance center; screws.

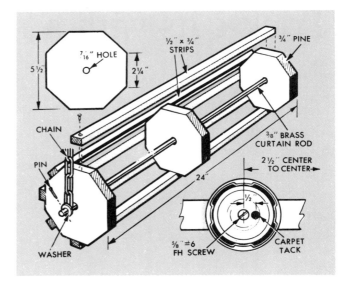

Curved grooves and slots can be formed with the power unit locked in the rip position and the saw arm swung right to left. Clamp work to the table and repeat passes

Trick cuts with a radial-arm saw

BY R. J. DeCRISTOFORO

Put your radial-arm saw
to work making all
kinds of cuts—
from bevels to coves
to circles and saucers.
These tips show you how

■ IF YOU'VE LOOKED upon the radial-arm saw as nothing more than a cutoff tool, you're in for a surprise. For, by fully utilizing its swiveling, tilting, swinging and sliding movements, you'll find yourself doing such a bagful of tricks with this versatile machine that its basic cutoff function will seem almost incidental.

Once you master a few settings, you can use the saw for jobs you'd otherwise have to do on a lathe, jigsaw, router—or by hand. In some cases, the way the tool performs suggests special decorative treatments you could achieve by no other means. The techniques demonstrated on these pages are only a starter. As you experiment with all of these various cuts, you'll be able to innovate many more of your own.

By setting blade in rip position and using a nail as a center pivot (below), you can rotate the workpiece against blade rotation and thus cut a perfect circle. Since the blade is always tangent to the arc, you are actually making a cove cut, but as this occurs in the waste only, the edge of the circular piece is cut square. Repeat passes, lowering blade about 1/16 in. each time. You cut completely to the work surface beneath the stock

Similar setup is used for cutting circular coves as for cutting circles. Saw blade is adjusted so that it is actually cutting a true cove instead of tangent to the arc. The greater the offset of the blade in relation to the circle, the wider the cove cut. Since the blade does as much scraping as it does cutting, full depth of cut must be made by repeat passes, the final one with the blade barely touching to produce the smoothest possible surface

continued

Saucer cuts are accomplished by swinging blade back and forth through power unit's tilt range in the crosscut position. Full depth of saucer shape is achieved by making repeat passes, and you can cut faster and deeper if you do the job with a dado. Be sure the workpiece is clamped securely and keep the hands away from the cutting area. Saw's tilt stop must be disengaged, of course, to permit unrestricted swing of power unit

Small circles can be cut in this unique manner simply because the power unit can be rotated 360 deg. Clamp the work and tilt the dado about 10 deg. Lower the dado slowly until it makes a small bite and then rotate the power unit a full circle. Repeat the step, taking a ⅛-in. bite each time until the cut is complete. If you plan to cut completely through, back up the work with a scrap piece to avoid cutting into the saw's wooden table

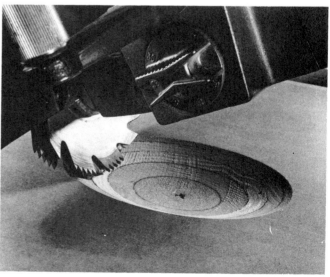

Limitless variety of fancy decorative cuts is possible through the saw's tilting action. The faceted surface you see here is accomplished with a dado by setting the power unit in the rip position and then tilting it 45 deg. Each pass produces a V-groove, so equally spaced cuts, with and across the grain, create a pleasing decorative surface. Smooth job results when the crossgrain Vs are made first; this is true in cutting with and across grain

Panel raising can be done in a more convenient manner on a radial saw than on a conventional table saw since the operation is done with the workpiece flat on the table. With the power unit set in the rip position and the desired distance from the fence, ⅛-in. deep shoulder cuts are made in the surface of the panel first, running saw cuts around the four sides. To "raise" the panel, the power unit is set for horizontal cutting, the saw tilted up a few degrees and the panel is fed past the slanting blade as it is guided along the fence. Blade height must be set so the cut ends at the very bottom of the kerfs. Since the blade must clear the saw's fence, support the work on an auxiliary panel to raise it above the fence

In another example of decorative "carving," power unit is set in the crosscut position and tilted 45 deg. To form one side of the gothic V-cuts you pull the dado. To cut the other, you turn the work end for end and push the dado across the work. A C-clamp attached to the saw's arm serves as a stop and establishes length of grooves. Spacing of each pair of cuts is assured by use of a stop block which is repositioned as the work is shifted

trick radial-saw cuts, continued

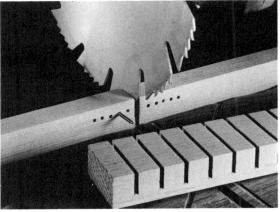

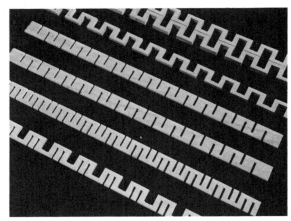

Examples of "dentil" type molding which are formed by kerfing as shown above, left. Some are made with a saw blade, others with a dado blade, still others by combining both. Cuts are made across grain of thick stock, then sliced lengthwise into thin strips. Top molding in photo results in joining two pieces edgewise. An endless variety of patterns is possible by varying spacing of cuts

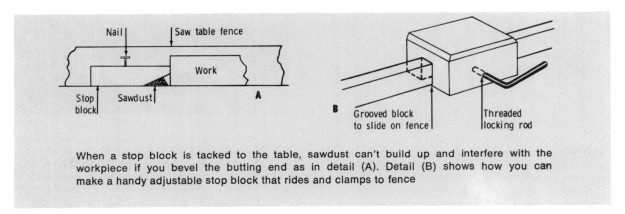

When a stop block is tacked to the table, sawdust can't build up and interfere with the workpiece if you bevel the butting end as in detail (A). Detail (B) shows how you can make a handy adjustable stop block that rides and clamps to fence

continued

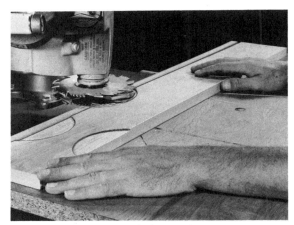

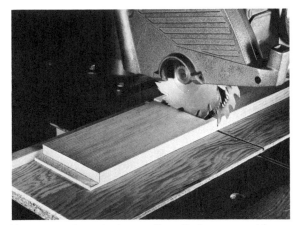

To form scallops with a dado, set the power unit in a horizontal cutting position and lower it so the dado just clears the fence. Feed the work slowly since the dado will tend to kick the work out of position. A C-clamp attached to the saw's fence will provide a stop against which you can brace the workpiece as you feed it. This basic cut can lead to many pleasing designs merely by changing the spacing between the units. Saw guard has been purposely removed to show operation more clearly, but for actual cutting it should always be in place as a dado in this position can be quite dangerous

You can perform dual operations that save considerable time by combining different blades on the saw's arbor. Here, a 6-in. dado and a 7-in. saw blade ganged together not only sever the workpiece but form an end rabbet, both in one pass. Likewise, two saw blades of equal diameter spaced apart with washers will cut kerfing time in half. Surface kerfing with twin blades spaced apart will also add a decorative border to wall plaques, drawer fronts, etc. When end-rabbeting with ganged blades in the manner pictured above, you protect the saw's table with a scrap of ¼-in. plywood. Pull the saw slowly through the stock to get a smooth, splinter-free cut

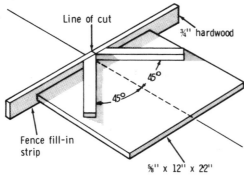

Line of cut

¾" hardwood

45°

45°

Fence fill-in strip

⅝" x 12" x 22"

Eight-pointed diamond star is an example of the different decorative rosettes which can be assembled of pieces cut from triangular strips. Here the saw's arm is swung to a 45 deg. setting and the power unit is tilted to match the bevel of the strips. Segments are "chopped" off in quantity by making the first cut with the stock placed to the left of the blade, then shifting it to the right-hand side to make the second cut. In each case, the blade must be in exact line with the topmost point of the first cut. Work finishes out smoothest when you make the cut slowly

Best way to cut miters is to use a mitering jig and forget the 45 deg. setting of the power unit. The jig (detailed above) fits the slot of the saw's regular fence and is aligned with the blade so the line of cut splits it down the middle. It's the only practical way to cut compound miters. Edges of stock are pre-beveled and then workpiece is stood on edge and held firmly against fences of guide as work is cut

See also: bench saws; circular saw blades; picture frames; saber saws.

trick radial-saw cuts, continued

Differing from table-saw technique, cove cutting here is done from the top side of the workpiece and fed to tool along saw's fence. Either a blade or dado may be used. For the widest cove, the saw is set for simple cross-cutting and the blade tilted 10 deg. to the left

Then it's located over the center of the work, adjusted to take a ⅛-in. cut and locked. The workpiece is fed repeatedly from right to left as if being ripped. Width of cove is varied by changing angle of blade. Edge coves are made by varying blade angle and tilt

METAL STRIP CLAMPED TO FRONT TABLE

GRINDING WHEEL

WHEEL MUST CLEAR

KNIFE

FRONT AND REAR JOINTER TABLES

Surface grinding on a radial saw

BY BEN QUAN

If the work is stationary, you can put your radial-arm saw to work grinding jointer knives and sharpening chisels

■ SURFACE GRINDING to a plane surface, also any grinding job where the work can be stationary and the wheel moved, can be done with your radial saw. Three examples are pictured above, the photo and detail at the right showing one way to grind jointer knives. Set the jointer on the saw table and then level it so that the travel of the wheel face is parallel with the bevel of one knife, as in the detail. Then clamp a straightedge to the jointer front table in a position that will hold the cutterhead with the knife bevel in position as in the detail. Loop a strong cord over an Allen wrench which is inserted in the setscrew in the pulley and tie it around the slide projection at the front of the table as pictured. Then lower the overarm of the saw until the grinding wheel just touches the knife; make a pass or two and again lower the overarm slightly. Continue the

procedure until the knife edge tests sharp throughout the length. Repeat the setup for the remaining knives, turning the jointer head and locking as before.

To grind a bevel on a cutter, chisel or plane iron, clamp it to a piece of plywood which is in turn clamped to the saw table as in the upper left-hand photo. Once the work has been located, just back the rotating wheel slowly until it touches the bevel. An advantage of this method is that the curvature of the wheel will hollow-grind the bevel slightly. To grind a surface, clamp the work in a drill vise as in the lower left-hand photo and place the vise against the fence. Then lower the grinding wheel to a light contact and make as many passes as are necessary to finish-grind the entire surface.

It's best to use a fine-grit wheel.

A saw
can sharpen itself

BY MANLY BANISTER

Here is a clamp-on vise
that fits any make of saw
and holds any saw blade
for accurate semiautomatic
machine sharpening

These front and rear views of the saw-sharpening vise show its blade arbor, adjustable to take various blade sizes, and its slip shoe, which holds it to the saw table for the initial adjustment

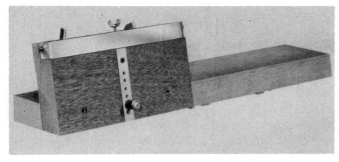

OWNERS OF RADIAL-ARM SAWS can throw away their file when it comes to sharpening the blade. With this clever clamp-on "filing" vise you can machine-sharpen the blade with the accuracy of the saw itself. It will handle any type blade of any diameter from 6 in. up to 10 in.

Here's how it's used: First remove the wood fence and the lift-out leaves from the table and slip the vise over the edge of the table at the right-hand end. The shoe clamp on the vise makes it fit snugly, yet permits shifting. Mount a ½ x 6-in. vitrified grinding wheel (100 grit, grade N) on the saw arbor, swing the radial arm 90 deg. to its normal cutoff position and replace the blade guard. Grade N is a medium-grit wheel. Avoid using a soft stone as it wears down too fast.

Now with the teeth pointing to the right, place the blade on the arbor of the vise and carefully adjust both the blade and the vise so that the area to be ground on each tooth is parallel with the *face* of the grinding wheel. Clamp the blade lightly to the vise and, in turn, clamp the vise to the saw table with a C-clamp. This done, slide the adjustable stop finger into position, two teeth *behind* the tooth to be ground, and hold the finger against the tooth by sliding the stop block against it.

make a trial pass

For a trial pass, set the depth of cut so the wheel barely touches the tooth, then lower the arm a little so the wheel just removes the bright spot left on the tooth by the initial jointing operation. To "file" each tooth, you simply pull the wheel slowly across it once, then push it back. As each tooth is ground, the C-clamp holding the blade is loosened, the stop finger moved back and the blade rotated ahead two teeth before repositioning the finger and reclamping the blade. Continue around the blade until you have ground every tooth. Then flop the blade in the vise and grind the remaining teeth in the same way. Here you use the second finger stop, and you'll find it necessary to shift the vise to realign the teeth under the wheel. If the blade to be ground has been hand-filed a number of times and is possibly out of round, it should first be jointed by mounting the blade backwards on its arbor and rotating it *by hand* against a stone placed on the saw table until there is a bright spot on every tooth.

As for making the vise, it's best to cut the wood parts from hardwood, and to use aluminum for all the metal parts—particularly finger

The blade is held in "filing" position by a small C-clamp which is loosened as each tooth
is ground. No attempt should be made to hold the blade by hand, since
the vibration would sting the fingers and could result in a chipped wheel. While the blade
guard is shown removed for the sake of clarity, it should always be in place for utmost safety

stops, to avoid damaging the teeth. The base
block is notched at an angle to support the blade
bed at a 10-deg. slant and additional support is
provided by a block placed directly in back of
it. The top edge of the blade bed is first rabbeted,
and then a dado is run across its face to receive
a 4½-in. strip of flat aluminum. Five holes are
drilled and tapped in the latter to receive the
adjustable saw arbor. The end-view drawing at
the right gives the correct spacing of the holes
in relation to the top of the vise. Clearance holes
are drilled in the wood directly behind the tapped
holes to a depth of about ½ in., and the strip
is held in its dado with two No. 8 x ¾-in. flathead
wood screws. The arbor itself is held by a ¼-
20 x 1-in. machine screw. Since a small C-clamp
is used to anchor the blade as each tooth is
ground, a flat strip of aluminum is screwed to

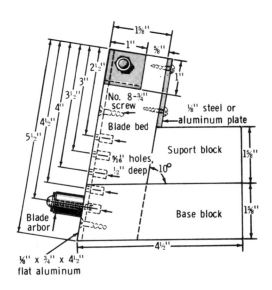

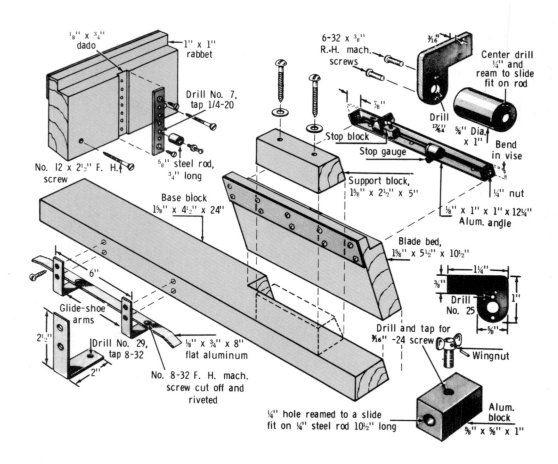

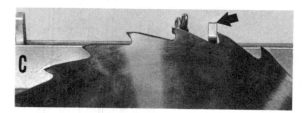

The four photos at the left show the relative position of the tooth to be ground and the stop finger setting for different diameters and types of blades. The arrow in each case indicates the stop finger. Blade (A) is a combination blade from a 7-in. Porter-Cable saw, while (B) is an 8-in. blade from a Stanley. Blade (C) is a 30-tooth, 10-in. one from the DeWalt on which it is being sharpened. Blade (D) is a 28-tooth, 10-in. coarse-cutting Craftsman brand. The vise works on all of them

the back of the blade bed to protect the wood from clamp marks.

The two stop fingers and the single stop block slide on a ¼-in. rod which is supported by a bracket formed from a length of aluminum angle. This is cut overlong so that its ends can be notched, drilled and bent 90 deg. to support the threaded ends of the rod. The angle is held in its rabbet with three No. 8 x ¾-in. flathead wood screws.

The spring slide shoe attached to the base block serves to hold the vise temporarily to the saw table while positioning it under the grinding wheel. Once set, a sturdy C-clamp is used to anchor the overhanging vise to the table.

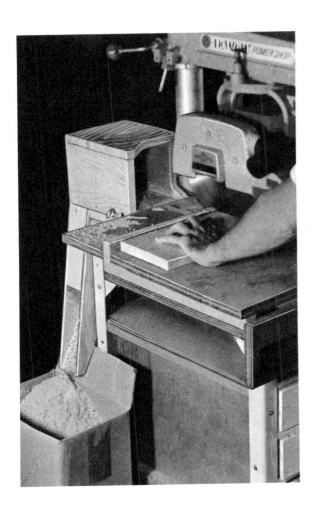

Trap the dust from your saw

BY ART YOUNGQUIST

■ EVEN WITH a shop-type vacuum cleaner attachment clamped to the discharge spout of a radial-arm saw, you can't catch the sawdust that piles at the rear of the saw. But it's easier than you might realize to have a clean shop. All that's needed is a chute with a box-shaped top. The force with which the blade throws the sawdust clear of the work is utilized to direct the dust into the top of the chute, from where it is funneled into a cardboard carton.

Making the chute may not require the purchase of any material since it can be built from scrap-size pieces of ¾-in. solid stock and ¼-in. plywood cut to the size shown below. The catcher is positioned behind the saw blade and is attached to the table frame of the saw by a crossbar and wingnut. The dimensions given will be found suitable for most radial-arm saws, though you may find that the table thickness of your saw requires a change in measurement so that the catcher will fit on the table properly.

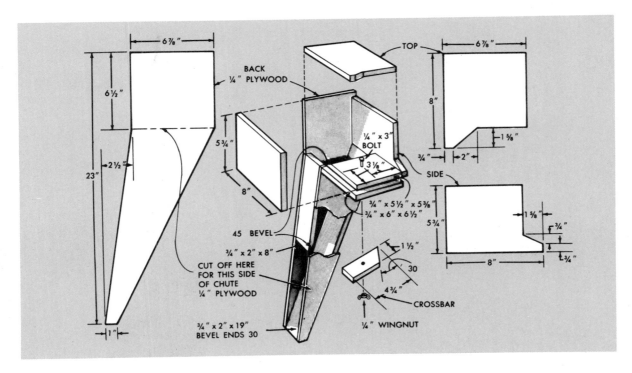

Electric brake for a radial saw

BY DR. JOHN D. GRIFFITH

Press a button
and eliminate the irritation
of waiting for the whirring blade
to coast slowly to a stop

■ WAITING IMPATIENTLY for the blade of your radial-arm saw to coast to a stop can be for the birds. Not only is this an irritating waste of time, but a coasting saw blade can be the source of a serious injury.

These are two reasons why you should take the time to add the electric brake described here to your saw.

Here's how it works: After the saw's motor is shut off, the brake button is pressed. This puts a silicon rectifier and a resistor in series with the motor's leads and the line, which in turn converts AC to DC. Direct current added to the fields of the motor causes the armature to slow down, and the more DC you induce, the quicker the motor will come to a stop.

The unit shown places about 12 amp of DC current to the fields, which is safe against overload on motors ranging from ½ to 1½ hp. The brake cannot be used on DC or small universal motors.

All components tuck neatly in a Minibox measuring only 2⅛ x 3 x 5¼ in. You should watch to see that no connections touch when the cover goes on, and plan to locate the glowing ceramic resistor so there is ample space around it. There's no need to worry about which end of the silicon

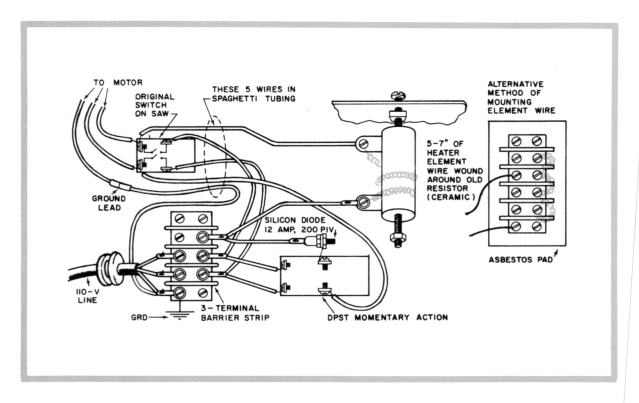

TO MOTOR

ORIGINAL SWITCH ON SAW

THESE 5 WIRES IN SPAGHETTI TUBING

ALTERNATIVE METHOD OF MOUNTING ELEMENT WIRE

5-7" OF HEATER ELEMENT WIRE WOUND AROUND OLD RESISTOR (CERAMIC)

GROUND LEAD

SILICON DIODE 12 AMP, 200 PIV

ASBESTOS PAD

110-V LINE

GRD →

3-TERMINAL BARRIER STRIP

DPST MOMENTARY ACTION

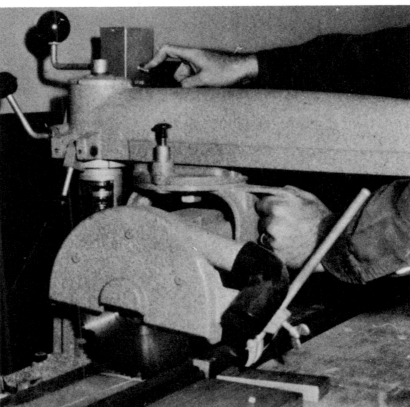

rectifier is cathode or anode for it works equally well even when installed in reverse position.

The resistor, which you make, is nothing more than a 7-in. length of ¼-in. heater-element wire (B & S 20-ga. 1.1 ohm), wound around a ½ x 3-in. high-value ceramic resistor. If you have trouble finding this, you can use a piece of ceramic from a lead-in insulator. Attach the ends of the element wire to the original terminals of the resistor, but do not solder them; either use lock washers or crimp-on lugs.

The silicon rectifier does not need a massive heat sink for occasional operation if you use one having the rating indicated. This hookup will work nicely with a heavy copper wire and spade lug as your heat sink. Since rectifiers have two current ratings (continuous and peak), watch out for "bargain" units in which the 12-amp rating actually turns out to be the peak (1 cycle) rating. Such units will literally explode when subjected to 12 amps for even a few seconds.

To install the brake, disconnect the line cord to the motor and rewire it as a line cord to the Minibox, following the diagram and making sure that you connect the ground wire to the box itself. Now fish the 5 wires from the box to the saw's motor through a 36-in. length of spaghetti tubing and attach the leads as shown in the diagram. The important thing is not to reverse leads 3 and 4 to the motor switch; if you do, you will blow a fuse as soon as you switch on the motor.

Test the completed brake with the blade securely tightened on the mandrel. Note the number of seconds it takes for the blade to coast to a stop. If *more* than 8 seconds, keep shortening the length of the resistance wire, but don't try for a quicker stop as sudden braking action could loosen the saw blade.

PARTS LIST

1—2⅛ x 3 x 5¼" Bud Minibox
1—Silicon diode, 12 amp. 200 P.i.v.
1—7" length of ¼" coil, B & S 20- ga. heater element wire (1.1 ohm/inch)
1—D.p.s.t. toggle switch; off, momentary on
1—Barrier strip, 3-terminal
Assorted hardware, grommets

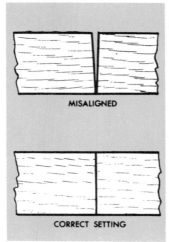

MISALIGNED

CORRECT SETTING

■ WITH THE TILT gauge set at its normal 90-deg. position, here's a simple check you can run in about one minute to determine the accuracy of the miter-gauge setting on a table saw or the angle setting on a radial saw in making a square cut. Set the miter gauge, on the radial saw, to 90 deg., place two short lengths of 1 x 4 stock, one on top of the other, and cut through both. Then stand them on edge, swing one piece, still on edge, through 180 deg. and butt the cut ends together. If there's a V-shaped opening as in the upper detail, then you will need to reset your miter gauge, or the angle setting on your radial saw, until you get a true butt joint as in the lower detail. Use a hollow ground blade for greater accuracy.

Two tips for your radial saw

■ WANT TO ADD an adjustable stop to your radial-arm saw for duplicate cutoff work? You can make a dandy one which screws to the top of the fence from four common awning fittings, a short piece of steel channel and a 10-ft. length of ½-in. thin-wall conduit. The four awning fittings are slit down the center with a hacksaw so they will clamp tight around the conduit when fitted with thumbscrews. Two of the fittings are brazed together, back to back; the other two are brazed to the steel channel as shown. The conduit is cut into 7 and 3 ft. sections: the long piece is held by the two fence clamps; the 3-ft. section becomes the stop rod.

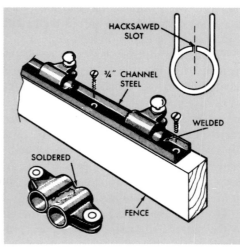

HACKSAWED SLOT

¾" CHANNEL STEEL

WELDED

SOLDERED

FENCE

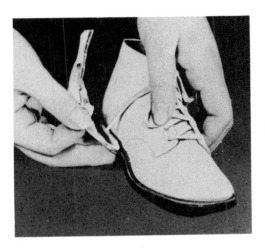

You'll find white shoes easier to polish if the sole edges are first covered with cellophane tape. This results in neat edges and the tape is easily removed from the sole when you're done.

Empty spice bottles having an inner snap-on plastic cover as pictured above make excellent salt and pepper shakers for picnics and cookouts. The screw-on metal caps prevent the contents from spilling.

SAND-AND-GLUE

A glass door knob that becomes loose is easy to make tight again. Simply remove the knob from the door, pour sand into the gap between the ferrule and glass. Then flow glue on top of the sand while supporting the knob.

Squeezing the contents from a tube of toothpaste or shaving cream is neatly done with a turnkey formed from a length of stiff wire. Bent to the shape of a hairpin, the turnkey is placed over the crimped end of the tube.

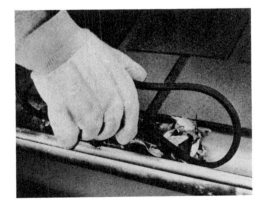

The discarded fan belt from your car makes an excellent gutter cleaner. Being flexible yet firm, the belt is easily formed to the shape of any gutter and enables muck and leaves to be scraped out quickly.

Have trouble keeping track of thumbtacks in your shop? Here's a good idea to keep them handy. Buy a large cork and mount it in a convenient place. Then whenever you find a thumbtack, stick it on this holder.

Mask out those naked radiators

BY RALPH TREVES

■ NOTHING DETRACTS from a well-furnished room like a naked radiator squatting under the window—or an ugly pipe climbing up a corner. The room above is cursed with both of these eyesores, but you'd never tell it because the problem corner has been masked with built-ins.

An attractive counter is built along the wall to windowsill level. It's designed to match adjacent cabinets. The countertop is notched around the steam-riser pipe, and the portion of this pipe that runs on up to the ceiling is hidden by an L-shaped screen made by simply nailing two boards together edge to face. In place, it suggests a structural column, but one that doubles nicely as a pole lamp.

The portion of the counter that covers the radiator has attractive louvers to coax cold air currents off the floor and up along the radiator vanes. The heated air passes into the room through slots cut in the top.

In the arrangement shown here, the corner end of the radiator cabinet is enclosed only partially to permit access to the shut-off valve. This gap is concealed by a shorter cabinet set at right angles to it, which slides away when heat adjust-

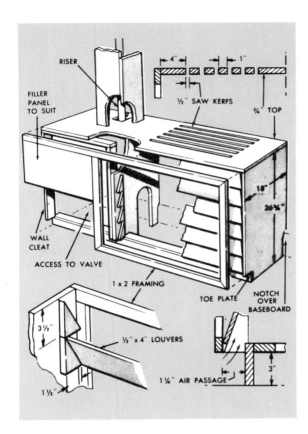

RISER

FILLER PANEL TO SUIT

½" SAW KERFS

¾" TOP

18"

26¾"

WALL CLEAT

ACCESS TO VALVE

1 x 2 FRAMING

TOE PLATE

NOTCH OVER BASEBOARD

3½"

½" x 4" LOUVERS

1¼" AIR PASSAGE

3"

1½"

An exposed steam riser is tucked behind an L-shaped housing that doubles as a lamp pole

Air slots in the top of the cover can be cut on a table saw with ganged blades or by running a saber saw between ½-in. holes, above

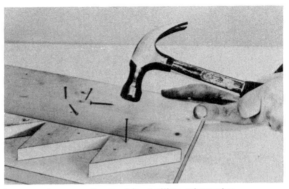

Louver steps are formed by nailing triangular blocks to the inner faces of two end panels. The louvers are tacked to the front edges

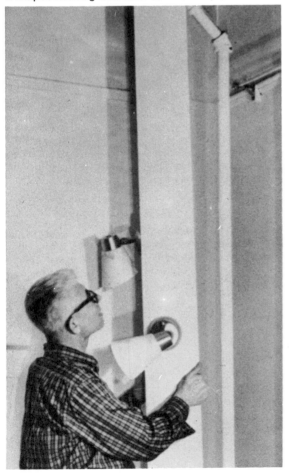

ment is necessary. You may wish to make a similar provision at the opposite end if access to an air-release valve is needed.

Construction requires no cabinetmaking skill. As shown above, assembly is by means of simple butt joints. The panels are ¾-in. plywood; the framing is all 1 x 2s, except for the louvers and toeplate. The latter is nailed at right angles to a 1 x 2 stiffener that is installed in two pieces—one nailed between the inner faces of the end panel and partition, the other between the partition and wall.

Assemble the front frame before fastening it to the panel edges. Note that the bottom frame member is supported only at the ends to provide an air passage behind the lowest louver. Therefore, it's best to assemble and apply the frame as a unit, after the louvers are in place.

You can simply wire the L-cover around the riser if you turn small screweyes into the rear faces of the boards.

See also: home improvement; remodeling; repairs, home.

How to improve radio reception

■ COMES A TIME when your a.c.-d.c. table radio may not sound as perky as it used to. The reception may be too weak and the static too strong. Buzzes, rattles or hisses may emanate from the speaker. Just turning the volume control may create scratchy sounds and the dial may not be pinpointing the station you want.

Remove the radio from its cabinet and replace the knobs on their proper shafts. Pull all tubes and test them at the local radio shop or drug-store. With good tubes, you are ready for the ten-step tuneup that will restore the set to almost new performance. Whenever you test with power on, use an insulated screwdriver. Old-timers may have their arms calibrated in volts, but play it safe by keeping one hand in your pocket!

See also: electronics; intercoms; oscillator, audio; preamplifier, stereo; radios, auto; radio, stereo FM; shortwave receivers; tester, radio; transistor radios; transmitter, FM; transmitter meter; tuners, FM.

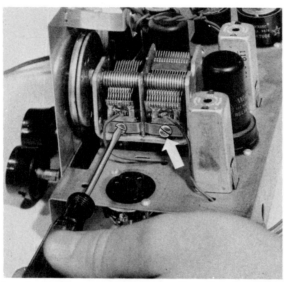

Locate trimmers on sides of capacitors. Set dial at station whose kilocycle frequency is known (check newspaper listings). Then adjust front trimmer (left above) until station is strongest at correct dial setting. (Tube was removed for photo purposes)

Repeat operation on rear trimmer, adjusting for best volume, then checking a few stations. For best compromise, on both front and rear trimmers, repeat for several stations. When you're working with the power on, be sure to use an insulated screwdriver

Tuning slugs are at top and bottom (under chassis) of two IF transformers. Turn carefully, one at a time, listening for maximum volume. Turn lightly; forcing will damage the transformer

If your radio's pilot lamp doesn't work, it means that the rectifier tube will burn out faster than it normally would. The lamp holder will snap out with a slight squeezing of the fingers

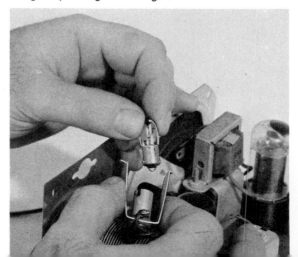

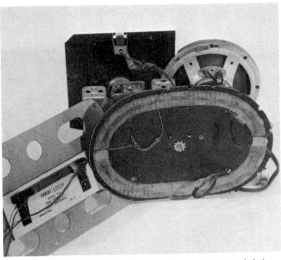

If your radio uses a wire loop antenna (above right), substitute a ferrite antenna (left). This will improve reception. You'll find that longer ferrite rods will give you the best performance

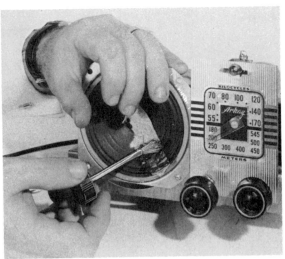

Minor tears produce scratchy sounds in the loudspeaker. Solve the problem by patching the cracks with several layers of tissue paper, using household cement or loudspeaker cone cement

For accurate tuning, the dial-cord tension should extend the spring slightly. A loose cord causes the pointer to jump. Cord slippage can be corrected with an application of dial-cord dressing

Use a pipe cleaner and a spray-can of contact cleaner to remove dust particles, which cause resistance. For more room to work in, unmesh the capacitor plates. Be careful not to deform the plates

To lubricate the capacitor for smoother tuning, use a light machine oil on the bearings, both at the front and rear. Also oil all moving control shafts. Be sure not to get any oil on the wires

If a special injector is available, use a liquid contact cleaner in order to provide a smoother noise-free action on the controls. Some solutions come equipped with an eyedropper syringe

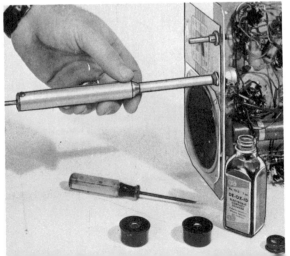

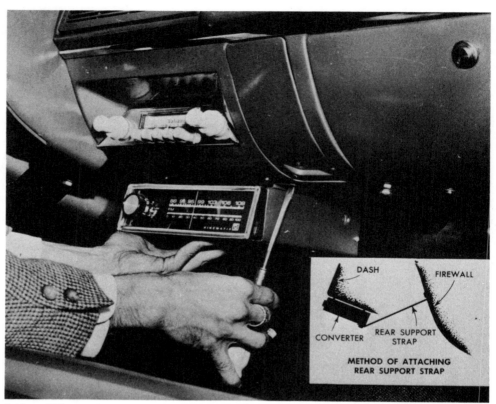

Add an FM converter to your car radio and enjoy better programming, fewer commercials and static-free reception. In this picture, the FM converter is being installed under the dash

Convert your car radio to AM-FM

BY LEONARD FISH

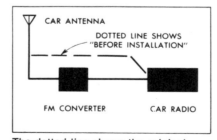

The dotted line shows the original AM radio installation. The solid line shows the FM converter added to the antenna circuit

■ MORE AND MORE American motorists are realizing the benefits of FM in the car. Better programming and fewer commercials, obvious advantages, are only a small part of the reason.

The automobile, with its sparkplugs, generators, relays and contactors is a notorious producer of static. Static is a sharp increase in amplitude, with no noticeable effect on frequency. Standard car radios are AM (Amplitude Modulation) receivers and as the AM receiver depends on changes in amplitude to operate, these crashes, fizzles and spittings come out of the loudspeaker. FM (Frequency Modulation) receivers are totally oblivious to these amplitude changes. As static cannot affect the frequency, FM is a "natural" for static-free reception in cars.

The chief objection to FM automobile radios in urban areas in the past was the fading in and out of the signal as the car was driven through areas of tall buildings. In recent years, however, many major urban FM stations have installed new types of antennas which radiate the signal better and eliminate the annoying fade-out. Now you can enjoy FM auto reception even in congested cities.

To install an FM converter in your car, use the mounting bracket supplied with the converter as a drilling template. Hold the bracket under the dash and carefully mark the required mounting holes. Feel behind the dash to be sure no wiring will interfere, then drill holes.

Find a screw head, nut or bolt which is located high in the center of the firewall. If the screw or nut can be removed without releasing some other part of the car, use this to attach the rear support strap as shown in the diagram. If not, drill a hole in the firewall and insert a screw. Again, make sure you don't interfere with any existing components on the other side of the firewall.

After attaching the rear support strap, mount the bracket to the FM converter using the sheet-metal screws provided. Holding the converter with one hand, attach the protruding tabs of the bracket to the dash, using the sheet-metal screws provided with the converter. Locate the small mounting hole under the rear side of the converter. Line this up with one of the holes in the rear support strap. Using another sheet-metal screw, pull the support strap tight and attach its free end to the back of the converter.

Making the Hookup. Trace the coaxial wire from the car's antenna to where it plugs into the car radio. Disconnect this wire from the car radio by gently tugging. Connect the coaxial plug at the end of this wire into the coaxial jack at the side of the converter. You will notice two wires coming from the rear of the converter. One of these (B) is fitted with the same type of plug as was just inserted into the converter. Insert this plug into the car radio antenna jack. The other wire from the converter (A) terminates in a ring lug and may be interrupted by a fuse.

To make sure your converter will shut off when the ignition switch is off, locate a source of battery voltage which will not be "ON" unless your ignition is on. Possible places are the cold side of the ignition switch itself, the heater or turn signals. Attach the small ring lug at the end of the wire to the voltage source. This completes the internal installation of the unit. Now adjust the antenna to a length of 30 in.

Should you desire to operate the radio as an ordinary AM unit, switch the converter to OFF. This automatically connects the antenna directly to the car radio. To hear FM stations, turn both units on and tune the AM radio to about 900 kc. Then tune the FM stations with the converter.

See also: electronics; oscillator, audio; radio repair; AM; tester, radio; tuners, FM.

For FM reception, set antenna length at 30 in. Add scribe marks for resetting if antenna is moved

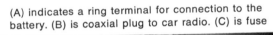

(A) indicates a ring terminal for connection to the battery. (B) is coaxial plug to car radio. (C) is fuse

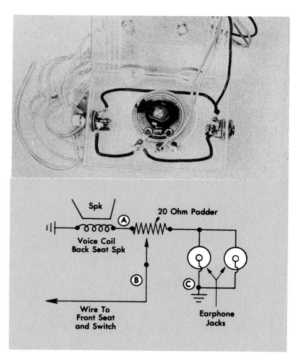

Above left, an adapter for use in the back seat. The knob controls volume, and jacks at sides receive earphones. Internal wiring is shown, top, right

Radio earphones for back seaters

BY HOMER L. DAVIDSON

IF YOU HAVE YOUNGSTERS who insist on raucous music and clatter from the car radio throughout a long trip, here's how to keep the rest of the family happy. Build a small adapter unit that enables a couple of earphones to be operated at the back seat. Only the plugged ears need to hear the racket. There's a volume control for adjusting earphone level and to restore the speaker to normal operation at will.

The circuit is built into a plastic box large enough to accommodate the jacks and control. With care, the mounting holes for these items can be made with the tip of a hot soldering iron gently applied to the plastic. Follow the illustrations for the internal hookup and you should end up with three leads emerging from the adapter, each about 1 ft. long. If the car has a rear-seat speaker, these wires are run through the rear

shelf into the trunk compartment. If you don't want to drill extra holes, remove a speaker-mounting screw and use the exposed hole.

Next step is to open the trunk lid and locate the rear-seat speaker terminals. Disconnect the single wire you find there (the other is a short ground connection) and splice it to the wire marked "B" in the schematic. Now connect wire "A" from the adapter to the free speaker terminal. The remaining wire, "C," is fastened under a speaker-mounting bolt to achieve a good electrical ground.

If your car has no rear speaker, installation is a bit more lengthy. All connections are the same as shown, but you'll have to run long extensions of wires "A" and "B" underneath the car floor from the front speaker to the adapter location at the rear seat.

PARTS LIST
1 Plastic Box 2⅞ x 2 x 1 in. or Equiv. MS-158
1 20-OHM Wirewound Dual Spk. Fader Control MS-187
2 Earphone Jacks, Miniature, Come with Earphones
2 Earphones, Argonne AR-47, 6 OHMS
Misc. Wire, Metal Screws, Knobs. Etc.
All Parts Obtained From Lafayette Radio

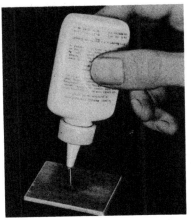

To avoid replacing the cap each time on a squeeze bottle when using small amounts of glue repeatedly, drive a nail through a block of wood and use it as a stopper for the spout.

A man's belt lends a helping hand, above, when placing a dry-cleaning bag over a garment. The buckle end of the belt is dropped through the hole and the hanger hooked onto it.

RUBBER BAND

Ever spend several frustrating minutes searching for the end of the thread on a spool? There is usually a slot in the rim of the spool, but this has a tendency to chip out. You'll solve this problem by wrapping the spool with a rubber band. Catch the end of the thread under the band. This also prevents the thread from unwinding accidentally when you pick it up.

This nontip caddy for a can of paint, above, is a detergent carton with a cutout made in the center of one side to receive the can. The carton also serves as a brush rest.

To prevent soil from being washed away when watering a newly planted shrub, slit aluminum-foil pie tin radially and center it on the shrub trunk as shown above.

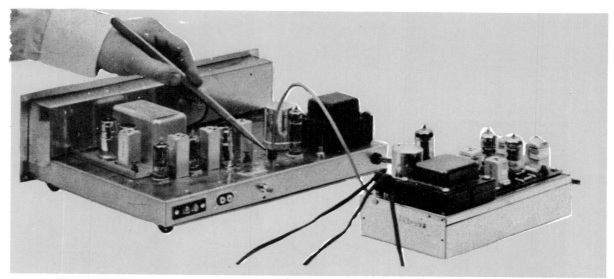

There's only one connection to make to the FM tuner. Take the shielded lead with the phono plug on the end and push it into the multiplex jack

Adapt your stereo for FM

BY LEONARD FELDMAN

If you have a stereo
    amplifier and an FM
tuner, you can receive stereo
    broadcasts with this adapter

■ MANY FM RADIO STATIONS have upgraded their programs by broadcasting in stereophonic sound. Take advantage of these FM stereo broadcasts by connecting this compact adapter to your present FM tuner and stereo amplifier. It will add a new dimension to your radio listening enjoyment.

The 2-tube circuit includes a neon indicator that lights when you're tuned to a stereo broad-

cast. Then there's a silencing circuit that cuts off the tuner unless you are tuned to stereo. Best of all you get the full 20–15,000-cycle response that the station is transmitting.

There is one decision you have to make before you start. Do you need a power supply? If you can tap off 6.3 volts *a.c.* at 0.6 *amp* and 180 to 200 volts *d.c.* at 7 *ma* from your existing equipment, you won't have to bother building one. If these voltages are not available, add on the power supply circuit shown in the schematic.

The schematic diagram shows the wiring in detail and the parts list can be filled by most electronics supply houses.

Your most difficult job will be aligning the adapter after it is completed. You'll need two things for this: a stereo program being broadcast and an audio *a.c.* vacuum-tube-voltmeter (*vtvm*).

Start off by connecting the adapter's input plug to the FM tuner's multiplex output jack. Then turn on the tuner and adapter and tune to a station you know is broadcasting stereo. Watch the tuning indicator on the FM tuner and adjust for the strongest signal.

Now connect the audio *a.c. vtvm* to either end of transformer T1's primary and slowly adjust the slug in the transformer for a maximum reading on the meter. Then, leaving the meter connected to the same spot, adjust L3 and L2 for a maximum voltage reading. Work back over T1, L3 and L2 at least three times. Disregard the neon lamp which will light before maximum reading is reached.

Next, connect the left and right outputs of the

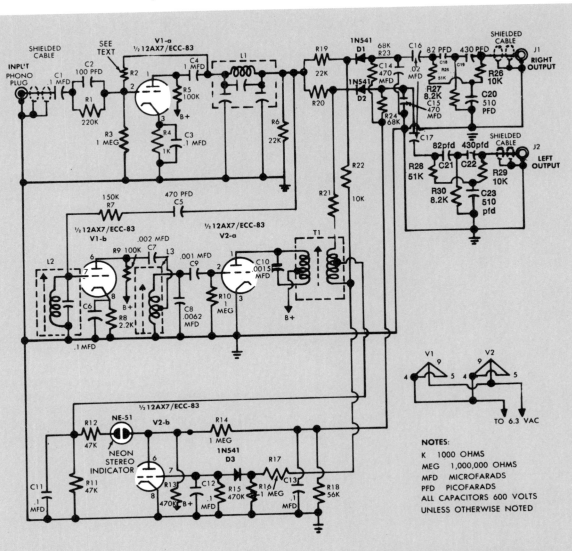

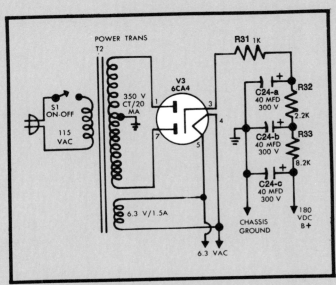

Complete circuit of the 2-tube multiplex adapter. There are four stages as each tube is a dual triode. Note the automatic neon stereo indicator lamp

You need this power supply only if you can't tap off the needed voltages from your tuner or amplifier. It can be built right onto the adapter chassis

NOTES:
K   1000 OHMS
MEG   1,000,000 OHMS
MFD   MICROFARADS
PFD   PICOFARADS
ALL CAPACITORS 600 VOLTS
UNLESS OTHERWISE NOTED

This closeup of the adapter shows how the power transformer, rectifier and filter capacitor can be mounted at one end of the chassis when a little power supply is necessary

stereo adapter, continued

Parts List

R1—220,000 ohms
R2—3 megohm pot (see text)
R3, R10, R14, R16, R17—1 megohm
R4, R31—1000 ohms
R5, R9—100,000 ohms
R6, R19, R20—22,000 ohms
R7—150,000 ohms
RR8, R32—2200 ohms
R11, 12—47,000 ohms
R13, R15—470,000 ohms
R18—56,000 ohms
R21, R22, R26, R29—10,000 ohms
R23, R24—68,000 ohms
R25, R28—51,000 ohms
R27, R30, R33—8200 ohms
All resistors, ½-watt carbon, 10% tolerance
C1, C3, C6, C11, C13—0.1 MFD
C2—100 PFD
C4—1 MFD, 100 volts, molded paper
C5, C14, C15—470 PFD
C7—.002 MFD
C8—.0062 MFD
C9—.001 MFD
C10—.0015 MFD
C16, C17—.02 MFD
C18, C21—82 PFD
C19, C22—430 PFD
C20, C23—510 PFD
C24—Three section electrolytic. 40—40—40 MFD, 300 volts
All capacitors ceramic rated at 200 volts or better unless noted
V1, V2—12AX7/ECC83
V3—6CA4
T1—Miller transformer #135
T2—Power transformer: 115-volt primary; 350-volt 20-ma ct. and 6.3-volt 0.6 amp. secondaries
L1—Miller coil #1358
L2—Miller coil #1351
L3—Miller coil #1356
J1, J2—phonojacks
D1, D2, D3—1N541 diodes
S1—spst toggle switch
Neon lamp assembly including NE-51 lamp
Phono plug, 5-foot length of shielded cable, two 9-pin miniature tube sockets, 5 x 6 x 2 inch chassis

adapter to an unused pair of inputs on your stereo amplifier and listen for separation (how isolated one channel is from the other). Use a 3-megohm potentiometer for R2 and adjust it for maximum separation. From this point on no further adjustments will be needed.

The automatic nature of the adapter can now be tested. Tune across the FM band and note the complete absence of sound until you hit a station broadcasting in stereo. If you tune rapidly, the neon indicator may blink once or twice as you hit transient noise peaks between stations. This is normal and should be disregarded.

Another built-in feature of this adapter is that it will reject any stereo signals that are too weak to give good reproduction. So if a signal is picked up and heard, it will be reasonably strong and sound good. Nevertheless, if you prefer to listen to weaker stations, even though they may be noisy, you can lower the rejection point by decreasing the value of R17, the 1-megohm resistor connected between T1's secondary and D3.

See also: electronics: oscillator, audio; preamplifier, stereo; radio repair, AM; radios, auto; tester, radio; transmitter, FM; tuners, FM.

Don't waste sandpaper by tearing the sheet and using the pieces separately. Here's a way to fold the sheet to four thicknesses and form a pad with four fresh sanding surfaces. Lay the sheet with the abrasive side up and crease it at the center. Then cut to the center along the fold. Turn the sheet over and fold the A section over the B section. Then fold A and B over section C and finally fold section D over the first three. After the exposed sides are worn, refold again, beginning with the D section. You'll find that this idea really saves sandpaper. Try it next time you have a big sanding job.

Use this sliding ring and stake to support spreading plants. Stakes are cut from 1 x 2 stock to a length of 4 to 6 ft. and one end of each is pointed so that it will drive easily. The sliding ring is formed from heavy wire and normally should be about 15 in. in diameter. Opposite the splice a self-locking loop is formed in the wire as detailed.

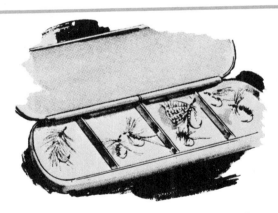

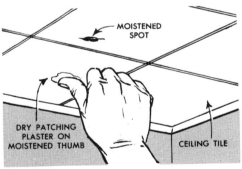

Trout and bass flies won't get their hooks into you if they're kept in a left-over spectacle case. Or, maybe you'd just like to keep those choice flies separate for use as a last resort when the fish refuse the bugs you've been feeding them. The case should be of the metal type with a leather-ette covering. The spring cover should close with a snap, just as it did when new. You can divide the case into compartments by making separators of stiff cardboard, cutting them so that they fit the curvature snugly and cementing them in place.

Ever wonder what to do about holes and gouges in your ceiling tile? It seems like such a bother to replace the whole tile. It's really not necessary. You can patch a dig in ceiling tile by using dry plaster or talcum powder. Just dampen the damaged area with a sponge or wet cloth and then thumb the dry powder into the depression. Brush away the excess with a flick or two of a whisk broom. Repeat if necessary to bring the patch to the level of the surrounding area. A patch made in this way will dry without any sheen, matching the surface finish of the tile perfectly. Work carefully and your guests will never know that the tile has been patched.

Pikes Peak railroad in HO-gauge

This interesting little HO train climbs and descends Pike's Peak continuously, while you run the rest of the layout on schedule

The engine and car ride level up and down the mountain due to wedge-shaped construction of the frames. The car and engine were always painted in bright, attractive colors

■ THERE IS NOTHING QUITE LIKE an unusual piece of equipment to add interest to your HO-gauge layout—particularly if it is an authentic copy of an historical engine. This engine and car, patterned after the famous Pikes Peak cog railroad, was built by avid model railroader, Frank Beatty, to liven things in the mountains that surrounded his layout.

While designed to operate without a cog, the model climbs easily and descends a 15-deg. grade. Reversing at each end is accomplished when the engine contacts bumper switches at the top and bottom of the incline. These switches automatically reverse the rotation of the motor in the engine, sending it up or down the incline.

Two rheostats control the speed of the train. One operates as it climbs the incline, and the other works as it backs down.

After you've built these two gems, you can use a little extra imagination and make the proper scenery for them. A little "waiting room"

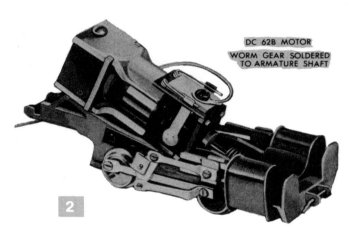

DC 62B MOTOR

WORM GEAR SOLDERED TO ARMATURE SHAFT

2

Here is the engine chassis complete, ready for installation of the cab, boiler and accessories

Pikes Peak railroad, continued

station can be located at the bottom of the incline. At the top you might build a resort hotel, an observation platform complete with tiny telescopes, and a second station. For humorous detail, consider incorporating a twisting, tortuous highway paralleling the railroad up the incline. On it you can place tiny automobiles, some with engines boiling over (a tiny fluff of cotton or angel's hair will look like steam coming from the radiator), others with flat tires (and a line of waiting cars behind them).

To make the frame of the locomotive, cut out the parts with a fine-toothed hacksaw, following the full-scale patterns shown in Fig. 3. The main section of the frame is made of ½ x ½-in. channel brass, and should be shaped by slow and careful work with a file. To complete the motor mount, cut the two cover pieces out of ¹⁄₁₆-in. brass plate. The bearing plate is next. Cut this plate from ¹⁄₁₆-in. brass and solder two small

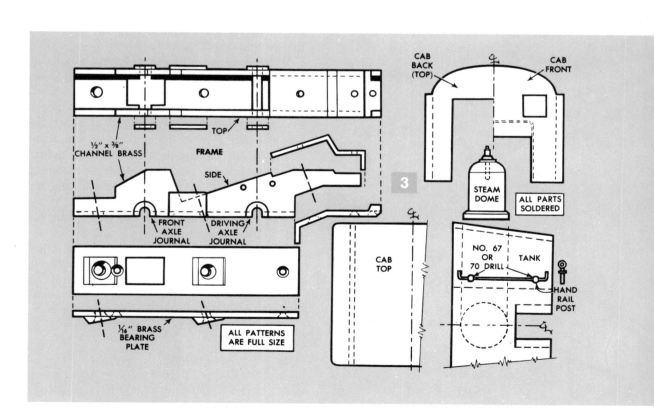

wedge-shaped pieces to the underside of the plate, Fig. 3. These blocks support and align the base-plate screws, which in turn hold the motor in place. The wheel axles float in journals which are formed by drilling the channel frame at the points indicated and sweat-soldering brass washers over the holes. Washers are later filed off flush.

The motor, a d.c. 62B Pittman, is held in place on the main frame by screws extending through the frame and into the motor mount. The worm gear on the armature shaft meshes with the gear on the axle. The worm gear must be purchased separately. It should fit snugly on the armature shaft; but, if the fit is too snug, it will be necessary to reduce the diameter of the shaft with fine emery cloth. The gear can be pressed on the shaft by using a drill press to exert a steady, even pressure. After meshing the worm and wheel accurately, cut off the shaft

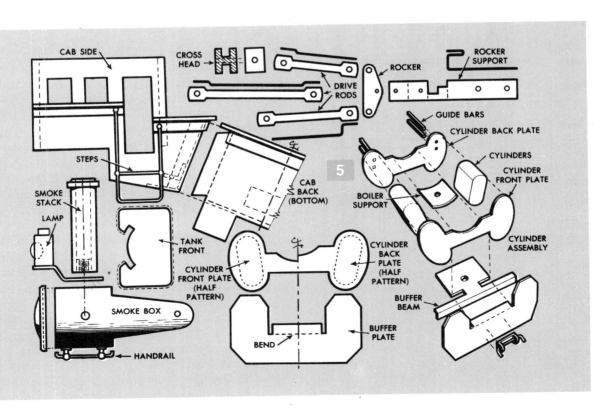

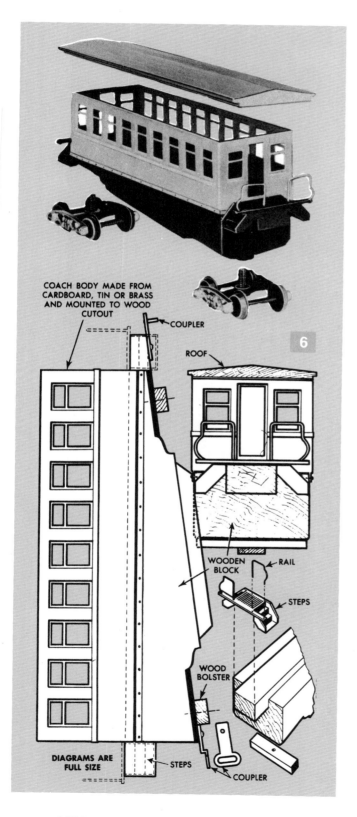

COACH BODY MADE FROM CARDBOARD, TIN OR BRASS AND MOUNTED TO WOOD CUTOUT

COUPLER

ROOF

6

WOODEN BLOCK

RAIL

STEPS

WOOD BOLSTER

DIAGRAMS ARE FULL SIZE

STEPS

COUPLER

projection. Two sets of 36-in. scale wheels, the front set geared and the rear set plain, may be purchased from a hobby shop. The wheel axles drop into the journals and are held in place by the base plate. On one side the wheels are insulated from the rails to prevent shorting out the circuit. Wheels on the other rail conduct current to complete the circuit. The cylinder assembly should be made from .012 or .010-ga. sheet brass. Use a pair of sheet-metal snips to cut out the parts and follow the full-scale patterns given in Fig. 5. Shape the pieces over wooden forms and solder them together.

The drive-rod assembly is put together with small rivets, which are available at most hobby shops. Using the full-scale patterns, cut out the pieces. Use No. 0-80 machine screws and No. 0-80 side-rod screws in the drive-rod assembly. Their positions are shown in Fig. 4. The riveted parts should fit together snugly, but the rivets must not be drawn so tight that they prevent free movement. A good stunt is to place a piece of paper between the two parts when riveting and later pulling it out. This will keep the rods from binding but still make a snug fit. As you assemble the parts, keep checking them to make certain everything fits together properly and operates smoothly. The frame, cylinder and drive-rod assemblies and the motor are shown in position in Fig. 2.

the cab comes next

The cab of the locomotive is next. Using the full-scale patterns presented in Figs. 3 and 5, cut out the parts. The dome of the steam whistle is machined from a solid piece of ⁵⁄₁₆-in. brass rod, and can be shaped either in a lathe or drill press. If you use a drill press, chuck the rod and use files to shape it. The smoke stack is a short length of ⅛-in. brass tubing, and the bottom end is filled with solder, drilled and tapped for a No. 4-36 machine screw. Solder also is added to the top of the stack and filed to the shape shown in Fig. 4.

Use a piece of ⅝-in. brass tubing to form the body of the boiler. Then cut out the front boiler plate from sheet brass and peen it to a convex shape, Fig. 4. The handrail posts can be picked up at a hobby shop, and at the same time get enough steel wire for the boiler hand rails. Once you know the wire size, drill the posts, push the wire through the holes and shape the rails, following Fig. 3.

All the other cab parts are cut from sheet brass and shaped over wooden forms. Rough

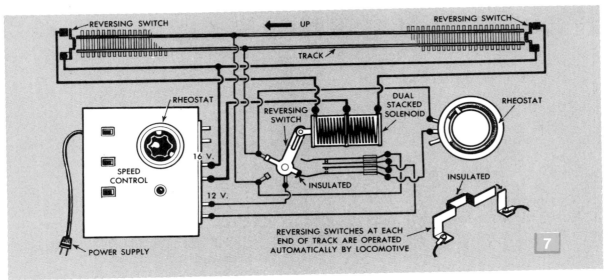

The electrical circuit includes two rheostats to control speed when the train reverses direction

cut the windows and doors first by drilling holes within the scribed openings and then filing to size. It is best to form such openings and other duplicate parts two at a time by sweat-soldering the parts back to back. This method assures identical units and the parts are easily separated when completed by heating. When assembling the parts, you'll do well to first spot-solder the pieces so you can check the fit before final soldering. As you solder, it is a good idea to use a heat sink (wet cloth) on sections already soldered.

The passenger-car details are shown in Fig. 6, and the patterns are all full size. Starting with the base, cut it out of a wooden block. Top of base and step supports are easier to form from a separate piece of wood. Insert this piece into a groove cut in the base, then shape the entire

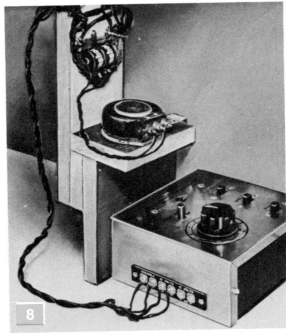

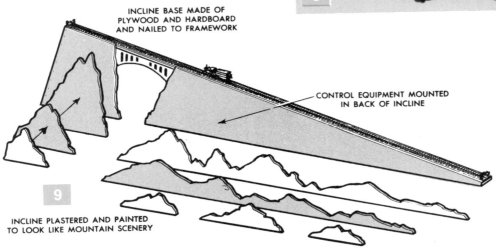

INCLINE BASE MADE OF PLYWOOD AND HARDBOARD AND NAILED TO FRAMEWORK

CONTROL EQUIPMENT MOUNTED IN BACK OF INCLINE

INCLINE PLASTERED AND PAINTED TO LOOK LIKE MOUNTAIN SCENERY

base as one piece. The roof either can be purchased from a hobby shop or cut out of wood. The coach body may be made of metal, cardboard, or wood. Even the sides of an old model coach may be used. You'll probably want to purchase the steps, two sets being needed. Fasten them to the platform ends of the wooden base. Cut off short lengths of steel wire for the step railings and form them as in Fig. 6.

attaching the trucks

Next, attach two sets of double trucks to the base. These also must be purchased from a hobby shop. The couplers are cut from sheet metal and a small rod soldered to one of them. Screw the couplers to the wooden base and nail two wooden bolsters in the positions shown, Fig. 6. Finish the locomotive and coach in any color you like. You may want to paint the cab and body of the locomotive red, the headlight yellow and leave the whistle a polished brass. Underparts are best painted a dull black—the same goes for the smoke stack. Model coaches usually are painted bright colors—a color that contrasts with the engine is best. Fig. 1 shows the finished job.

The length of the incline may be as long or short as you want to make it. Just mount the HO-gauge track on a 1 x 4 wooden base and nail vertical supports to the incline at 2-ft. intervals. To create the mountains effect, nail additional vertical supports to the framing and slant them outward. You can use scraps of wood, hardboard or other paneling material to cover the framework, Fig. 9. Scrap material is glued and nailed to the base, creating whatever scenic background is desired. For texture and form, a spackling compound is applied to the surface and then the entire background is painted. Figures, trees and other background accessories are added to make the scene realistic. It's up to you how simple or elaborate you care to make it.

Besides the standard power supply, which includes terminals for both 16-v. and 12-v. direct current and a rheostat, you need a second rheostat and a reversing switch, Fig. 7. A dual-stacked solenoid is included with the reversing switch. Also, at each end of the track, a bumper contact switch is closed automatically by the train. These are momentary switches that are activated every time the train bumps the insulated side of the contacts, Fig. 7. All of this equipment, with the exception of the bumper

Material List

LOCOMOTIVE

1 d.c. 62B Pittman motor
1 Worm gear
1 pr. 36" scale Kemtron, L 636, geared wheels
1 pr. 36" scale Kemtron, L 635, plain wheels
8 pc. Hand rail posts
   Wire for rails
1 pc. Channel brass, ½"x½"x4"
1 pc. 6"x12" .012 or .010-ga. sheet brass
2 pc. 6"x12" .008-ga. sheet brass
1 4-36 1½" machine screw
2 0-80 side rod screws, short
2 0-80 side rod screws, long
5 2-56 F.H. machine screws
1 2-56 R.H. machine screw
1 pc. ⅝"x1½" brass tubing
1 pc. ⅛"x1" brass tubing
1 pc. 5/16"x½" brass rod

PASSENGER CAR

2 pr. Steps
1 pc. Wood roof, 4"
1 pc. Wood base, 6"
1 Metal coupler
2 Sets Boxcar truck wheels
   Sides of car—make from metal, wood or cardboard
   Wood for car base and bolster

TRACK INCLINE, MISCELLANEOUS

1 B50 Rheostat, 50 watts
1 Tenshodo reversing switch
1 Power supply, model 3 Throttle Pack
3 pc. HO-gauge track, 3 ft.
4 pc. Track joiners
1 pc. 3/16"x4" brass rod
5 lb. Spackle
   Bell wire for circuit
   Lumber for incline framework
   Scraps of hardboard, wallboard, etc. for the mountain scenery
   Nails, screws, solder and paint

switches, may be purchased from a hobby shop or an electrical supply source. The complete setup, Fig. 8, may be mounted under the incline base, Fig. 9. Bell wire should be used to hook up the switching circuit. Follow the wiring diagram given in Fig. 7, soldering all connections to assure good contact.

Friends of the builder of this little engine, seeing it in operation on his layout, protested that they thought the original Pikes Peak locomotive *pushed* its car up the incline, while his *pulled* it. Of course, the prototype locos push the car. You can make yours do either, push or pull. If you join the *pushing* school, all you have to do is change the coupler arrangement.

Use a slightly longer coupler bar, of the type shown in the lower part of the drawing on page 2074. Attach it to the wooden base of the car. Mount a coupler pin on the front of the locomotive's cow catcher.

See also: pool tables; road-racing, model.

Build your own power rasp

BY W. CLYDE LAMMEY

Own a hedge trimmer or a saber saw? Make it do double duty by harnessing it to a rasp or file, using one of these five basic adapter designs

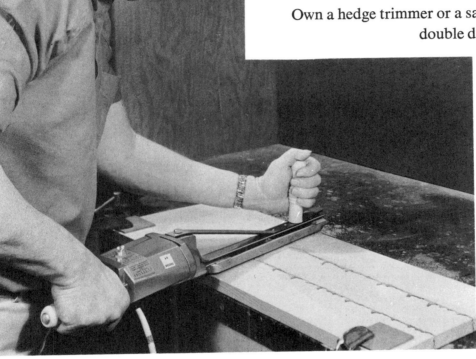

Here's a great new use for a hedge trimmer's powerhouse: a powered rasp that will speed up your cutting work. Converting the tool back for hedge trimming is easy, too.
The electric rasp or file will take the tedium out of such jobs as smoothing down glue joints, knocking sharp edges off panels or shelves, and shaping or scalloping stock

■ WITHOUT ANY ALTERATION of the tools themselves, most electric hedge trimmers and saber saws will take a simple, efficient bracket that converts them for power filing of metals or rasping of wood. The five attachments you see detailed here are adaptations from originals developed for possible industrial use by Marnie Averitt while a student at the Illinois Institute of Technology.

These adaptations have been simplified so that you can build any of them to fit your own saber saw or hedge trimmer from readily obtainable materials such as flat steel, standard screws

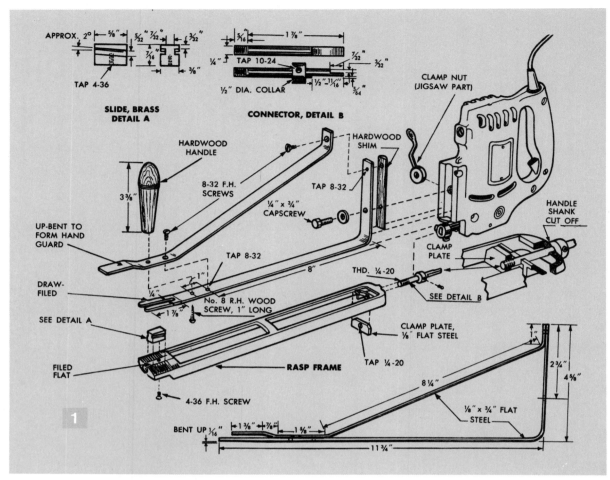

A bracket couples the rasp frame to saber saw. This is a Black & Decker Model U-40

and a few small conversion parts easily made from scraps of brass.

The rasps and files used are the newer type consisting of a handled frame to which special blades and files are attached. The unit is sold under the name Surform. Two types of blades are available, one for working wood, the other for nonferrous metals such as aluminum, brass and copper. The blades are available in flat and convex shapes.

The files are strips of steel with one surface impregnated with carbide grains in various grit sizes. Both the rasps and files cut exceptionally fast and smoothly when powered by a jigsaw or hedge trimmer. The latter is better adapted to filing operations due to the somewhat slower speed, but both work equally well when driving the wood and metal-cutting blades.

A good look at the detail drawings will give you the general idea of how the adaptations are made. But after a closer look at the details and photos you will also note that each one differs

in application. Minor changes in dimensions and manner of attachment must be made in each of the five adaptations detailed due to variations in the jigsaws and hedge trimmers.

Compare, for example, the adaptations in Figs. 1 and 2, in which the brackets are fitted to two well-known makes of saber saws. Do the same with those detailed in Figs. 4 and 5, and you'll see the variations necessary when fitting the adaptations to two makes of hedge trimmers. In Fig. 3 you see the attachment fitted to an older type of saber saw.

Saber saws of the type detailed in Figs. 1 and 2 have retracting blades, that is, the blade retracts on the down, or idle, stroke. Because of this construction it was found necessary to bend the arms of the yoke at the end of the carrier up about $\frac{1}{16}$ in. and also file the grooves in the slide at an angle of about 2 deg. This permits the outer end of the rasp frame to ride upward on the out stroke and tends to pull the rasp into the work on the in, or power, stroke. This contributes to faster cutting action and also results in smoother operation.

One important point in connection with fitting the brass slide, detail A, Fig. 1 (a variation of it is detailed in Fig. 3), is to file it to a free, sliding fit in the slot in the carrier. If the fit is even slightly snug, it may bind or seize in operation and cause breakage. Also, the slide must be well lubricated with a heavy oil to reduce wear.

Brass has been specified for the slide—and for wear parts in the hedge trimmer adaptations—simply because it is a more compatible metal for use where wear parts are in sliding contact. Mild (low-carbon) steel can be substituted.

soleplate must be removed

In fitting the carrier arm to the jigsaws in Figs. 1 and 3, note that in both instances the foot, or soleplate, must be removed. On the newer-type unit, Fig. 1, the soleplate tilts from 0 to 45 deg. on a trunnion. On the older type, Fig. 3, the plate is pivoted. On the third type, Fig. 2, the plate is also pivoted but need not be removed, as the openings in the plate permit attaching the carrier arm with a single screw turned into a tapped clamp plate.

In Fig. 1 the carrier arm is fitted into the trunnion by means of a hardwood shim and held by a single capscrew turned into the original clamp nut supplied with the saw. A hardwood handle is fitted to the carrier on all three units. No need to turn a handle. If you don't have a lathe, buy a large file handle, cut off the ferrule and drive a screw up into the wood.

The type of connector used on each saber saw must be made to fit the original blade chuck, or, as in Fig. 3, the chuck must be removed and a counterbored coupling substituted. In all instances the connector is fitted into the end of the rasp frame by first cutting off the handle shank close to the end of the frame, drilling a hole and slotting the lug so that the threaded end of the connector can be turned into a tapped hole in a clamp plate (as in the cutaway view, Fig. 1, and the cross section, Fig. 2).

The slide is filed to fit snugly in a groove filed across the corrugated finger pad at the outer end of the rasp frame and is held in place with a 4-36 F.H. screw passing through a countersunk hole centered on the bottom of the groove as in Figs. 1 and 2.

The same general assembly is used when fitting the adaptations to the hedge trimmers, Figs. 4 and 5. The exceptions are detailed in Figs. 4 and 5 and the photos picturing the as-

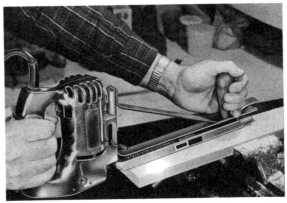

A flat-blade rasp can be used as a plane. Harnessed to a saber saw, it cuts fast. Due to the housing's overhang, the cut is made from both ends of the stock

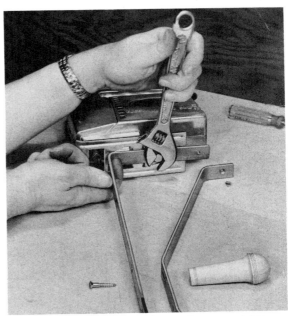

The two brackets that form the carrier arm quickly attach to the saber saw model detailed in the drawings on page 2078

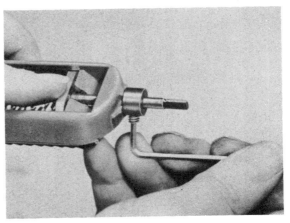

A connector is needed to fit the chuck of the saber saw. It goes in frame where handle shank is cut off

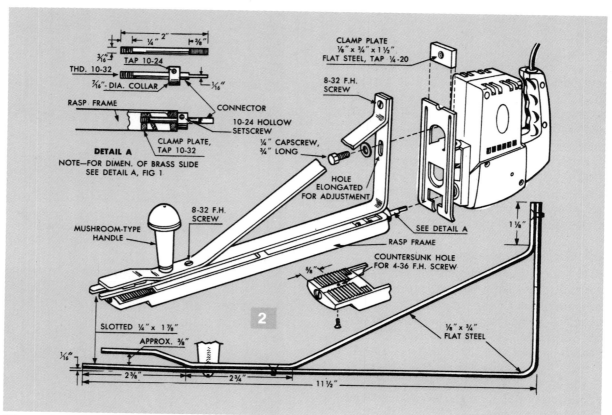

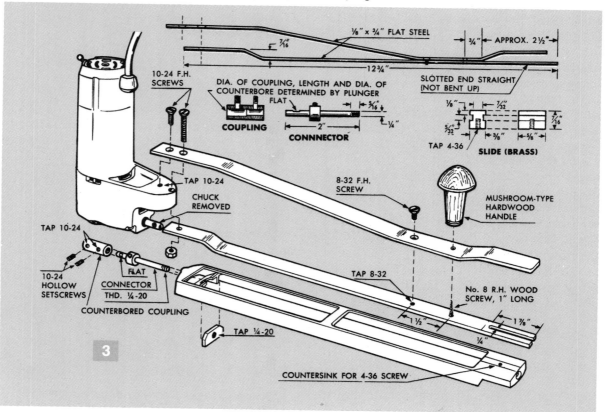

Other makes of saber saws require adaptations in the carrier arm design. The assembly above, for use with Sunbeam's model H-29 saw, is similar to the one on page 2078. The connector fits directly into the blade chuck. For older saws, below, replace the chuck with a specially made coupling

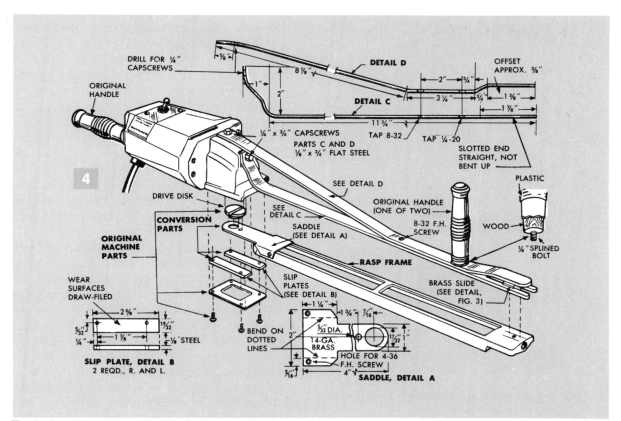

The hedge trimmer assembly sketched above is designed for Dormeyer's model HT6GR, which has a round drive disk. The different housing of PET's Starflite model 1370, below, requires a spacer block between the bracket and the yoke. Study your trimmer carefully before starting conversion

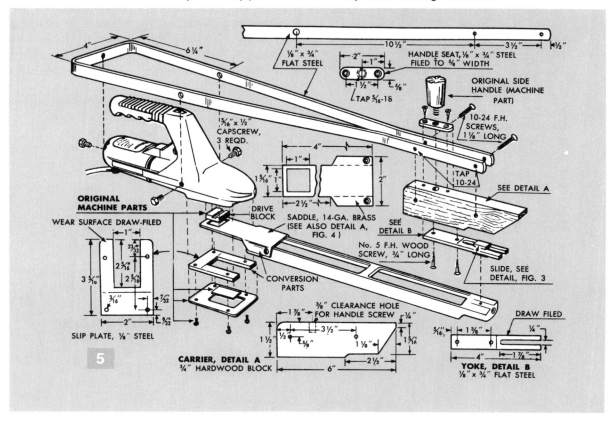

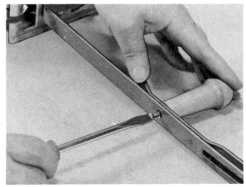

A turned handle is attached near the end of the carrier arm with a single wood screw. Note the yoke at the tip of the arm

A brass slide that rides in a yoke at the outer end of the carrier arm is fastened to the rasp frame with a small screw

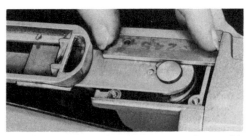

After fitting the saddle, the next step is to add slip plates at each side before replacing the saw's bottom plate

sembly of the drive hookup to the rasp frame. The conversion parts, Figs. 4 and 5, substitute for the original sickle and sickle bar of the trimmer and must be made and fitted with care. Note that in one, Fig. 4, two slip plates, or wear plates, are required as substitutes for the sickle bar while in the other adaptation a single U-shaped plate is used.

On the first trimmer the drive block is round, while on the other it is square. Care must be taken when making the saddle to see that the openings for the drive blocks duplicate those in the original sickle. There must be no binding at any point in the assembly of these parts. Lubricate them at the time of assembly.

By following one of the five adaptations (with some probable variations) you should be able to convert any saber saw or trimmer now on the market. But keep in mind that manufacturers sometimes make minor changes in current models, so—even if you own one of the five machines we've chosen as representative—do some checking before you grab a hacksaw and cut materials according to the dimensions given here.

Also, remember that the dimensions of the bent parts of the carrier arms can only be close approximations due to the radius bends. The latter are much easier to make by hand than are right-angle bends, but in assembling you very likely will have to do a little adjusting, possibly even rebend a part or two, in order to get things to fit right and the whole assembly to operate smoothly. However, flat steel in the sizes called for can be bent and rebent easily, so correcting minor errors should be no problem.

Before operating any of the saber saw adaptations make sure the chuck screws are tight.

See also: filing; grinding; saber saws.

This is a bottom view of the trimmer detailed in Fig. 4, page 2081. It shows how the saddle, attached to the rasp frame, fits over the drive disk. Opposite end of frame has a brass slide that rides in yoke of the carrier arm

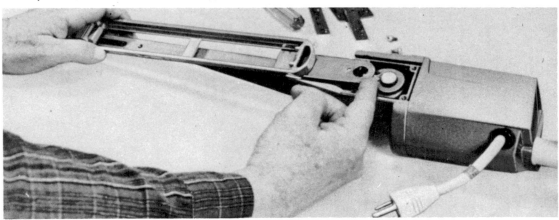

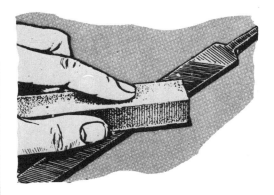

A sponge-rubber ball will keep the cord tight around your bundle of dowels. Drill two holes through the ball and thread a piece of strong cord through one hole, then double it back through the second hole to form a loop. Knot the end to keep the cord from pulling out of the hole, then slip the bundle of dowels through the loop. A slight pull on the free end will cinch the cord and friction of the rubber keeps it taut. As you use the dowels a tug on the end of the string will pull it up tight.

In fine work on some of the softer metals such as brass there are times when you need to make a very smooth cut with a new file, one that has never been used. You'll get a much smoother cut if you take time to go over one face of the file lightly with a fine oilstone. This puts a slight bevel on the teeth and also levels any high tooth that may be present. Mark this face of the file with a drop of paint or a square of tape so that it is easily identified and used only for special jobs in the future.

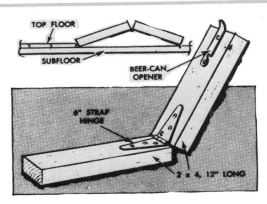

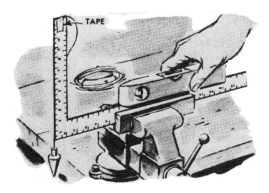

In nearly every bundle of hardwood flooring there will be at least one or two boards that are warped or bowed slightly, just enough to make it difficult, if not impossible, to get a tight joint when laying. But if you have the simple floorboard jack detailed, these pieces are no problem. The jack consists of two 12-in. lengths of 2 x 4, a strap hinge and a beer-can opener assembled as detailed. In use, you place the jack as shown in the side view with the point of the opener engaging the subfloor. Pressure at the hinge forces the floorboard into place.

If a carpenter's framing square is dropped accidentally and you question its accuracy, here is one way to check it before putting it to use on a job where work must be accurate. Clamp the beam of the square lightly in a vise, padding each jaw with a short piece of soft wood to protect the surfaces. Fasten a plumb line with a piece of tape to the upper end of the tongue of the square and let this drop over the vertical edge. Now place a level on the beam of the square and tilt the square until level. If the plumb stays in contact the square is true.

Record changer troubles you can cure

BY WALTER G. SALM

Is wow or rumble destroying the
sound? Aren't your records dropping?
Isn't your changer shutting off after
the last record? Here's how you can
solve these problems easily

■ THEY'RE COMPLICATED—or so you might think. Record changers look as though they should never be touched but actually there's nothing mysterious about them. Every gear and cam has its own specific purpose, and a little careful probing will reveal it clearly. Once you know what each part does, repairs are relatively easy.

Turntable. If the turntable doesn't turn, is slow or stops only during cycling, the trouble is in the drive train or the turntable is binding or scraping. Clean all friction-drive surfaces with carbon tetrachloride and be sure that all rubber-

to-metal contact points are free of grease. One missed spot can gum up the works. Give all metal-to-metal surfaces a dab of a light grease.

If the turntable seems to bind or scrape, check for missing washers, or races, above or below the ball bearing in the spindle well.

Wow. This is another fault that appears with age. It is caused when the turntable does not run at a constant speed, but slips or slows down periodically. Check the rubber drive (it idles between cycles) wheel that rotates the turntable. If the rubber is hard and has a slippery surface, it must be cleaned or replaced. Use carbon tetrachloride to clean the rubber wheel and the inside of the turntable rim. If replacement is required, most electronic supply houses carry a line of parts.

Sometimes excessive stylus pressure will cause wow, distorted sound and excessive record wear. Check this with a stylus pressure gauge. You might make certain the changer is level, too.

Rumble. This is common in low-cost changers

1 To remove the turntable, pry or push off the U-clamp at the base of the spindle and lift the turntable with a rocking motion. Some changers use a rubber retaining ring

2 An idler drive wheel can cause noise and cycling problems. It also is held in place by a U-clamp. Use a small screwdriver to pry off and release the idler

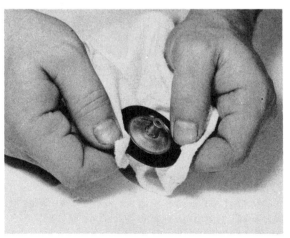

3 With the U-clamp removed, the idler wheel lifts right off. Inspect it for hard, cracked rubber, flats which look like dents, slippery outer rim, or any other damage

4 Clean the idler surface with carbon tetrachloride to remove all traces of oil or grease. If necessary, liven up the drive surface by rubbing with a pencil eraser

5 Clean the center shaft hole and mounting shaft. Then place a dab of grease on the bottom of the idler wheel hole. Do not get any grease on the rubber surfaces

6 Thrust bearing slides off the spindle; should have a washer above and below. Clean and then regrease. Check it for smooth operation after you finish the reinstallation

7 A changer with a removable spindle requires that the spindle be seated properly. Be sure it engages the mechanism in the well. Rotate the turntable by hand to check

8 Stylus pressure is important. Too much of it can ruin records and needles, and too little can cause skipping and poor reproduction. Check this with a pressure gauge

repairing changers, continued

and, to some extent, in more expensive units. Flats on the idler wheel are often at fault. These flattened portions of the drive surface are caused by prolonged contact with the turntable rim at the same point when the machine is turned off. The only cure: replace the idler wheel.

Another cause of rumble is a thrust bearing that's not turning properly. It may need only cleaning and lubrication.

Stylus. If the needle tends to jump or repeat grooves, look for a worn stylus. If it is worn and causing these difficulties, it has already done great

damage to your records; and a new needle also may jump in grooves worn by the old stylus. Replacement is the only solution.

Pickup. One frequent problem is a pickup arm that doesn't land the needle in the lead-in groove. It may lead outside or inside of this groove, or completely off the record. Almost every changer has an adjustment, usually a screw at the rear of the pickup arm or on the arm's supporting pedestal. This one is strictly trial-and-error, and you'll have to keep changing the adjustment until you get it right.

Shutoff. All record changers have an automatic shutoff. It is usually triggered by the record-leveling arm—the arm that swings over the top

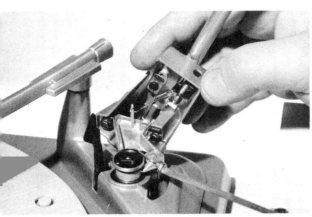

9 The needle setdown adjustment usually is found at the pivot point of pickup arm. The final setting is a trial-and-error procedure until the proper setting is found

10 A perpendicular style alignment is checked with a mirror in record-playing position. The double image in the mirror must appear as a straight, perpendicular line

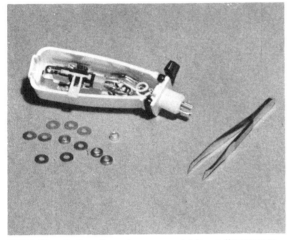

11 Plug-in heads make any cartridge adjustments relatively easy. Just remove the head from the pickup arm and loosen the mounting screws that hold the cartridge

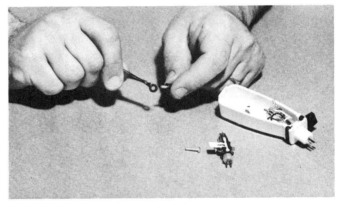

12 Brass shim washers slip under the cartridge around the mounting screw and compensate for tilt. Brass washers are a must because iron ones can cause magnetic distortion

of the record stack and balances the disks. When the last record drops, this arm pushes a small lever underneath the turntable mechanism. When the changer starts to cycle after the last record has played, this shutoff lever is depressed, the pickup arm drops onto its rest, the idler wheel disengages from the turntable rim (in some models) and the control switch flips off.

The usual cause of shutoff failure is simply that the balancing arm doesn't drop far enough. Dirt in the shaft, lack of lubrication or improper operation of the shutoff lever are the common reasons. Try moving the balancing arm up and down. If it moves freely and drops far enough, your trouble is in the linkage below; cleaning

and lubrication are in order. If it tends to stick and doesn't always drop all the way down (past the spindle pusher mechanism), remove the shaft assembly, clean out the well with carbon tet (pipe cleaners to the rescue again) and clean the shaft itself. Use a very thin coat of grease on the shaft and work the shaft around as you re-insert it to spread the lubricant. If the shaft won't come out without major surgery, try a few drops of light machine or turntable oil alongside the shaft.

If a shaft gets bent from abuse, the only solution is replacement with new parts.

See also: high fidelity; high-fidelity center; needles, phonograph; phonographs.

When disassembling the rectifier plates, first mark the positive side of each lightly with ink or paint to avoid error when reassembling. Be careful not to remove the washer

Convert to a full-wave rectifier

BY ROBERT MICALS

■ IF YOU NEED a full-wave rectifier for an experimental circuit and have only half-wave units in the catch-all box, these can be converted to full-wave easily.

Remove the plates from the hollow brass rivet by drilling one end off the rivet. Avoid scratching the positive surfaces.

Insert a screw in the fiber tube on which the plates were mounted and reassemble the plates as in the diagram. Add three solder lugs between the plates (¼-in. washer 1½-in. tongue). Use a lock washer and nut on the screw after the plates are in place. You can double the current capacity by using two plates between taps.

See also: battery chargers; electronics.

Assemble according to the diagram at the right. Be sure the plates face the right direction. The new rectifier (below) is shown at left. Note the jumper soldered to the two positives

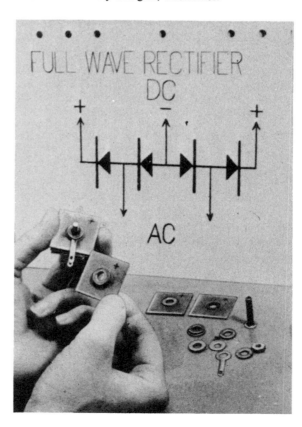

On new work it's often helpful to finish each part individually. It's one sure way to avoid sags and drips

Surface preparation for a new finish

BY W. CLYDE LAMMEY

The quality of the surface you prepare determines the quality of the finish you get. Here are some helpful pointers

ORDINARILY YOU JUST sand the wood smooth and slap on a finish of your choice. Or, if it's old work, you take off the old finish, sand lightly and refinish. But usually there are important steps in between. Neglect these and you may turn up with a final finish that doesn't look right.

"What," you ask, "did I do wrong?" Nearly every finisher has ended up at some time or other with this baffling question. Maybe, just maybe, the answer is in what you *didn't* do.

So you've sanded and sanded the surfaces of that pet project until they seemed perfectly smooth when viewed at all angles in good light. Or are they?

Dust the surfaces again and take another look. On some woods it's most difficult to see minute surface defects after thorough sanding. There can be tiny scratches, humps and hollows, even dents you may have missed. This is especially true of the light-colored woods when in the "white" (unfinished), such as maple and birch.

The instant you touch a clear finish or stain to such woods, out come unlooked-for scratches, and there may be low ridges and shallow hollows that cast shadows and give the finished surface a cloudy appearance in spots.

When very slight, these defects just can't be

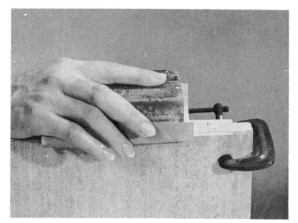

Sand end grain with blocking on each side and at the edges, clamping all the blocking securely in place. Use an unpadded sanding block

Use a felt-padded block for fine sandpaper and also when softening (rounding) corners. The padded block leaves a radius on a corner

Behr-Manning Company

Brush filler across the grain, allow to "flat," then wipe off across the grain. Sand lightly after the filler is thoroughly dry

If you're not sure about the presence of fine scratches, dampen the surface. This will show up any you've missed when sanding

seen on light woods and even some darker woods. But you can feel them. Wipe your forefinger to remove any dust and run that sensitive tip over the surface. You can feel, and locate, even the slightest hollows or ridges, and you can detect fine scratches you can't see. Scratches are likely leftovers from the sanding steps, but there also may be slight ripples, usually across the width, which were left by the surfacer when the boards were planed to finish dimensions. These, too, are difficult to detect.

Such defects are likely to show up under any finish—clear, stain or opaque. You just have to continue the sanding until the sand-and-finger-check technique shows unmistakably that the surface not only looks smooth; it *is* smooth, with no ripples, hollows, ridges or shallow dents.

Such a surface will usually take that perfect finish you're after.

And have you "softened" all the sharp, right-angle corners? Softened is a finisher's and cabinetmaker's term describing a slight rounding of all sharp corners on new work. No finish will remain the full thickness of the film on an unsoftened corner. It will sag away, usually on the down side and leave the wood partially, if not fully, exposed. Unsoftened corners also give the work a rather raw, half-done look. You do this rounding over with fine sandpaper, using a block with a felt pad so the paper will form a radius on the corner instead of a flat. It must be done with some care so you end up with a slightly rounded corner of a uniform radius.

If you're still not sure about the smoothness of some areas, it's usually permissible, on new work, to dampen the surface slightly. This generally will reveal any fine scratches that would otherwise escape notice. It also will usually trap any dimples or unnoticed dents. The latter, also some short, shallow hollows, can generally be

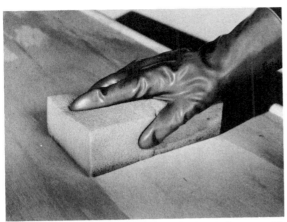

Some discolorations can be bleached out. Sponge off residues, allow the surface to dry, then sand to remove the raised grain

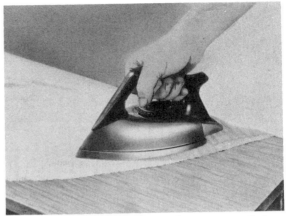

Dents and short, shallow depressions can usually be ironed out. Wet a cloth, spread it over the affected area and iron it dry

Wilson-Imperial Company

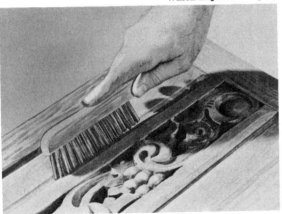

Old relief carvings and moldings difficult to sand effectively can often be smoothed satisfactorily with a wire brush

After a thorough sanding, coat any parts made from fir plywood either with white shellac or a sealer especially prepared for the purpose

"leveled" by dampening a cloth, laying it over the affected area, and ironing it dry. As a rule this trick works on both old and new work.

But you'll have to sand dampened surfaces. Wetting, even slightly, will raise the grain and leave a new roughness that must be sanded out.

On old work you must be on the lookout for rather deep scratches, dents, cracks and discolorations. True, on some old pieces these age and use marks are desirable. You may prefer to apply your new finish right over them. Then again, maybe not. Any scratch or age crack not too prominent or too wide can be eliminated by using any of the prepared fillers. Clean all loose material and dirt from a crack before filling. Then knife the filler into the opening, pressing it in tightly. Round the top of the filler slightly above the surface and then sand flush after it hardens.

Any cracks to be left as is may take the stain (if stain is to be used) or finish more deeply than the adjacent surfaces and thus turn up a darker color along the edges. To prevent this, "wash" the edges with a thinned coat of white shellac before staining or finishing.

Nicks, digs or gouges should, of course, be filled unless preservation is desirable. Treat undesirable dents as previously described.

Big cracks and discolorations are something else. Often it is possible to trim large cracks to a wedge shape. Then cut a wedge from matching wood and tap it into place over glue. Sanding flush and staining generally gets you by with an acceptable repair. Ordinary age discolorations may or may not be desirable. Often they must be bleached out, and here one must be careful. Sometimes it is necessary to bleach out a whole top or a panel in order to get a satisfactory job.

See also: finishes, furniture; finishes, removing; finishes, urethane; finishes, wood; painting; staining, wood.

Projects to solve home problems

Many times it's the
small, but much needed,
projects like these
that make the big difference
in comfortable living

■ TRANSFORM YOUR HOME in two days? Not quite, but the extra time that these weekend projects might take can add a lot of livability to a home.

Like all remodeling jobs, the projects illustrated on the following pages were designed to solve specific problems. Most of these—storage space, privacy, sleeping arrangements for guests —are common problems found in almost every home. However, the novel solutions that are shown have three things in common—ingenuity, simplicity and low cost.

For example, take a look at the "bare-faced entryway" on page 2093. The problem here was an entrance opening directly into the living room, a relatively common situation in many homes. The owner of this house wanted to screen off this entrance from the living room to form an entrance hall or foyer where guests could remove their wraps before entering the room.

He could have accomplished this in a dozen different ways—adding a regular plastered parti-

tion, a closet partition, a bookcase-room divider, a floor-to-ceiling screen—but, instead of choosing any of these common solutions, he constructed a door-height translucent screen, installed it with overhead beams which gave the illusion of a ceiling and continued it along the door wall behind the couch. As you can see from the drawing, the result is a modern entrance hall which looks like it was part of the original design of the house.

This entryway project illustrates two of the most important rules of remodeling—don't be afraid to be different, and plan your project to fit in with the surroundings. This is especially true today because of the many different kinds of building and finishing materials available to you. These include wood and vinyl paneling, plastic sheeting in various decorator designs and colors, a wide variety of paint and stain finishes, cabinet hardware, lighting fixtures, and so forth. Also, you can buy many ready-to-finish cabinets and shelving that could fit your project to a tee. Since World War II, there have been more than 500,000 items added to the building materials line!

Almost any of the projects shown on these pages can be easily modified to match your present decorating scheme. The sliding louvered screens on page 2097 may look starkly modern in the drawing, but if you stain them maple or cherry and add a scrolled cornice they will blend easily into an Early American room setting. Most any decor can be mixed, as any good interior decorator will tell you.

Now is a good time to take a look at these exciting projects and start planning your own weekend special. We've included detailed drawings of each of the projects to make the job go easier for you. Each can be modified quickly to match your situation.

Bare-faced entrance becomes an attractive entryway when you screen it off from the living room with this divider which doesn't shut out all of the available light. Designed by Manny Shein, Chicago, it is made by mounting flat fiberglass panels in a frame of 1¼-in. sq. stock and quarter round. For a dramatic effect, give the wooden frame two coats of flat black enamel. Sand with fine grit sandpaper between the coats for the smoothest job

continued

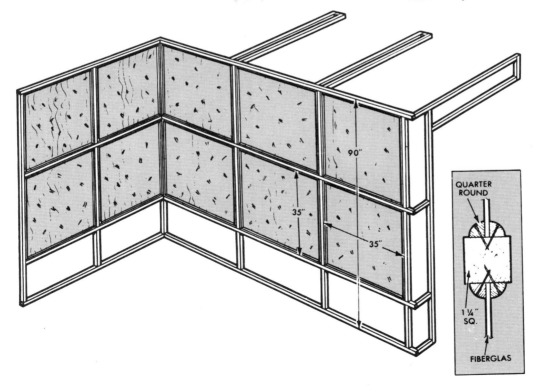

90"

35"

35"

QUARTER
ROUND

1¼"
SQ.

FIBERGLAS

A cluttered vanity yields to convenient order when you organize it with these slide-away storage shelves. Pinch-hitting as a medicine chest for a fixed-mirror vanity, the pull-out shelves work like vertical drawers on smooth roller-bearing tracks. Like having two medicine cabinets that slide in and out (below), these "shelf-drawers" alongside the knee-hole in the vanity take over most of your storage needs. The shelves have been designed to fit various drug and sundry items that will set on them. The mirror is installed with screws and clips; the molding around it is nailed to the studs. Countersink the nails, fill the holes and paint or stain the molding to match the cabinet finish. The necessary hardware is standard throughout the design details

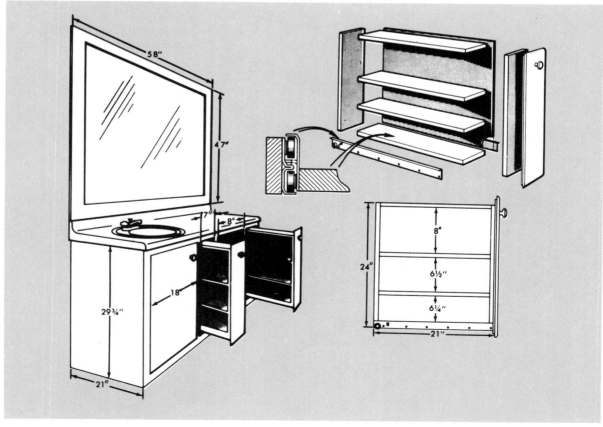

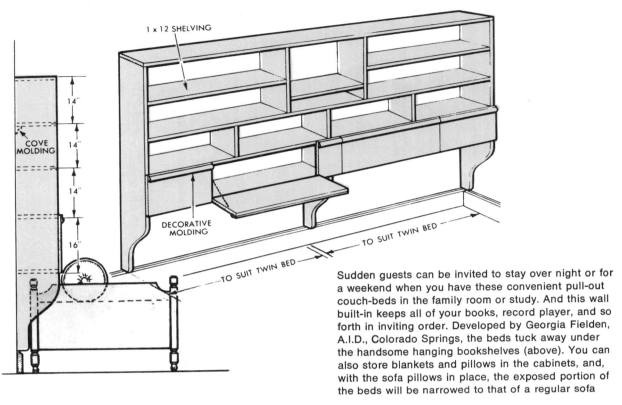

1 x 12 SHELVING

14"

COVE
MOLDING

14"

14"

16"

DECORATIVE
MOLDING

TO SUIT TWIN BED

TO SUIT TWIN BED

Sudden guests can be invited to stay over night or for
a weekend when you have these convenient pull-out
couch-beds in the family room or study. And this wall
built-in keeps all of your books, record player, and so
forth in inviting order. Developed by Georgia Fielden,
A.I.D., Colorado Springs, the beds tuck away under
the handsome hanging bookshelves (above). You can
also store blankets and pillows in the cabinets, and,
with the sofa pillows in place, the exposed portion of
the beds will be narrowed to that of a regular sofa

continued

remodeling projects, continued

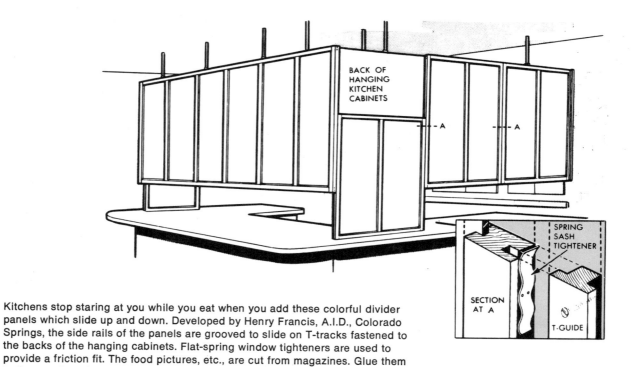

BACK OF
HANGING
KITCHEN
CABINETS

A   A

SPRING
SASH
TIGHTENER

SECTION
AT A

T-GUIDE

Kitchens stop staring at you while you eat when you add these colorful divider panels which slide up and down. Developed by Henry Francis, A.I.D., Colorado Springs, the side rails of the panels are grooved to slide on T-tracks fastened to the backs of the hanging cabinets. Flat-spring window tighteners are used to provide a friction fit. The food pictures, etc., are cut from magazines. Glue them to the panels and protect them from wear with a smooth coat of varnish

Where rooms have a wide cove molding at the ceiling, small windows acquire architectural importance and a real sense of unity when the same molding is used for window cornices. The floor-to-ceiling window screens, below, slide past one another. The screens ride on continuous flat-metal rails, as the drawing below shows. The screens can be painted an accent color to go with the other colors in the room, or they can be stained, if you have Early American decor. If you paint them, use two coats for the best results, and sand between coats

continued

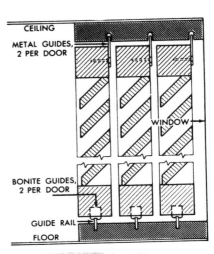

Pop-eyed picture windows lose their glaring ability when you cover them with this floor-to-ceiling screen, which is detailed above. Three fixed-louver panels let in just the right amount of sunlight, or they slide open sidewise to provide access to the windows to let in air or for cleaning. Designed by John Galbraith, A.I.A., San Gabriel, Calif., the panels here were custom built. Similar panels can be purchased at most retail building material outlets or home stores. They also can be bought through mail order houses. When you measure for the panels, be sure to subtract the thickness of the track at the floor and ceiling

Labels on illustration: SWIVEL CASTER · SPECIAL BRASS CATCH

remodeling projects, continued

Roll the wind and glare off of your porch with this adjustable privacy screen. The accordion arrangement of hinged shutters on coasters was designed by Bunts and Kelsey, A.I.A., Colorado Springs. The handsome screen consists of five stock louver panels hinged together alternately and then to a corner of a patio porch. Raised off the floor by stilted casters, the screen still admits gentle breezes when closed. Three special catches you can buy engage the slots in the post to keep the screen tightly shut. When the screen is folded back, it is kept secure by a dog leash. The screen can be painted an accent color to go with your patio furnishings, or paint it the color of the trim on your house

Straddling a low paneled wall 28 in. high, this king-size eating counter which measures 44 x 72 in. can accommodate as many as seven persons. An 18 x 72 in. piece of plywood was first centered and attached to the top of the stud wall and braced on each side with metal shelf brackets spaced 6 in. apart. Then the counter was attached to the base and covered with high-pressure plastic laminate. Exposed wood was stained

continued

Space-wasting card table setups tuck away out of sight in this easy-to-build hollow room divider. It was designed by William McConnel, Covina, Calif. The hollow divider is large enough so that an entire card-table and chair set will fit into it, without wedging against the sides. Unit can be larger for more chairs

The divider is built around an inner framework of 1 x 2 stock which may be faced on each side with hardwood-faced plywood or prefinished hardboard with a wood grain design. Or if it is to be painted, use regular Douglas fir plywood or hardboard. Hardwood should be used for the trim around the top of the unit

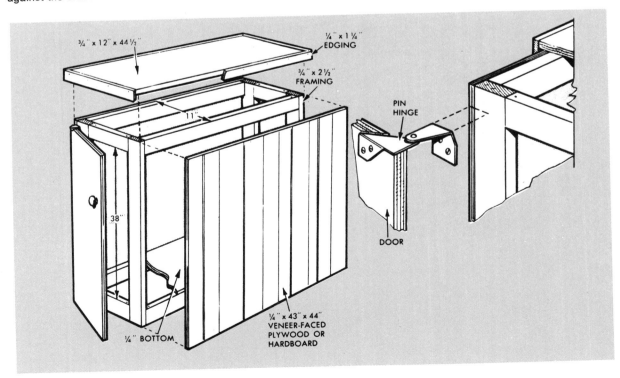

3/4" x 12" x 44 1/2"

1/4" x 1 1/4"
EDGING

3/4" x 2 1/2"
FRAMING

11"

PIN
HINGE

38"

DOOR

1/4" BOTTOM

1/4" x 43" x 44"
VENEER-FACED
PLYWOOD OR
HARDBOARD

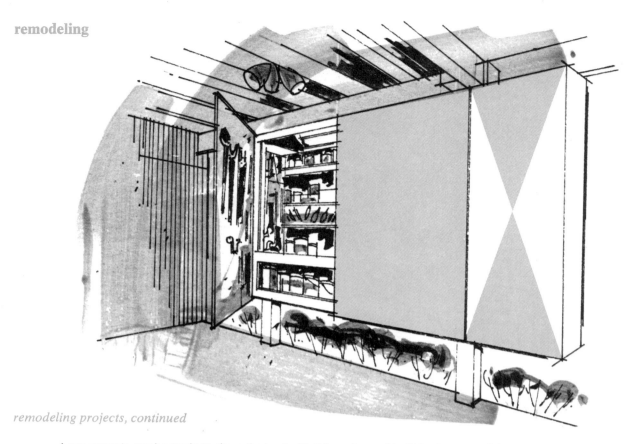

remodeling projects, continued

Lazy carports can be made to share the load with this under-roof built-in storage wall for tools and garden and household supplies. The cabinet is waterproof and it is built around the support posts. The cabinet consists of a simple plywood-covered framework of 2 x 4s. Use exterior grade plywood for this project. Masking tape is used to set off paint designs

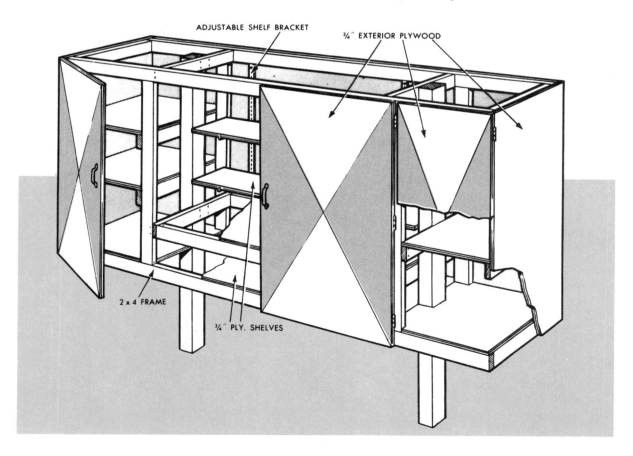

ADJUSTABLE SHELF BRACKET

¾" EXTERIOR PLYWOOD

2 x 4 FRAME

¾" PLY. SHELVES

continued

When you're pinched for space in a small room, consider replacing that full-width door with two narrow louvered doors. These will require less clearance to open and close, allowing you to locate furniture nearer the door. And apart from saving space, such doors will dress up an otherwise dull room. The doors are simply hinged to the present door jambs. Paint them to match the trim or room decor. The decorator door pulls are fastened to the center rail. Three hinges for each panel should be used; put one near the top and bottom and one in the center

This kitchen desk—popular in today's kitchen planning—is flanked by shallow louver-door cabinets to provide a handy spot to park kitchen appliances. Typical cabinet joinery is used throughout construction. The plywood top is made extra thick by using a hardwood edging of 1 x 2 stock. The top and edging are then covered with a bright-colored plastic laminate. The laminate used here is a different color than the cabinet below. However, a matching color can be used, if you prefer. The top is fastened to the cabinet with screws driven in from below, after the laminate is on

remodeling projects, continued

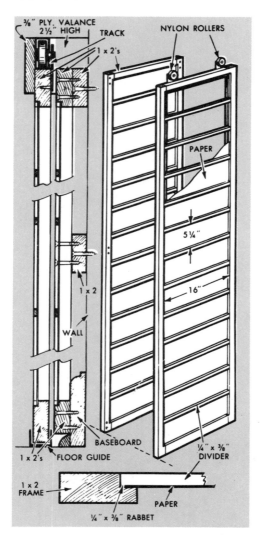

Sliding Shoji screens help to dramatize a small window. The outside panels are stationary; the sliding inside panels roll on nylon wheels over a steel track hidden behind a plywood valance board. Make all the panels the same, rabbeting 1 x 2 outside framing stock to hold the white drafting paper and the cross strips. Cut the paper to fit inside the rabbets and glue it into position. When the glue has dried, paint the divider strips with flat black enamel. Then nail them into position and touch up nailheads

Waste storage space in your kitchen soffit can be easily turned into a shallow box cabinet for holding canned goods or other small items such as seldom-used dishes and serving equipment. You can make the cabinet one can deep, as shown below, to fit an opening cut in the face of the soffit. Nail it to the soffit framing. Plywood, painted, can be used for this. Or use hardwood-faced plywood to match the finish of the kitchen cabinets

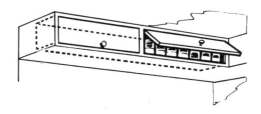

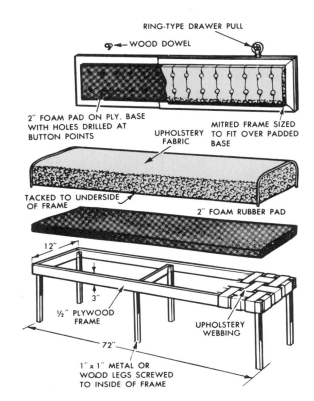

RING-TYPE DRAWER PULL

WOOD DOWEL

2" FOAM PAD ON PLY. BASE
WITH HOLES DRILLED AT
BUTTON POINTS

UPHOLSTERY
FABRIC

MITRED FRAME SIZED
TO FIT OVER PADDED
BASE

TACKED TO UNDERSIDE
OF FRAME

2" FOAM RUBBER PAD

12"

3"

½" PLYWOOD
FRAME

UPHOLSTERY
WEBBING

72"

1" x 1" METAL OR
WOOD LEGS SCREWED
TO INSIDE OF FRAME

Is your entry hall too small for a normal-width bench?
This slim hallway bench, designed by Georgia Fielden,
A.I.D., requires only 12 in. of space and uses a wall-
hung backrest. The base is standard upholstery construction—a wooden frame, upholstery webbing and
foam-rubber pad are covered with upholstery cloth.
For a simpler back cushion, you can mount the rubber pad on a ½-in. plywood panel and cover it with
upholstery cloth. If you do this, omit the tufting

continued

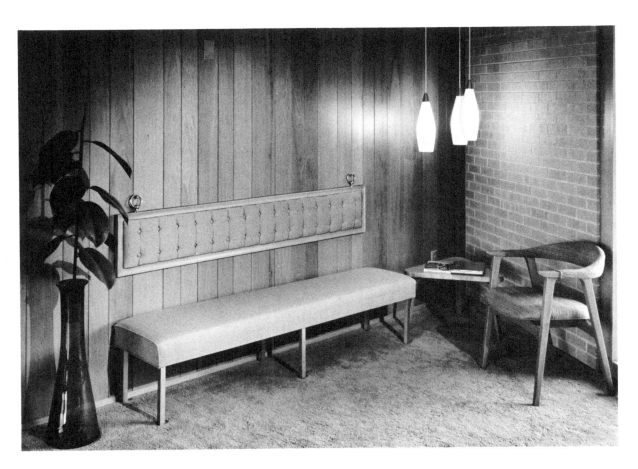

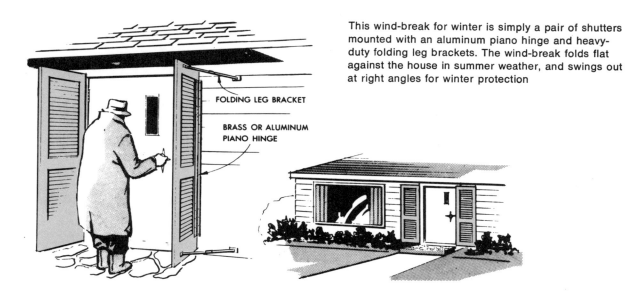

This wind-break for winter is simply a pair of shutters mounted with an aluminum piano hinge and heavy-duty folding leg brackets. The wind-break folds flat against the house in summer weather, and swings out at right angles for winter protection

FOLDING LEG BRACKET

BRASS OR ALUMINUM PIANO HINGE

remodeling projects, continued

Built-in drawers can reclaim that inaccessible space in deep closets. Before opening the wall, check to make sure that you don't run into heating ducts or wiring. The knock-down drawers are available at lumberyards, or you can buy them via mail order

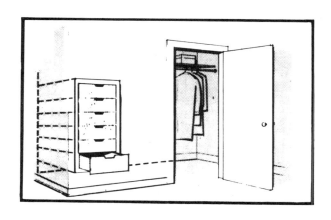

This two-way linen closet is an easy conversion when the closet forms a part of the bathroom wall. Simply cut a rectangular opening between the studs, frame it with 1-in. lumber and finish with a trim color to match the bathroom door. Prime-paint the lumber first

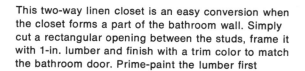

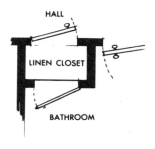

HALL

LINEN CLOSET

BATHROOM

Clear up clutter on closet floors by adding a shoe shelf with individual compartments for each pair. Lower the pole enough to allow mounting an extra shelf 6 in. below the existing shelf, then cut the shoe shelf and dividers from ½ in. plywood and nail it into place. If the present shelf is too low, add a new shelf above it for more storage space. Line the shoe shelf with old carpeting for luxury

See also: attic remodeling; bathrooms; building; closets; dormers; home additions; measurements; remodeling, exterior; remodeling, ideas; remodeling, shortcuts; windows, picture.

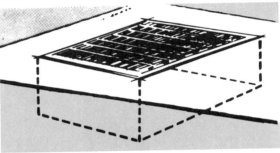

This foot scraper grate over a shallow pit is a great idea if you're adding a new stoop. The grate lifts out so you can clean the pit when it's full

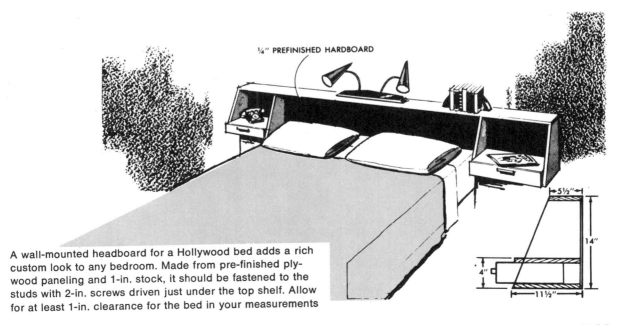

¼" PREFINISHED HARDBOARD

A wall-mounted headboard for a Hollywood bed adds a rich custom look to any bedroom. Made from pre-finished plywood paneling and 1-in. stock, it should be fastened to the studs with 2-in. screws driven just under the top shelf. Allow for at least 1-in. clearance for the bed in your measurements

5½"
14"
4"
11½"

Why live in a "carbon-copy" home?

Even the most attractive home can look drab
if surrounded by identical houses. But, with
these ideas, you can transform any look-alike
house into a truly distinctive home of your own

Development Bungalow Converts Into . . .

YOUR HOUSE doesn't have to look like your neighbor's any more than you have to drive the same car he does, or wear the same clothes. And yet, to look at the face of America, dotted with look-alike row and development houses, you would almost think we were a nation of carbon-copiers. We aren't. It's just that few of us have the funds to insist on a personalized home design when we start house hunting.

Not that homes such as the Cape Cod and the ubiquitous modern split-level don't provide comfortable shelter at a good price. But their attractiveness fades when they are grouped with others of the same design.

You don't have to live in such a carbon-copy home indefinitely. It can be transformed into some truly distinctive living, as the illustrations here and on the next four pages show. They were developed by Architect William J. Ward to serve as a source lode of ideas.

Try them for size or as departure points for your own concepts.

an Inviting Contemporary

continued

A LONG, LOW SILHOUETTE replaces the original boxy shape. Extending the front gable 8 to 10 ft. shelters the entry and provides a welcome sunshade for the living room. Opened-up glass areas with floor-to-ceiling windows admit more light to the interior.

An added louver vent in the front gable airs out the attic, makes the house cooler in the summer while helping to prevent moisture problems in the winter. The use of one siding material gives the front a more harmonious look; the narrow strips make the house look bigger, lower

the silhouette. A new concrete front patio under the gable should extend 3 to 5 ft. beyond the new roof. The planter at the edge of the patio slab adds a distinctive touch. The materials should cost about $2000—including the carport. (Note: this figure can vary with location.)

Structural changes should be at a minimum, as the roof extension ties in with the existing gable. To lower the cost, you could apply the siding yourself—in most cases right over the old. If necessary, the patio, carport, planter and the roof extension could be omitted from the design.

Story-and-a-half Modern Transforms Into..

■ BRICK VENEER, applied to the front only in this remodeling, hides a miscellany of old sidings. (The foundation must be widened, but existing stone facing peels off readily.) Front steps are removed, and the plot re-graded slightly. Entry is now taller, wider, has double doors. Formal doors on both house and garage are actually flush doors with applied molding.

Flat pilasters about 3 in. thick go over the brick. Colonial double-hung windows (8 over 12) replace random mixture of sizes and styles. Fireplace and chimney are optional, but desirable in this treatment. Low picket fence and dentilling on fascia are important finishing touches. Estimated cost of $3500 to $4000 includes labor for the brick veneer and chimney.

Split Level Modern Converts to Rural Contemporary

a Formal Georgian Cottage

continued

■ EXISTING GARAGE moves forward here, creating a new family room at rear. Cupola on roof adds warm New England touch while providing ventilation. On bedroom wing, the greatly enlarged, bold glass areas brighten the interior while giving the exterior a dramatic vertical accent.

In main wing, an attractive bay replaces original strip of double-hung windows. A slate or flagstone walkway now connects front entry with garage. Roof has been carried forward to cover walkway and to make the house appear closer to the ground. Bedroom wing can be brought forward to meet the new roof line, as shown, but this step is not essential.

The entire house is re-covered with natural stone or split concrete block and vertical-grooved siding—preferably cypress or cedar. Extensive structural changes, most of which might be best done professionally, plus an estimated $10,000 materials cost, make this an expensive conversion. However, a good part of this cost should be recoverable in added resale value.

Two-Story Box Becomes ... a Portsmouth Junior Mansion

MINOR CHANGES can effect striking transformations. The simple step of removing the front porch and dormer alleviates a cluttered, gaping facade. The living-room windows give way to the attractive box bay which adds character and admits more light. The corner pilasters add stature, height and dignity.

The widow's walk could be merely implied by an ornamental railing; the chimney is enlarged with sheetmetal falsework around the existing brick. The new windows, doors and shutters need only minor structural changes.

Changes to the house alone should run about $2000 for materials. The optional garden house and breezeway will cost an additional $1500 to $2000.

Cape Cod Becomes ... an Early American Dutch Style Home

THIS ORIGINAL HOUSE was a good but common design. Jutting dormers were removed in front, shed dormers were added in the rear to increase light and usable headroom upstairs.

The side porch is replaced by a covered way, leading to a new garage with a storage room or studio upstairs. The way can be left open or enclosed to become a storage room or laundry. The roof is extended 2½ ft. front and rear by tying in with the existing rafters. Deepen windows by shortening the cripples. Brick veneer covers clapboards; picket fence should be removed or replaced with informal rail type. Materials cost: about $6000 up.

See also: building; dormers; garages; home additions; measurements; porch; remodeling; remodeling ideas; remodeling shortcuts; windows, picture.

REAR VIEW

2111

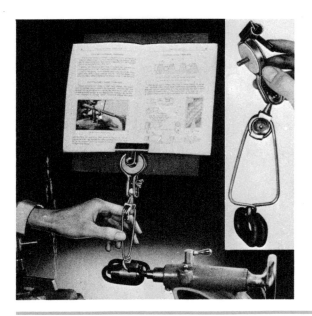

When working from plans, charts or magazines you will find that the spring clamp of a photoflood reflector makes a dandy holder. For example, when working at the lathe, a drill chuck inserted in the tailstock sleeve provides a convenient clamping surface. The rubber-covered loops of the spring clamp will hold it securely wherever placed. A plywood disk about ½-in. thick is cut to fit in the pinch clamp which normally grips a lamp socket. A ³⁄₁₆-in. stovebolt passing through the wood disk holds a spring paper clamp and a square piece of hardboard which supports the copy for quick, easy reference.

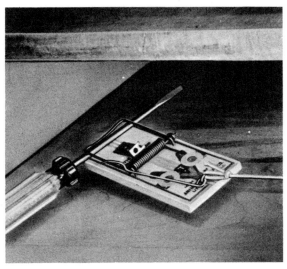

While it does not happen very often, occasionally small tools or parts are dropped in hard-to-reach spaces. Retrieving them can be very frustrating. A magnet is not always available and will not attract all materials but a mousetrap will grab with finality. Simply tie a string of suitable length to the staple holding the trigger and set the trap. Lower the trap into the confined area close to the fugitive part or tool and dangle it until the bait pan contacts the object. This will spring the trap, the jaw will grab the runaway and up it comes.

Finding the center of a disk or other round stock is easy and can be done quickly with a thin paper. Place the disk on it, trace the outline with a soft pencil and cut it out. Fold this in half twice, the second time lining up the two halves of the first crease, to give you two creases crossing each other at right angles as indicated in the photograph. Now carefully lay it flat on the work and using any pointed tool, pierce the disk at the intersection of the crease marks. This will give you the center of the round stock and you continue from there.